The Collected Essays of
Josephine J. Turpin Washington

The Collected Essays of Josephine J. Turpin Washington

A BLACK REFORMER IN THE POST-RECONSTRUCTION SOUTH

Edited by

RITA B. DANDRIDGE

University of Virginia Press

CHARLOTTESVILLE AND LONDON

University of Virginia Press
© 2019 by the Rector and Visitors of the University of Virginia
All rights reserved
Printed in the United States of America on acid-free paper

First published 2019

ISBN 978-0-8139-4212-4 (cloth)
ISBN 978-0-8139-4213-1 (ebook)

1 3 5 7 9 8 6 4 2

Library of Congress Cataloging-in-Publication Data is available for this title.

Cover art: Josephine J. Turpin Washington's 1886 graduating class, Howard College.
(Courtesy of the Moorland-Spingarn Research Center, Manuscript Division, Howard
University, Washington, DC)

Contents

Acknowledgments

As I reflect on those who have supported me in this small but demanding project, I am reminded of John Donne's adage "No [wo]man is an island." To all those who have assisted me in bringing this manuscript to completion, I give thanks.

Special thanks go to my Virginia State University colleagues Leah Thomas, Gary MacDonald, and Michael McClure, who read several drafts of the proposal and introduction during our monthly meetings as a writing group. I thank them immensely for their encouraging words and constructive comments that moved the project forward.

I am indebted to my dear friend Patricia Fleming, who drove many miles to archives and libraries with me. Without her assistance with long-distance driving, the manuscript would still be incomplete.

The archivists and staff at several libraries and institutions are due thanks: Christina Jordan Dunn, Acting Director, Goochland County Historical Society; Heather Dawn Beattie, Museum Collections Manager, Virginia Historical Society; Meaghan A. Alston, MLIS, Manuscript Division, Moorland-Spingarn Research Center, Howard University; Joellen El Bashir, Curator, Moorland-Spingarn Research Center, Howard University; Catherine Curry, Reference Librarian, Jacksonville Public Library, Florida; Arlene Balkansky, Reference Specialist, Newspaper and Current Periodical Reading Room, Library of Congress; Dana Chandler, University Archivist, Tuskegee University; Howard O. Robinson II, Archives Coordinator, Levi Watkins Learning Center, Alabama State University; and Glenda Puckett, Archivist, Alabama Department of Archives and History. Their knowledge and assistance led me to new discoveries about the works and life of Josephine Turpin Washington.

I extend special thanks to Dave Grabarek, Circulation and Archival Assistant, Library of Virginia, for speedily retrieving reels of difficult-to-obtain African American newspapers and for enlarging print copies of newspaper articles.

To the librarians at Virginia State University, I express gratitude for their kind outreach from the time I entered the portals of Johnston Memorial Library until I left. Special thanks are extended to Nelson Jefferson, Library Assistant; Anthony Lewis, Circulation Assistant; and Louveller Luster, Collection Development Librarian.

And, finally, I thank University of Virginia Press, my first choice for a publisher, for its interest in my manuscript.

Introduction

Josephine Turpin Washington (1861–1949) is a unique voice in African American literary studies.[1] Her post-Reconstruction uplift essays span many subjects, making her a significant contributor to an emerging black press in the nineteenth century. Born free in slaveholding Goochland, Virginia, Washington began her essay writing at Richmond Colored Normal School (now Armstrong High School) in 1877, where she published her first temperance essay, "A Talk about Church Fairs," now lost, in the *Virginia Star*, the first Richmond newspaper printed by a black. In 1880, she entered Richmond Institute (now Virginia Union University), a seminary purposed to train men for the ministry, where she read her essays before the Literary Society of Richmond Institute and published "The Benefits of Trouble" in the *Virginia Star*. The youngest-known post-Reconstruction black Virginia writer of published essays, Washington was considered "one of [the] most brilliant and accomplished writers."[2] An embodiment of racial and gender progress, in 1883 she enrolled at Howard College (now Howard University) and published a dozen essays, among which were "Higher Education for Women" and "A Plea for the Co-Education of the Sexes," in which she argues for women's coeducation and higher education, since women in Virginia lacked access to coeducation in higher education. After graduating from Howard College in 1886 as the only female in her graduating class and marrying Dr. Samuel Somerville Hawkins Washington, an 1886 Howard Medical School graduate and West Indies native,[3] she moved with him to Alabama, where she taught at various newly formed black colleges,[4] engaged with other black women working for racial uplift, and became a significant leader in and relevant writer about Alabama's Federation of Colored Women's Clubs (FCWC).[5] The quality and content of Washington's writings assisted the development of the black press in a historical era when few African Americans were literate. Written within the historical context of post-Reconstruction racial and gender uplift, Washington's essays are significant for their contributions to an emerging black press as they disrupt the nineteenth-century African American literary canon prioritizing slave narratives; they pave the way for the race womanhood ideology depicted in later nineteenth-century African American women's novels; they link to biblical scriptures and to European and American literatures to support racial uplift ideology; and they serve as guides, articulating the responsibilities and aesthetic standards that will allow the black press to establish a reputable literary sphere.

Historical Context: Post-Reconstruction Era
and Racial and Gender Uplift

The Post-Reconstruction era (1877–1920) is often referred to as the nadir of African American life. Blacks faced a precipitous erosion of gains won during the 1865–77 military occupation of the South. Southern states, formerly associated with the Confederacy, defied the Fifteenth Amendment of 1870 that had granted suffrage to black men. Extralegal voting activities were prominent. A dual, unequal educational system was established; Black Codes were instituted; trade unions ostracized blacks; race and gender stereotypes were promoted; and violence, including lynching, accompanied the indignities of Jim Crow law. Race-based discrimination became legal with the 1896 Supreme Court decision in *Plessy v. Ferguson*. The "separate but equal" mandate used to support Louisiana's segregated public transportation system became the legal justification for racial segregation throughout the South. These egregious harms debilitated and impeded the social progress of the majority of blacks. Reduced to second-class citizenship, they struggled to attain self-sufficiency, while white America transformed itself into an impressive empire with expanded transportation systems, industrialized markets, annexed territories, and the explosive growth of European and Scandinavian emigrants. The black middle class, whom W. E. B. Du Bois much later would label the "Talented Tenth," committed itself to uplift the race and shield it from others' negative perceptions. One of the Talented Tenth, Washington shaped the conversation before Du Bois. Whereas Du Bois included only men among his Talented Tenth workers, Washington, as a woman writer, responded to an aggressive post-Reconstruction program of racial and gender uplift that African American conventions, churches, and presses facilitated.

Negro conferences played a major role in racial uplift efforts. They identified and found solutions for racial issues. An excerpt from the proceedings of the National Negro Conference held in 1879 in Nashville, Tennessee, reads: "We are to a great extent the architects of our own fortunes, and must rely mainly on our own exertions for success. We, therefore, recommend to the youth of our race the observation of strict morality, temperate habits, and the practice of economy, the acquisition of land, the acquiring [of] agricultural education, of advancing to mercantile positions and forcing their way into the various productive channels of literature, art, science, and [mechanics]."[6] The proceedings detail earnest avenues for racial uplift, the focus of the National Negro Convention since its inception in Philadelphia among free blacks in 1829, in response to northern white violence against southern black migrants in the North. Character building, education, employment, land ownership, and participation in the arts were as much the racial levers for blacks' strides toward middle-class status in 1829 as in 1879. These were factors identified as keeping at bay crime, state dependency, chronic unemployment, and ignorance.

Josephine Turpin's 1886 graduating class, Howard College: Kelly Miller Sr.,
seated left; Josephine J. Turpin, *center*; William Palmer, *seated right*. (Courtesy
of the Moorland-Spingarn Research Center, Manuscript Division, Howard
University, Washington, DC)

Women's clubs and their conventions were the germinating seeds for some
of Washington's essays. The most notable were the Alabama Federation of Colored Women's Clubs (FCWC) and the Sojourner Truth Club, which focused on
literary interests. Organized 19 December 1899, the State Federation of Colored
Women's Clubs was a chapter of the National Association of Colored Women's
Clubs (NACWC), the successor of the National Conference of Colored Women,

which was formed in 1895, when a group of concerned black women, under the leadership of Josephine St. Pierre Ruffin of Boston, Massachusetts, protested against the racial accusations of John W. Jacks, the white president of the Missouri Press Association. Jacks had written to Florence Belgarnie, secretary of a former antislavery society in England, "For the most part [black women are] ignorant and immoral, some exceptions, of course, but they don't count."[7] A white feminist with an interest in blacks and contacts with Ida B. Wells, an antilynching crusader and writer, Belgarnie sent the letter to Ruffin, editor of *Woman's Era*. Ruffin sent a copy of Jacks's letter to black women's clubs and associations nationwide and attached to it a leaflet calling an urgent meeting in Boston, 29–31 July 1895 and challenging black women to take action against others' indictments of them. The convention's minutes described Jacks's missive as "a most indecent, foul, and slanderous letter, traducing American womanhood."[8] The attendees at this convention, known as National Conference of Colored Women, resolved to "denounce [Jacks] as a man wholly without a sense of chivalry and honor, and bound by the iron hand of prejudice, sectionalism and race hatred, entirely unreliable and unworthy [of] the prominence he seeks." As a result of this convention, the National Conference of Colored Women expanded and became the National Federation of Afro-American Women, an organization devoted to the needs of black women and the race.

With "more than 1,000 clubs, representing about 150,000 women," the Alabama FCWC had racial and gender uplift as its raison d'être.[9] At its 1910 meeting in Auburn, Alabama, at which Washington was present, the Federation presented a symposium on "Our Work," "Its Aims," "Its Workers," "Its Accomplishments," and "Its Needs."[10] The group resolved to scrutinize shortcomings in the race, plan for improvement, and execute results.

Washington's essays, inspired by her association with Alabama's Federation of Colored Women's Clubs, became signature pieces that focused on multiple racial and gender uplift concerns. In "Impressions of a Southern Federation," Washington wrote about the organization's Sixth Annual Meeting in Mobile, Alabama, and named the Federation's agenda issues in her essays—"The Mission of Motherhood," "How to Help Our Boys and Girls," "Problems of Negro Womanhood," and "How to Help the Fallen." She recorded the Federation's saving of money and charitable giving to construct black hospitals and schools. In "Child Saving in Alabama," she decries the incarceration of black boys with adult criminals, a primary concern of black mothers. To improve the circumstances of black youth, Washington and other black women members of Alabama's Federation of Colored Women's Clubs built Mt. Meigs, a reformatory school for black youth in Montgomery County.

Washington's essays, written when she was a FCWC member, are significant because they corroborate FCWC's belief in the moral imperative for racial and gender uplift work. "Child Saving in Alabama" (1908) asserts that the main purposes of club women "are to relieve suffering, to reclaim the erring, and to advance the cause of education."[11] The essay then details the agonizing struggle of the Alabama chapters of FCWC to find and finance humane accommodations for young black males found guilty of misdemeanors and sentenced to salt mines and adult prisons. Washington's "Four Years' Growth" (1908) confirms the women's arduous task of inciting moral sentiment for a reformatory project, squeezing money from meager purses to acquire it, buying land at twenty-five dollars per acre at Mt. Meigs to erect it, and collecting materials to furnish the five-bedroom reformatory. "Four Years' Growth" then acknowledges the Committee on Resolutions as saying, "We pledge ourselves anew to the work of child saving, realizing that in our young lives the hope of the race and that when we save the boy or girl of today, we save the man or the woman of tomorrow."[12] With a focus on safeguarding children, the essays articulate the club women's moral commitment to racial and gender uplift as essential to post-Reconstruction work.

"Impressions of a Southern Federation" (1904) notes the clubs' work to offer uplift in other areas of neglect. Club women raised money for charity, in order to provide food, fuel, and medicine for the ill. They paid tuition for students to attend private schools where public schools were overcrowded. Members made garments for the poor, gave clothing from their wardrobes, and furnished a room for the infirm in the charity ward of the local hospital. The essay adds: "Nor do [the members] make the giving of alms the limit of their service. They seek to elevate the tone of life in their communities; they stand for 'purity, for progress, for philanthropy, for peace.'"[13] "Impressions of a Southern Federation," "Child Saving in Alabama," and "Four Years' Growth" document Washington's commitment to racial elevation and her participation in community uplift efforts. In asserting a moral commitment to assist the less fortunate, Washington and her cohorts worked in conjunction with the black church, where most of the clubs' meetings were held.

Historically, the black church has played a major role in promoting racial uplift. After Emancipation, for instance, northern black independent churches sent representatives south to address the challenges that newly freed slaves encountered. Church representatives distributed food to freedmen and freedwomen, mediated their marital disputes, found employment for them, set up southern black independent churches, and founded schools. Better educated than most of their southern counterparts, northern black religious leaders seemed to have had a more focused vision of racial uplift needs. They also had access to more resources.

The African Methodist Episcopal Church, representing the oldest black denomination in America, was instrumental in establishing private schools for African Americans. It opened schools in the South for black men training for the ministry. Morris Brown College, named after the second AME bishop, was established in Atlanta, Georgia, in 1881. Another school, Brown Theological Institute, first chartered in 1872, was founded in Jacksonville, Florida, in 1866; it closed in the 1870s, reopened in 1883, and was renamed East Florida Conference High School and then Edward Waters College after the third AME bishop. These private AME Church schools made it possible for southern black men to obtain a higher education, which white public schools denied them. Their racial uplift curricula stressed spiritual, moral, and intellectual growth.

The AME Church pressed for blacks' uplift at the same time that white religious denominations also opened schools for blacks. The Seventh Day Adventists established Oakwood University in Huntsville, Alabama, in 1897. Catholics founded Xavier College in New Orleans, Louisiana, in 1925. The Baptist American Home Mission Society founded Richmond Theological School for Freedmen in Richmond, Virginia, in 1865, where, as a student, Washington wrote her earliest essays. The overall mission of these schools was to provide male leaders to advocate for a more just and humane world and for the elevation of the African American race.

Washington supported the black churches' educational uplift mission in her essays. She advocated a "moral aim" in education and quoted the black theologian Phillip Brooks as saying, "I do not know how any man can stand and plead with his brethren for the higher life unless he is perpetually conscious that round them whom he pleads there is the perpetual pleading and the voice of God Himself."[14] Washington urged that education should be pursued with an ethical consciousness, but her essays on education aimed higher than the goals of many black churches—to establish schools to train black men for the ministry. Her important treatises on higher education and coeducation criticized the lack of education available to women in church schools and emphasized the need for their education during a progressive educational reform movement in America.

The educational reform movement in nineteenth-century America brought many changes. Education was transformed from a private to public enterprise, from educating the rich to teaching the poor, and from patriarchal home instruction to maternal schooling. Samuel Bowles and Herbert Gintis argue that "manufacturers and merchants spearheaded the public-school expansions to instill in future workers a respect for law and authority necessary in the newly emerging capitalist economy."[15] The problem is that workers were predominantly male and white, and so were the teachers. Black and white women faced an uphill battle to overturn nineteenth-century patriarchal assumptions that the male was intellectually superior to the female,[16] that girls were unfit to study certain subjects, and that "the menstruating female, engaging in brain work, [made] herself susceptible to a host of ills," including "periodic hemorrhage, amenorrhoea, menorrhagia, dysmenorrhea, hysteria, anemia [and] chorea."[17] Even by blacks otherwise aggressively advocating a more just society, a black woman with an education was considered less deserving of a ministerial post in the AME Church than a man with equal learning. The historic case of Jarena Lee, who studied for the ministry but was denied ordination, is a case in point.[18] Jarena Lee believed that God had called her to preach. When she confided in Rev. Richard Allen, minister of the AME Church in Philadelphia, that she had received the call, Lee relates that he answered, "As to women preaching . . . our Discipline knew nothing at all about it . . . it did not call for women preachers."[19] Educating the female and helping her to attain public work were considered subversive to America's social order.

Thus, black women encountered gender exclusion in higher education. This discrimination came on the heels of the limited learning that southern whites felt was appropriate for blacks given their menial societal roles. Within post-Reconstruction African American schools, black women met with few opportunities for higher education that led to their receiving the baccalaureate degree. Expected to become wives and mothers, they were excluded from the planning of some early black colleges that the Baptist Missionary Association founded to train black male ministers. Predominantly black Lincoln College and Biddle College (now Johnson C. Smith University) did not admit women. When opportunities for higher education were present, the number of black women graduates fell below that of black males. In his study of black colleges from 1850 to 1898, W. E. B. Du Bois reports that "252 women," compared to "2,272 men," had obtained baccalaureate degrees.[20] Of these, 82 women had received degrees in northern white institutions.[21] The disparity between the graduation rates for black men and women was often attributed to limited postgraduation job opportunities for black women in southern black communities that prioritized the hiring of black men with families. As Jeffrey Williams argues, it was necessary for black men "to assert African American manhood and citizenship" and manifest their possession of "the intellectual and literary skills necessary for African Americans to contribute their own authoritative voices as equals to the nation's ongoing civic discussions."[22] Thus, many black women became discouraged, anticipating that their chances for utilizing their educational credentials might be thwarted. Opposed to this gender injustice, Washington insisted, "The very fact that woman has a mind capable of infinite expansion, is in itself an argument that she should receive the highest possible development."[23] Moreover, she cautioned young women to stay in school and graduate to prevent future regrets of "lost opportunities," especially if they were to marry poorly. She believed that young black women's personal efforts to improve themselves were necessary to elevate the race and women.

Washington's essays on education had an important place in the conversation about women's education in the nineteenth century. "Higher Education for Women," "A Plea for the Co-Education of the Sexes," "Teaching as a Profession," and "A Plea for the Moral Aim in Education" advanced the theme of women's

rights to a higher education and embraced the thinking of leading female re-
formers arguing for women's education based on their need and their intellectual ability for it. Among these women activists were Mary Mason Lyon,[24]
Emma Hart Willard,[25] Mary Julia Baldwin,[26] Anna Julia Cooper,[27] Lucy Craft
Laney,[28] Charlotte Hawkins Brown,[29] and Mary McLeod Bethune.[30] Black and
white women did not see their issues as united. Women generally sought educational reform to improve their status in America and to render themselves
more efficient and independent in their homes. Black women further aimed
to educate themselves to escape poverty and to lend service and uplift to the
race. Owing to the limited educational opportunities for black women, Washington argued, "the broad and true conception of the feminine[31] sphere is not
that bounded by men's prejudices and ideas of propriety, but a sphere appointed
by God and bounded by powers He has bestowed."[32] Her moral perspective
called into question the very idea of establishing Christian schools that excluded
women. But more importantly, her essays voiced a common belief in the black
community that education is the lever for success in America.

To serve the black community, African American presses likewise transported the written message of racial uplift. After the Civil War, black presses
began to flourish in the South. The periodicals they produced addressed uplift
relevant to the majority of blacks still residing in the South. Education, fru-
gality, temperance, landownership, and moral leaders dominated the pages of
affordable five-cent weeklies and monthlies. These periodicals welcomed the
uplift writings of the first generation of educated southern black women journalists, Washington among them. She and her female contemporaries Victoria
Earle Mathews (1861–1907) from Georgia, Mary Church Terrell (1863–1954)
from Tennessee, Alice Dunbar (1875–1935) from Louisiana, Mary Virginia Cook
(1868–1945) from Kentucky, Anna Julia Cooper (1858–1914) from North Carolina, and Ida B. Wells-Barnett (1862–1931) from Mississippi brought female
perspectives to black print culture and a desire to achieve both racial and gender uplift. The essay form allowed quick and frequent responses to public and
private issues and contributed to the timeliness of black print.

As a concerned journalist, Washington penned relevant uplift responses to
the post-Reconstruction nadir in African American life. In nationally published
black newspapers, her essays advised women on character building, pressed
for stability in black families, warned against racial mediocrity, exhorted race
heroes, acknowledged white friends of the race, insisted on higher education,
and pleaded for Christian morality. She extolled teaching as an honorable profession and reading poetry as a means to elevate the soul. She denounced war
and advocated support of the national government, even as blacks lost their
political positions in the South. Whether Washington wrote in the *People's
Advocate, Globe, Colored American Magazine,* the *A.M.E. Church Review,* or the
Virginia Star, she was always concerned about the race's future. She was as ad-

amant about saving the African American child as she was in extirpating "Negrophobes" dissembling as friends of the race. In "Anglo Saxon Supremacy" she warns, "We cannot with surety classify either our friends or our enemies by sections, but we recognize them when we find them."[33] Recognizing enemies was crucial to racial and gender uplift; it identified obstacles in the race's move toward progress. Washington insisted on blacks' vigilance, self-help, and moral conduct as the means to dispel others' negative perceptions of black men and women. This urgent desire to achieve something better for African Americans was deeply infused in Washington and enabled her to respond forthrightly to uplift missions of African American conferences, churches, and periodicals.

Literary Context: The Evolution of the Black Press and Washington's Essay Contributions to It

The first African American press evolved in 1817 with the founding of AME Book Concern, the publishing house of the AME Church.[34] Its beginning reveals the historic interest that religious organizations took in black print culture. Early black publications related to church law, hymnals, and proceedings. As print culture developed and as the race advanced in education, literary forms appeared in print. This print culture, as Frances Smith Foster assesses it, "became a primary tool in constructing African America, in ensuring the protection and progress of the 'race' or the 'nation' not only in defending themselves from libelous or ignorant attacks by other Americans but even more for constructing individual and group definitions and for advocating behaviors and philosophies that were positive and purposeful."[35] A lifelong member of the AME Church and a contributor to two AME publications—the *A.M.E. Church Review* and the *Christian Recorder*—Washington found these church journals appropriate conveyances for her racial uplift essays, purposed to construct individual behavior for a more positive group identification in the post-Reconstruction South. Expressive of her interests in all aspects of black life, Washington's essays bring a literary dynamism to the evolving black press in four specific ways: as disrupter of the nineteenth-century African American literary canon; as a precursor to the race womanhood ideology depicted in later nineteenth-century black women's novels; as links to biblical scriptures and to British and American literature; and as a guide to the black press, noting its aesthetic needs and responsibilities in its endeavor to establish a reputable literary sphere.

First, Washington's essays complicated the notion that the male-dominated and exclusionary slave narrative is the preferred genre representing post-Reconstruction African American literature. Many post–Civil War slave narratives aimed to uplift the race through education or the ministry. Most were written by men. The more familiar are James Lindsay Smith's *Autobiography of James L. Smith, Including, Also, Reminiscences of Slave Life, Recollections of the War, Education of Freedmen, Causes of the Exodus, etc.* (1881); Booker T. Washington's *Up from Slavery* (1901); Francis Frederick's *Autobiography of Rev. Francis Frederick of Virginia* (1869); and Josiah Henson's *An Autobiography of the Rev. Josiah Henson from 1789 to 1876* (1876). These were important narratives manifesting the authors' progress as ex-slaves and their missions to uplift others. Yet, as Eric Gardner affirms, "Slave narratives were not *all* of nineteenth-century literature. That field of texts did not simply include a handful of bound books that focused on men and, less often, women becoming unbound from American slavery, though such texts, again, were crucial."[36] Just as crucial were the unrecognized or forgotten African American serialized novels, short stories, poems, and essays, the authors of many of which had not been slaves.

Washington complicates the prominent position of slave narratives because her more inclusive essays were written from the perspective of a freeborn black woman whose concerns involved a broader vantage point than did slave narratives. Not restricted to subjects related to education and clerical duties, Washington's essays expanded from one's civic duty to the government, to the remedy for international war, to women's right to work in the public sphere, to child saving, to social responsibilities, and to the benefits of reading literature. Her essays exceeded the two-part narrative arrangement (slavery, freedom) of post–Civil War slave narratives to admit formats of argumentation and proposal. Culturally relevant, content worthy, and aesthetically written, Washington's essays are among the recovered literary pieces necessary for reforming a restricted nineteenth-century African American literary canon.

Second, Washington's essays paved the way for the race womanhood ideology depicted in later nineteenth-century African American novels. In doing so, they helped to invalidate "the true womanhood" ideology as the only doctrine to follow for black women's progress. Tied to the "cult of domesticity," the traditional view of "true womanhood" framed a nineteenth-century, middle-class value system for white women, detailing their relations to home, family, and work.[37] Pivoting around four traits—domesticity, piety, purity, and submissiveness[38]—the "true womanhood" theory promoted the spiritual and domestic woman and supported patriarchal superiority in the home. Black women were excluded from this construction of womanhood, owing to their history of slavery that classified them as chattel property and denied them marriage rights.

The true womanhood ideology proved to be insufficient for black women. In her attempt to reframe the work that nineteenth-century black women were doing, Brittney C. Cooper, a gender studies critic, opines, "Black women did not have the luxury of confining their advocacy for the shaping of Black moral, social, or intellectual life strictly to the domestic realm."[39] To define a gendered race leadership, Cooper summons a "race womanhood" ideology, a term she borrowed from Pauline Hopkins's 1902 essay "Some Literary Workers." Cooper argues that there was a "codified . . . set of practices and discussions which Black female race leaders had been engaging in since the early 1890s."[40] Primary among the practices Cooper lists are obtaining an education and engaging in uplift work. Although Cooper does not mention any writer using race woman-hood ideas before the 1890s, Washington was more than twenty years ahead of Pauline Hopkins in setting forth her ideas for race women.

In addition to advocating education and racial uplift work, Washington was concerned about the psychological and physical effects that might impact black women should they fail to improve themselves. Young girls dropping out of school and marrying poorly doomed themselves to a life of misery, including loneliness, depression, poverty, physical exhaustion, and poor health. Unlike Brittney Cooper, who looks beyond the home for "the shaping of black moral, social, or intellectual life," Washington locates the home as the important start-ing place for black girls to elevate themselves to avoid "lost opportunities."

As a race woman, Washington found the "true womanhood" ideology limited in the 1880s. It did not take into consideration all the characteristics necessary for the race work that needed to be done to ready masses of young black women for competent work in the private and public spheres. To prepare black women for racial uplift work, Washington stressed personal nobility and education. In "Notes to Girls, No. 1," she writes: "It is for you who are daily maturing [in] character to emulate the brightest examples, and to strive to show womanhood in its highest nobility. These early girlish days of comparative ease and irrespon-sibility are given you to fit yourselves for a broader place of action."[41] "A broader place of action" is the public space beyond the domicile in which women have historically functioned as mothers and wives, dependent on and subject to the whims of the male head. In the public sphere, nobility coupled with educa-tion were requisites for uplift leadership. In "Higher Education for Women," Washington argues, "The possession of a higher education multiplies woman's bread-winning opportunities."[42] With an education, a woman has many oppor-tunities to work in uplift situations. Inside the home, she can "be a fountain of knowledge to her family"; outside the home, she can aid others. In the compro-mised home situations in which many young black women found themselves, nobility and education were necessary assets to achieve race womanhood.

Washington's emphasis on nobility and education in her 1880s "Notes to Girls" prefigures the protagonists' reliance on these resources to combat adver-sity in the novels of Pauline Hopkins and Frances Harper. In presenting their young mulatto protagonists, Hopkins and Harper situate them in dangerous domestic situations. In *Contending Forces*, fifteen-year-old Mabelle Beaubean must endure the misogynist hatred of a white uncle, who kidnaps her and places her in a New Orleans brothel to support his lifestyle. The uncle's motives repudi-ate the idea that a female with Negro blood possesses any purity, as he reasons, "What does a woman with mixed blood, or any Negress, for that matter, know of virtue? It is my belief that they were a direct creation by God to be the pleasant companions of men of my race."[43] Reinventing herself as Sappho Clark, the protagonist presents an outward demeanor of nobility, doubly manifested in the domestic transformation she makes in decorating her room in white as a symbol of purity. Ready for uplift service, she publicly acknowledges her abandoned son and vows, "I will take a mother's place and do my duty."[44] In Frances Harper's *Iola Leroy,* Iola's deficit in the home is a submissive mother whose obedience to her racist husband forbids her to inform Iola of her Negro identity. Iola's less than noble attitude toward Negroes is rehabilitated upon her discovery of her true racial identity at a white prep school. Turning to racial uplift as teacher and nurse, she strives "to be [a] moral and spiritual [force] among a people who so much needed [her] helping hands."[45]

Similar to Washington's essays, *Iola Leroy* and *Contending Forces* suggest that deficits in the home often retard a noble and intellectual upbringing in black females. Triumphing over a domineering patriarchy and learning a lesson from a submissive mother hasten the racial and gender usefulness of female youth. As uplift agents, Iola and Mabelle undergo the real-life struggles nineteenth-century black females encountered. Drawn from a revised image of true white womanhood, they don the mantle of "true race women" while mirroring the young girls receiving advice in Washington's prophetic essays.

Washington's third literary contribution to the black press is her use of world literatures to support her uplift argument that blacks are not alone in their uplift struggles. She employed the classics (Aristotle and Plato), the English (William Shakespeare, Matthew Arnold, and Thomas Babington Macaulay), the Americans (Ralph Waldo Emerson, Henry Longfellow, and Mark Twain), and women (Felicia Hemans and Elizabeth Barrett Browning). She borrowed from the Bible, women's articles, and contemporary journals. From all these, she culled the idea that mankind has been historically and universally concerned about the betterment of the human condition. The details informed black press readers of humans' avid struggle for improvement, often with the intent to fulfill a spiritual need, to obviate social adversity, to correct personal failings, or to foster industry. Washington's borrowings are valued as a source of strength and self-preservation to African Americans in times of adversity.

Washington's literary adoptions also provide uplift models of responsible citizenship in her essays. "Paul's Trade and What Use He Made of It" offers the biblical account of Paul as a model laborer and responsible citizen. A Jewish tent maker by trade, Paul used his business in Corinth to support himself and to drive out commercial sycophants. He even preached in the temple, lived by the gospel, and remained circumspect in his personal life. Paul had been reared according to the wisdom of a rabbi's maxim: "He who does not teach his son a trade, teaches him to steal."[46] The proverb teaches that one's failure to support himself precipitates hunger and renders him a parasite to others.

The young Washington wrote "Paul's Trade and What Use He Made of It" in 1884 in response to many African Americans' reluctance to accept industrial education as a means to elevate the race. Ironically, this aversion to manual labor coincided with the rise of industrial education as a college curriculum for blacks, first at Hampton Institute and then at Tuskegee Institute under Booker T. Washington's leadership. Booker T. Washington argued, "I plead for industrial education and development for the Negro not because I want to cramp him, but because I want to free him."[47] His detractors W. E. B. Du Bois and Henry Monroe Trotter advocated a liberal education that included the classics and foreign languages. At the time, the majority of blacks knew little other than physical toil to survive, and many lived in segregated areas where whites denied them an education and equal employment in nonindustrial jobs. Washington's biblical model of Paul affirms the value of manual labor and supports her thinking that "physical labor is not incompatible with mental culture and a high degree of spirituality."[48] The lowliest jobs provide the laborer with opportunity to think about and start useful projects to benefit self and others. The result is a responsible citizenship in an improving community.

In "The Benefits of Trouble," Washington turns to Henry Wadsworth Longfellow's *Hyperion* (1839) for a model survivor of adversity in the character of Paul Flemming. Overcome with grief from his failed relationship with Fanny Appleton, Flemming is the autobiographical portrayal of Longfellow, who was consumed with sorrow over the 1835 death of his first wife, Mary Storer Potter, from a miscarriage. Both men used their overwhelming depression as a springboard to gallant undertakings. Flemming traveled to Germany; Longfellow translated German poetry and produced *Ballads and Others Poems* in 1841.

Flemming's declaration, "I will be strong"[49] announces his restoration. The catalyst for his renewal comes in the form of a ghostlike funeral tablet during his visit to a remote European chapel. The dead one seems to speak as Flemming reads the inscription: "Look not mournfully into the Past. It comes not back again. Wisely improve the Present. It is thine. Go forth to meet the shadowy Future, without fear, and with a manly heart."[50] The inscription pointing the way to Flemming's future leads him in the direction of a viable life and thus uplifts him.

In "The Benefits of Trouble," Washington uses Paul Flemming's response to adversity to argue that suffering brings strength. Suffering "trains courage," "secures self-control," and "makes us wise." Washington believes that "a noble character is best formed by the discipline of suffering."[51] Through discipline, one can elevate the self in physical, mental, and spiritual domains, thus increasing one's capacity to assist others.

In 1882, when "The Benefits of Trouble" was published, Washington, like Paul Flemming, faced adversity. The *Virginia Star,* the one newspaper to have published all of Washington's previous essays, went out of business. For a twenty-two-year-old teacher and writer giving uplift advice to an appreciative local community, the newspaper's demise must have been devastating. Strengthening her resolve to continue writing, Washington began to submit her articles to a variety of emerging black newspapers, thus minimizing anxiety from future downturns in the black publishing industry. Her strength proved to be advantageous; her essays were subsequently printed and preserved in most newspapers.

In addition to using literary models to make a case for racial uplift, Washington turns to poetry to argue for its uplifting benefits. Her reason for introducing poetry as an elevating medium is to appeal to those people "who pride themselves upon being what they call 'practical,' and who look with contempt upon anything verging on sentiment."[52] The "practical" are identified as those of the middle class interested in making money, playing the stock market, and deciding what to eat, drink, and wear. These people see nothing interesting in the *Iliad* and thus go "through life maimed in soul, dwarfed and incomplete."[53] Their obstructed self-elevation is regarded as a form of "blundering stupidity" not unlike that found in Mr. Gradgrind in Charles Dickens's novel *Hard Times* (1854).

A primary benefit of poetry is its capacity to transport one to a world beyond the intellect. Wordsworth identifies this sphere as the imagination. It possesses "The glorious faculty assigned / To elevate the more-than reasoning mind / And color life's dark cloud with orient rays."[54] Poetry's elevating agency allows one to suspend the woes of the common world and to put aside petty annoyances. The solace may be brief, but its reprieve is calming and uplifting.

Washington cites poets calmed by their own poetic musings as validation of poetry's worth. Confined to a hospital for psychotic behavior, the Italian poet Tasso "relieved the gloom of his lonely cell with the splendid scenes of his *Jerusalem*."[55] Bereft of his dear friend Arthur Henry Hallam, Alfred, Lord Tennyson wrote "In Memoriam" over a seventeen-year period. The poets' healings through their own verses empower others to seek comfort in poetry.

A second benefit of poetry is its humanitarian influence. Washington was especially cognizant of the role of poetry and songs in the troubled lives of African Americans and women. She refers to John Greenleaf Whittier's and Henry Wadsworth Longfellow's antislavery poems that "helped to break the chain which bound the slaves."[56] She saw value in "the rude rhymes of the oppressed, sung amid the toil of the field, [which] tended to ease the burden of pain at their hearts."[57] She cites Elizabeth Barrett Browning's blank-verse novel *Aurora Leigh* (1857) as one taking a stand against inhumanity and presenting "a nobler conception of womanhood."[58] Prioritizing human welfare, the poetry of Whittier, Longfellow, and Browning promoted social reform, just as the field songs salved the slaves' wounds.

A third benefit of poetry is its spiritualizing effect. It appeals to the soul rather than to corporeity. Edgar Allan Poe claims that poetry produces "an elevating excitement of the soul quite independent of that passion which is the intoxication of the heart, or of that truth which is the satisfaction of the reason."[59] Poetry stimulates the psyche and lifts one above the intellect and the passions. It can be especially beneficial to an oppressed race or gender because it stirs the soul to action and wills a moral ethos that transitions to the expectation of a liberating immortality.

The transportable, humanitarian, and spiritualizing effects of poetry are salves for racial and gender despondency. These beneficial results uplift the soul, spur serviceable humane work, and activate pious reform. Washington's essay borrowings from other literatures are significant for informing black press readers of poetry's benefits in the race's crucial uplift strategy. Her essays on poetry's benefits prove especially advantageous to the black press interested in expanding its print material to include the poetic genre.

Washington's fourth contribution to the black press is informing it of its aesthetic needs and responsibilities to uplift black print culture. The black press often provided the only outlet for the publication of African American novels, short stories, poems, and essays, and Washington's advice is indispensable to a publishing enterprise expecting to flourish in the American literary sphere. By 1889, when Washington published her essay "Needs of Our Newspapers: Some Reasons for Their Existence," fewer than a half dozen African American novels had been published by independent publishers, and two novels, William Wells Brown's *Clotel, or the President's Daughter* (1853) and Frank Webb's *The Garies and Their Friends* (1857), had the imprint of London publishers, owing to Brown's attack on Thomas Jefferson and Webb's assault on America's denial of mixed-race marriages. The first African American short-story collection did not appear until Alice Moore published *Violets and Other Tales* in 1895. Only two well known and often anthologized black poets, Phillis Wheatley and George Moses Horton, had offered their lyrics in bound volumes. David Walker published his essays in *The Appeal* (1830) in book form. With a paucity of black literature finding its way into single-authored books, black newspapers became the publisher-caretaker of most African American literature. As a frequent contributor to black newspapers, Washington became concerned about the self-limiting aspects plaguing some of the race's publications. In her essay "Needs of Our Newspapers: Some Reasons for Their Existence," she addresses these concerns under the categories of "intrinsic and extrinsic" requirements.

An inherent necessity for black newspapers, according to Washington, is to vet their contributors. "To secure the best writers" should be prioritized without concern for what people think. Washington writes, "Now, if people think that because they take a certain paper that paper ought to print any and all of their senseless effusions, [the sooner] they are disabused of this idea, the better for them individually and for the race collectively."[60] By publishing the best writers, the black press uplifts readers and elevates the status of black newspapers.

Washington further advocates "more original and less patent matter."[61] One sheet of original work "would accomplish more for the race" than several sheets of previously published material, even though more effort is required to produce the former.[62] Washington suggests that publishing material printed elsewhere offers no news and wastes the reader's time. In addition, original matter should include neither abuse of other writers nor excessive praise for modest endeavors. For the sake of racial elevation, publishers must be cognizant of and accountable for the material they publish.

What is published is as important as how it is published. Washington advocates "the improvement of the mechanical makeup of the paper." Misspelled words, subject-verb disagreement, omission and displacement of words, phrases, and parts of sentences cause better writers to shun publishing their works in certain newspapers. Greater supervision over copyeditors and typesetters could solve the problems.

Washington identifies subscriber support as the greatest extrinsic need of black newspapers. Support fails to come when newspapers show poor maintenance, print the same material, charge more than white-owned newspapers, and disparage black-owned businesses. Washington points to the excellent quality of the *New York Age, Detroit Plaindealer,* and *Cleveland Gazette,* but she never mentions the newspapers that did a poor job of publishing her own essays. Rather, she advises the African American editor not to be "discouraged because of imperfections, but persevere in his efforts to work out the salvation of his people."[63] After all, the black editor was critical to his paper's success in the American literary sphere, and Washington's "Needs of Our Newspapers" is a serious reminder to publishers of what to prioritize in their plan for survival.

The significance of Washington's essays can be gleaned from the historical context of racial and gender uplift in which they were written and from their literary contributions to an emerging black press. Written during the post-Reconstruction era, a time of debilitating racial and gender oppression, Washington's essays aligned with the uplift missions of women's clubs, churches, and the black press. They charted a Christian path toward progress, prescribing moral behavior, education, political duty, community service, rehabilitation of youth, and reasoned admonishment to those harboring race and gender prejudice. As literary contributions to the black press, her essays played havoc with the nineteenth-century African American literary canon prioritizing slave narratives; they paved the way for a gendered uplift ideology depicted in later nineteenth-century African American novels; they linked to biblical, British, and American literatures fostering Christian models applicable to blacks' uplift struggles; and they apprised the black press of its needs and responsibilities to achieve repute in America's literary arena. Relevant, insightful, and substantive, Washington's essays emerged from the pen of a unique writer who launched her career as a teenager when most blacks in the South could not read, write, or cipher. Her treatises are delivered from the perspective of a southern black Christian intellectual appealing to whites for common justice and advising members of her race and gender on how to rise above the commonplace. The recovery of these essays is long overdue.

The following sections comprise Josephine J. Turpin Washington's works on racial and gender uplift. Presented thematically and chronologically in eight annotated sections, Washington's essays provide a crucial understanding of how one southern black woman confronted race and gender discrimination: she demanded educational imperatives, supported a work ethic, and advised Christian benevolence to promote the uplift of African Americans and women.

Part 1, "Educational Imperatives," focuses on Washington's views regarding urgent educational reforms needed to elevate blacks and to empower women. These needs include the coeducation of the sexes, higher education for women, a moral aim in education, well-trained teachers, and students graduating from college. She writes from her own experiences of having to leave Virginia to obtain higher education in a coeducational setting and working in environments in which blacks demanded that black teachers be allowed to teach black students.

Expanding the educational imperatives theme, part 2, "Literary Enhancement," points to literature as a requisite for elevating the intellect and the person. Two essays posit that poetry "ennobles [a person's] whole nature" and fits [that individual] for the better performance of any duty ("The Province of Poetry" and "Holland's 'Kathrina'"). Her prose encourages black men to become "giants in intellectual strength, warriors in the cause of right and justice" ("Anglo-African Magazine"). The essays employ literature as an educational pivot to intellectual refinement that spurs race and gender elevation.

Part 3, "Gender Propriety," advocates a work ethic as a vehicle to woman's "highest nobility" and to racial uplift. Work is measured by the effort one takes to enhance one's character, whether by appearance or by activities. In "Notes to Girls" and in four other essays, two of which she writes under her pseudonym "Joyce," Washington characterizes work as Christian behavior that generates proper attire, domestic accomplishments, cleanliness, educational achievement, and self-respect.

Part 4, "Civic Duty," transforms work into a moral obligation. "What the Citizen Owes the Government" asks citizens to render all services to the government, including paying taxes and voting. Each citizen must "be ready to [do] every good work" for the good of the community. "The Remedy for War" argues that even though Christian civilizations have lessened the frequency of wars, the "inefficiency to accomplish desired ends" in war necessitates work to achieve a remedy. The essay proposes "a definite code of law for nations" and an internal tribunal to enforce the code. The author's aspirations for an international tribunal stem from Europe's incursions into Africa and Asia for colonization purposes and from America's fear that its place in global markets would be compromised.

Part 5, "Societal Responsibility," extends the work ethic to African Americans' duty to be socially mindful. They must be aware of their words so as not to offend others ("Unwise Talkers"); they must bear adversity while securing self-control and maintaining strength ("The Benefits of Trouble"); and they must be less "indifferent to the quality of . . . material [published] in colored newspapers" ("Needs of Our Newspapers"). Embracing a broad spectrum, from rules of self-conduct to accountability in newspaper production, the work ethic invests self-awareness in the racial uplift paradigm.

For their work productivity and moral standing, six self-made men, black and white, are celebrated in part 6, "Personal Tributes." These men are Wendell Phillips, orator; Frederick Douglass, abolitionist; Charles Dickens, writer; T. Thomas Fortune, founder of the National League; William McKinley, president of the United States; and William Paterson, president of the State Normal School in Montgomery, Alabama. Their industry to enhance their lives serves as an uplift model to follow.

Part 7, "Racial Defense," recommends Christian benevolence in the face of bigotry, which impedes racial uplift. "A Great Danger" advises Annie Porter to exercise kindness toward blacks rather than rail against what she perceives as their religious superstitions, sloth, and barbarism. The essay suggests that Porter's inattention to the race's improvement signals her "ignoble prejudices." "Anglo Saxon Supremacy" counters whites' lies inhibiting philanthropy to blacks from other, well-meaning whites. The essay summons the Christian spirit of benevolence and presumes that racial uplift cannot be achieved without whites' generosity.

Part 8, "Women's Club Work," highlights the Alabama State Federation of Colored Women's Clubs (FCWC) and its uplift projects. An organization in which Washington actively participated, the Alabama FCWC established "a reformatory for wayward [black] boys" to prevent their incarceration in prison with hardened adult criminals ("Impressions of a Southern Federation" and "Child Saving in Alabama"), and it assisted the fallen in the race ("Four Years' Growth"). Club women requested and received space in the *Colored Alabamian*, a local newspaper, to solicit donations for its uplift efforts ("A Card—To the Women's Clubs of Alabama"). The Alabama FCWC also needed its helpers' "constant cultivation of a prayerful, earnest and consecrated spirit" as much as it desired material goods to give to the impoverished ("12th Annual Meeting of the State Federation of Women's Clubs"). Christian benevolence is evident in the five essays in this section as a supporting factor in the uplift efforts of the Alabama FCWC.

The Collected Essays of Josephine J. Turpin Washington presents an African American woman's ongoing uplift efforts to make a difference in the lives of blacks during the post-Reconstruction era. These essays link to and expand the uplift endeavors in which blacks have historically engaged. Their emphasis on education, responsibility, and morality as levers to racial acceptance and progress are grounded in a racial uplift culture that African American churches, conventions, and conferences endorsed. Enlarging the tradition, *The Collected Essays* argues for the advancement of women as a necessary corollary to racial uplift.

Notes

1. For the sake of clarity, I refer to Josephine Turpin Washington throughout this volume by her married surname, Washington.

2. This editorial comment appears on the same page in the *Virginia Star* as does Washington's essay "The Benefits of Trouble."

3. Lamb, *Howard University Medical Department,* 226–27.

4. Washington taught at Selma University (1888–89), Tuskegee Institute (1893–96), and Lincoln Normal School, now Alabama State University (1900–1913).

5. Washington penned the anthem for Alabama's FCWC (see appendix A), and she dedicated "Cedar Hill Saved" to the organization (see appendix B).

6. *Proceedings of the National Conference of Colored Men,* 96.

7. "Address of Josephine St. P. Ruffin, President of the Conference," 32.

8. "Minutes of the First National Conference of Colored Women," 11. The following quotation can be found on the same page.

9. "National Association of Colored Women's Clubs," 1.

10. J. T. Washington, "12th Annual Meeting of the State Federation of Women's Clubs," 180.

11. Josephine T. Washington, "Child Saving in Alabama," 170.

12. Josephine T. Washington, "Four Years' Growth," 176.

13. Josephine T. Washington, "Impressions of a Southern Federation," 168.

14. Josephine T. Washington, "A Plea for the Moral Aim in Education," 27.

15. Bowles and Gintis, *Schooling in Capitalist America,* 178–79.

16. Charles Darwin, the leading nineteenth-century evolutionist, perceived woman as intellectually inferior to man. Before his marriage to his cousin Emma Wedgewood, Darwin regarded woman only as "a constant companion (friend in old age) who will feel interested in one, object to be loved and played with—better than a dog anyhow—Home, and someone to take care of house" (see Darwin, *The Autobiography of Charles Darwin,* 232–33).

17. Clarke, *Sex in Education,* 48.

18. Lee, *The Religious Experience and Journal of Mrs. Jarena Lee,* 11.

19. Ibid.

20. Du Bois, *The College-Bred Negro,* 55.

21. Ibid., 56.

22. Williams, "Racial Uplift," n.p.

23. Josephine J. Turpin, "Higher Education for Women," 3.

24. Mary Mason Lyon (1797–1849), a women's rights' activist. In 1837, she founded America's first female college, Mount Holyoke Female Seminary (now Mount Holyoke College), in South Hadley, Massachusetts. She offered a curriculum for women similar to that used in male schools. It included mathematics and science to enable women to compete in the competitive masculine world (E. Green, *Mary Lyon and Mt. Holyoke*).

25. Emma Hart Willard (1787–1870), a New England pioneer in women's education. In 1814, she opened a female seminary in Waterford, New York, despite the New York legislature's rejection of her proposal to do so. In 1821, she moved the seminary to Troy, New York, where the city council provided four thousand dollars for the purchase of a building for the school's use. Named the Troy Female Seminary, this independent boarding school offered advanced courses for females comparable to those offered in all-male colleges (A. Scott, "The Ever-Widening Circle," 3–5).

26. Mary Julia Baldwin (1829–1897), principal of Augusta Female Seminary in Staunton, Virginia, in 1863. It had been her alma mater, which the ravages of the Civil War threatened to close. Presiding for thirty-four years at the school, Baldwin developed a curriculum similar to that at University of Virginia for male matriculating students. Two years before her death, the school was renamed Mary Baldwin Seminary to commemorate her work. In 1923, the school was renamed Mary Baldwin College (Watters, *The History of Mary Baldwin College*, 65–88, 203, 313).

27. Anna Julia Cooper (1858–1964), a lifelong African American educator and defender of women's learning. As a young woman, she tutored students at St. Augustine's Normal School and Collegiate Institute in Raleigh, North Carolina, where she protested women's exclusion from upper-level courses designed for men studying theology. She taught at M Street School (now Paul Laurence Dunbar High School) in Washington, D.C., and later became president of Frelinghuysen University, an adult learning institution that extended an education to both sexes of poor, black working-class D.C. residents. In the 1930s, Cooper rented out her home at 201 T Street, NW, Washington, D.C., for the university to hold its classes. Her concern for African American women's education manifests further in her speech "The Needs and Status of Black Women," presented at the World's Columbian Exposition in 1893, and in her essay "The Higher Education of Women," published in *A Voice from the South* (1892). Cooper is honored on the United States' Forever stamp for her career as an educator and defender of women's rights (K. Johnson, *Uplifting the Women and the Race*).

28. Lucy Craft Laney (1854–1933), a distinguished African American educator. She founded the Haines Normal and Industrial Institute in Augusta, Georgia, in 1886. Intended as an all-girls' institution, the school opened to boys and girls owing to the chronic need for education among blacks in the region. She believed the sanctity of the home and the moral integrity of the black woman were educational keys to uplift the race (Patton, "Lucy Craft Laney, 226–27).

29. Charlotte Hawkins Brown (1883–1961) founded her own school in Sedalia, North Carolina, at nineteen years of age. The opportunity came after the American Missionary Association (AMA) closed the one-room school where she taught a class of fifty students. With the community desiring her to remain, she was given fifteen acres of land and an old building where she began work and named the school Alice Freeman

Palmer Institute after her white benefactress (Thompson, "Brown, Charlotte Hawkins," 172–74).

30. Mary McLeod Bethune (1875–1955) established Daytona Normal and Industrial Institute for Negro Girls in 1904 for the female children of black workers who had migrated to Daytona Beach to work on the East Coast Railway. With $1.50 and five female students, Bethune initiated a curriculum of reading, writing, arithmetic, and vocational training in sewing, husbandry, and household skills. In 1923, Daytona Normal and Industrial Institute for Negro Girls merged with the all-male Cookman Institute in Jacksonville, Florida, to become the Daytona Cookman Collegiate Institute. The curriculum expanded to include teacher training for women, while men studied for the ministry. The traditional curriculum for women also remained intact. The new school was renamed Bethune-Cookman College in honor of Mary McLeod Bethune and Alfred Cookman, a Methodist minister who financed the first building for Cookman Institute (Holt, *Mary McLeod Bethune*).

31. The original reads "feminize."

32. Turpin, "A Plea for the Co-Education of the Sexes," 11.

33. Josephine Turpin Washington, "Anglo Saxon Supremacy," 157.

34. Gardner, *Black Print Unbound*, 26.

35. Foster, "A Narrative of the Interesting Origins," 714.

36. Gardner, *Black Print Unbound*, 13.

37. For an overview of "True Womanhood" ideology, see Keister and Southgate, *Inequality: A Contemporary Approach to Race, Class, and Gender*, 228; Lavender, "Notes on the Cult of Domesticity and True Womanhood," 1–2; and Lindley, *You Have Stept out of Your Place*, 53.

38. Welter, "The Cult of True Womanhood," 152.

39. Cooper, *Beyond Respectability*, 13.

40. Ibid., 12.

41. "Joyce" [Turpin], "Notes to Girls, No. 1," 63. The following quotation is also found on page 63.

42. Josephine J. Turpin, "Higher Education for Women," 5.

43. Hopkins, *Contending Forces*, 69.

44. Ibid., 350.

45. This and the following quotation are taken from Harper's *Iola Leroy*, 200.

46. The maxim is a variation of the verse found in 2 Thess. 3:10.

47. B. T. Washington, "The Industrial Education for the Negro," n.p.

48. Josephine J. Turpin, "Paul's Trade," 109.

49. Longfellow, *Hyperion*, bk. 4, chap. 8, p. 370.

50. Ibid., 369.

51. J. J. Turpin, "The Benefits of Trouble," 103.

52. Josephine Turpin Washington, "The Province of Poetry," 48.

53. Ibid.

54. Wordsworth, "Weak Is the Will of Man," 134–35.

55. Josephine Turpin Washington, "The Province of Poetry," 55.

56. Ibid., 56.

57. Ibid., 56.
58. Ibid., 56.
59. Poe, "The Poetic Principle," 254. Poe capitalizes "Soul," "Heart," "Truth," and "Reason."
60. Josephine Turpin Washington, "Needs of Our Newspapers," 112.
61. Ibid.
62. Ibid.
63. Ibid.

Editor's Notes

The Collected Essays of Josephine J. Turpin Washington continues the legacy of recovering the hidden works of nineteenth-century African American women identified in the edited, multivolume *Schomburg Library of Nineteenth-Century Black Women Writers* published in 1998. I began accumulating Josephine Turpin Washington's works in 1989 with only three available historical references to her works: Irvine Garland Penn's *The Afro-American Press and Its Editors* (1891); Lawson A. Scruggs's *Women of Distinction: Remarkable in Works and Invincible in Character* (1893); and Mrs. N. F. Mossell's *The Work of the Afro-American Woman* (1894). The authors of these works were Washington's contemporaries and had read her essays; Penn and Scruggs were native Virginians, as was Washington. None provided citations for Washington's works they had read in various newspapers, and none indicated where these newspapers containing Washington's essays could be found. Although collecting Josephine Joyce Turpin Washington's essays presented enormous challenges, it was a labor of love. As I searched for her writings found mostly in post-Reconstruction African American newspapers and magazines, three challenges were foremost: locating, assessing, and editing her works.

Locating Washington's essays involved a three-decade search. In the late 1980s, I sat for hours at microfilm machines with right-hand cranks as I tediously searched for Washington's works in nonindexed newspapers. When I did find an essay of hers, I could barely contain my elation. Photocopying the work, however, proved nearly as arduous as finding the newspaper with her essays in it. *The People's Advocate,* an Alexandria, Virginia, African American weekly, published from 1876 until 1879, was one of several newspapers with six columns, measuring 17″ × 22″; it was an odd fit for the face of an 11″ × 17″ copier. Often segments of one page had to be copied numerous times in order to reproduce the entire page.

A daunting challenge was the search for Washington's first published essay, "A Talk about Church Fairs" (1877). Lawson A. Scruggs and Irvine Garland Penn cite this essay as having been published in the *Virginia Star* (1877–82), a weekly sold for five cents a copy. I discovered that most issues of this publication, the only African American newspaper published in Richmond at the time, were missing. The only other 1877 extant and nationally digitized issue of the *Virginia Star* is that for 8 September 1877. Washington's essay is not present in this September issue. Neither is it in the next extant issue, dated 14 December 1878.

According to Scruggs, Washington's essay "was a good thrust at intemperance, against selling wine at entertainments for church benefit." Irvine Garland Penn adds that the essay "elicited much favorable comment." Scruggs and Penn date the beginning of Washington's publishing career with this essay. However, my search for this work has yielded nothing.

A considerable effort was taken also to locate the *Industrial Herald,* an African American newspaper to which Mrs. N. F. Mossell claimed Washington contributed. Mossell writes, "Among [Washington's] most popular productions are probably the following: a series of descriptive papers written in *The Industrial Herald* of Richmond, during a six-weeks' stay in New York and Boston, in the summer of 1883." Mossell's quotation is found in Penn's *The African American Press and Its Editors,* but the newspaper cannot be found.

I abandoned the project until the turn of the twenty-first century, when I assessed the value of Washington's work and decided the essays have merit for several reasons. First, they present the unique voice of a post-Reconstruction black woman writer in African American literary studies, enabling scholars to expand their knowledge of African American history, women's studies, studies in black periodical writing, and southern regional studies. Second, the essays make significant contributions to an emerging post-Reconstruction black press, as they present Washington's observations and salient comments about race and gender progress in the South at a time when the masses of African Americans were still illiterate. Third, they identify Washington as a connoisseur of English and American literature, from which she has extracted providential sayings and moral characters to use as models in her racial and gender uplift instruction, thereby enhancing the literary sphere of the black press. Not only do the essays provide historical context for racial and gender ideology in the post-Reconstruction era in which they were written, but they also make a substantial contribution to African American literary studies and to black print culture.

After assessing the value of Washington's essays, I began editing them. Editing demanded careful attention, but I took a conservative approach. I have made corrections only when necessary. I took this path since nineteenth-century English differs considerably from twenty-first-century English and since the quality of many African American periodicals often fell short due to lack of staffing and to inadequate funding. I changed obvious typographical errors including misspellings (e.g., littlh to little), repeated words (e.g., and and), and missing double quotation marks at the end of a quoted passage. When part of an infinitive is missing, I inserted "to" in brackets. I also modernized archaic spellings (e.g., moulded to molded). These emendations are identified in the notes section. I also joined compound words (to day, some one, some how, and can not) to construct modern one-word spellings. Owing to the abundance of these compound words in Washington's essays, I changed the compound word to one word in the text without pointing to each one in the notes. All changes were made in the interest of clarity, consistency, and correctness.

Other peculiarities remain uncorrected. When a section of a sentence has been omitted or smudged beyond readability, I bracketed a question mark in the space. I left unchanged inconsistent punctuation of sentences leading to fragments and run-ons. I also left unpunctuated the introductory clauses not followed by a comma.

Washington quotes profusely from other writers, making it difficult to locate all of her sources. When quotations can be found, the source is indicated in notes. Washington's alteration of spelling in her use of others' works usually improves upon the readability of the work. For instance, she corrects the spelling in Edward Young's line in "Night Thoughts" which reads, "the needful auxiliars are our friends / to give. . . ." Washington writes, "needful [auxiliaries] are our friends / to give. . . ." When Washington emends the words of another writer, I bracket the word she changes in the related footnote.

This volume of Washington's essays has been culled primarily from newspapers. They represent the bulk of her extant essays. Missing from this collection are several essays referred to by her contemporaries that have failed to surface in this research project. Among those missing compositions are "A Talk about Church Fairs," "The Hero of Harper's Ferry," "The Afro-American in Literature," and "How Shall Our Girls Be Properly Employed and Protected?" These missing compositions do not mar the aim of this first edition of Josephine J. Turpin Washington's collected essays, which is to lay a firm foundation for future scholars, teachers, and critics inquiring about Washington's post-Reconstruction racial and gender uplift writings.

The three decades spent locating, assessing, and editing Washington's essays published in emerging black newspapers speak to the difficulty in recovering the hidden writings of nineteenth-century African American women. Despite the considerable time spent in recovering Washington's essays, the need for reclamation cannot be overemphasized. Washington's essays manifest an unparalleled achievement for a southern black woman contributing to a developing black print culture. They were instrumental in giving a literary character to black print while changing the assumed trajectory of nineteenth-century African American literary studies from a male-focused and genre-exclusive sphere to a female-inclusive and genre-varied field. Without the recovery of Washington's published essays, nineteenth-century African American newspapers would be less woman-focused and the canon of African American literature would be incomplete.

PART I

EDUCATIONAL IMPERATIVES

Higher Education for Women

JOSEPHINE J. TURPIN

The dense darkness, which for six thousand years, has enveloped woman's intellectual life, is rapidly disappearing before the rays of modern civilization. Advanced public sentiment says, "Let there be light!" and there is light; but it is not that of a brilliant noonday, rather it is the brightness of a rising sun, destined to flood the world with glory. There are still many, who, while advocating female education to a certain point, decry the necessity and propriety of giving to woman what is known as the higher education. By this term we mean that education which involves the same head-training, having for its banks the same general studies, deemed essential to our brothers; that education acquired only at the college and the university.

The very fact that woman has a mind capable of infinite expansion, is in itself an argument that she should receive the highest possible development. Man is placed here to grow. It is his duty to make the most of the powers within him. Has anyone the right to thwart him in these efforts, to shut him out from the means to this end, to say to him as concerns his educational training, "Thus far shalt thou go and no further!"[1] This being true of man specifically, is no less true of man generally. . . . Poets and novelists all agree in according to woman's heart; but, in the practical treatment of subjects, the fact should not be overlooked that she has also a head. The Martineaus,[2] Hemans,[3] Hannah Mores,[4] George Eliots,[5] and Mrs. Brownings[6] haven't failed to demonstrate this.

Admitting for the sake of argument that most women are intellectually inferior to most men; still, in the words of Plato "Many women are in many things

* "Higher Education for Women," *People's Advocate* (Washington, D.C.), 12 April 1884, 1.

1. A rewording of Job 38:11, which reads, "[Hitherto] shalt thou [come], but no further." All quotations from the Bible refer to the King James Version published by Regency in 1976.

2. Harriet Martineau (1802–1876), English novelist and social reformer.

3. Felicia Dorothea Hemans (1793–1835), a versatile and prolific English poet.

4. Hannah More (1745–1833), an English dramatist, social reformer, and tract writer.

5. George Eliot, pseudonym of Mary Ann Evans (1819–1880), a prolific English novelist.

6. Mrs. Elizabeth Barrett Browning (1806–1861), English poet whose well-known poem "Aurora Leigh" (1857) advocates for women's rights.

superior to many men."[7] Should not those who have capacity and inclination be allowed to receive this higher education? Should not those who have a gift be permitted to develop and exercise it? If a woman has a message for the world, must she remain dumb? God forbid that man should close the lips of one commissioned from heaven to speak! Who wishes that Mrs. Stowe[8] had not taken up her pen to depict the horrors of slave life? Yet had she desisted from such labors, probably she would have darned a greater number of stockings and sewed on more buttons. Would you have had Lucretia Mott[9] withhold herself from public life, from platform efforts as temperance reformer and antislavery agitator? Lucretia Mott!

> "Something God had to say to thee,
> Worth hearing from the lips of all."[10]

Woman molds and fashions society. Man's chivalrous deference gives her a preeminence and an influence here which carry with them a proportionally great responsibility. The better the training she has received, the better enabled will she be to perform the social duties devolving upon her. The more effective the intellectual armor in which she encases herself, the more prepared will she be to engage in the contests of [the] mind. Men adapt themselves to their company, and conversation in society does not rise above the level of its women. Is it not necessary that woman be ready to meet man upon equal intellectual ground? Is it not important that her mental equipment be not inferior to his own? No one would have social converse composed exclusively of discussions on the "elegies," or made up of quotations from the "little Latin and less Greek" learned in the schools; but the discipline gained by such scholastic training makes one undeniably brighter, wittier, more entertaining, capable of wielding a greater influence for good. The salons of the intellectual women of France afford numerous examples of what may be accomplished by woman in society.

Who has not heard of Madame Recamier[11] and Roland,[12] of Madame de

---

7. Plato, *The Republic*, bk. 5, p. 717.

8. Harriet Elizabeth Beecher Stowe (1811–1896), American novelist and author of the internationally known novel *Uncle Tom's Cabin; or, Life among the Lowly* (1851–52).

9. Lucretia Mott (1793–1880), American abolitionist and women's rights advocate instrumental in establishing the all-female Swarthmore College in 1864.

10. Bulwer-Lytton, *Clytemnestra*, stanza 11, p. 197.

11. Madame Juliette Récamier (1777–1849), famous French socialite who maintained a literary and political salon in Paris (*The Cambridge Biographical Encyclopedia*, 2nd ed. [1998], ed. Crystal, s.v. Récamier, [Jeanne Françoise] Julie Adélaide).

12. Madame Roland, born Marie-Jeanne Philipon (1754–1793), supported her husband in his political ambition to aid the Revolution rather than the monarchy; she was beheaded at the guillotine for treason (*The Cambridge Biographical Encyclopedia*, 2nd ed. [1998], ed. Crystal, s.v. "Rolande de la Platière, Jean Marie).

Le'vigne,[13] hated by Louis XIV, because of her wit; of Madame de Staël,[14] persecuted by Napoleon, who could not forgive her for being more clever than himself?

These women, when old and faded, still charmed by their grace and cultivation of mind. Loveliness of person is a rare gift, a precious boon to be duly
appreciated; but only mind is truly beautiful.

> "Mind, mind alone, bear witness earth and heaven;
> The living fountain in itself contains of beauteous and sublime.
> Here hand in hand sit paramount the graces."[15]

The possession of a higher education multiplies woman's bread-winning opportunities. This is a most important consideration. All women do not enter the
domestic state; and even many who do are afterwards so situated as to require
a resort to some means for earning their own living and that of others dependent upon them. What shall these women do? True, sewing is considered a
very respectable occupation, and nursing is certainly a most feminine; but some
women have no desire to sing "the song of the shirt,"[16] and possess no taste for
minding babies, least of all, those of other people. Besides both of these avenues
of female labor, as others of similar character, are overcrowded and but slightly
remunerative. I repeat it, what is to be done with these women, seeking the
means by which to earn their daily bread?

Will you give them this higher education, and thereby open doors to congenial and paying pursuits; or will you frown them down, and tempt to dishonor
by refusing the means of self-support? Quoting Plato again: "Neither a woman
as a woman nor a man as a man has any special function, but the gifts of nature
are equally diffused in both sexes; all the pursuits of men are the pursuits of
women also."[17]

13. "Madame de Le vinge" should be Madame de Sévigné (1626–1696), epistolary
writer during France's classic period of art and literature (*The Cambridge Biographical
Dictionary*, 2nd ed. [1998], ed. Crystal, "Sévigné, Madame de").

14. Madame de Staël, née Anne Louise Germaine Necker (1766–1817), a Parisian
writer and author of the novel *Delphine* (1802), which enraged Napoleon Bonaparte because it glorified divorce, liberalism, and Protestantism. A Catholic, Napoleon banished
Madame de Staël from Paris for her unorthodoxy (*The Cambridge Biographical Dictionary*, 2nd ed. [1998], ed. Crystal, s.v. Staël, Madame de.").

15. Akenside, "The Pleasures of the Imagination," 25. Akenside's version, with different
punctuation, reads, "Mind, mind alone [bear witness earth and heaven] / The living fountains
in itself contains / Of beauteous and sublime: Here, hand in hand/ Sit paramount the graces."

16. The original reads, "the the song of the shirt."

17. Plato, *The Republic*, bk. 5, p. 717. Plato's version reads: "[There is no special faculty
of administration in a state which a woman has because she is a woman, or which a man
has by virtue of his sex,] but the gifts of nature are alike diffused in both. All the pursuits
of men are the pursuits of women also, but in all of them a woman is inferior to a man."

While I do not fully agree with the ancient sage, in his comprehensive state-ment, I do believe that if a woman has a gift for a particular calling, and she is not debarred from that calling by the natural barrier of that sex, it is presump-tuous, nay more, it is unjust for man to attempt the restraining of her, and to say, You shall not enter the work whereunto God has called you; it is *unfeminine!* Even men with wise and statesmanlike views upon other subjects, turn fanatics upon this. They would not have a woman lecture, because it would make her too public, as if publicity would harm one whose only desire is to do good work in a good cause. They would not have her a physician, because she must study indelicate subjects, as if to a pure-minded person the contemplation of the work-manship of these bodies which God made, would be indelicate. They would not have her control a steamer, though she be fully able to do so; and though cir-cumstances make it the most convenient way for her to earn an honest support. Through blind prejudice, they endeavored to prevent Captain Mary Miller[18] from mastering her husband's boat on the Mississippi river.

Woman is for a helpmeet unto man. She is meant to be his assistant in every good work, and his companion in the fullest sense of the word. Properly to sus-tain this relation, she must have equal educational advantages with man.

Can there be perfect companionship between two people, one of whom is by far the intellectual superior of the other? Will not the one have thoughts, feelings, aspirations, which the other can neither sympathize with nor under-stand? Can the wife be truly a helpmeet for her husband, if her mind has not been equally broadened and deepened; if she is not capable of giving wise coun-sels and judgments for the furtherance of his aims? Verily, "two cannot walk together except they be agreed."[19]

Many an eminent man attributes greatly his success to the clear head as well as the loving heart of the woman[20] who was his wife. She is the power behind the throne, often more powerful than the monarch himself; hers is often the hand at the helm, moving noiselessly but most effectually.

There are many Caroline Herchels [*sic*][21] quietly aiding a brother or a hus-band on to fame.

18. Mary Millicent Miller (1846–1894) received her license as steamboat captain after competitors charged her husband, George, with illegally serving as pilot and captain of the *Saline* on the Mississippi River (Talbott, "Grave of Steamboat Captain [Mary M. Miller]," Explore KYHistory, http://exploreKYHistory.ky.gov/items/show/456).

19. This is an interpretation of Amos 3:3: "Can two walk together, except they be agreed?"

20. The original reads "women."

21. Caroline Herschel (1750–1848), sister and assistant to German-born astrono-mer William Herschel. With the telescope that William gave her, Caroline was the first woman to discover various comets. She also updated and corrected John F. Flamsteed's work related to the stars' position. In 1846, she was awarded a Gold Medal for Science (Hoskin, "Herschel, Caroline Lucretia," 824–25).

It is even more necessary that women be well educated than men, for they are to be the mothers of future generations.

Men make laws and institutions, but women make men. The child in the hands of its mother, is as clay in the hands of the potter. It is hers to "rear the tender mind," to direct the infant thought, to impress the growing character. Can there be a higher mission than this; can there be a more responsible position; can there be a calling requiring greater knowledge and wisdom?

An ancient philosopher says: "The most important part of education is right training in the nursery. The soul of the child in his play should be trained in that sort of excellence in which, when he grows up to manhood, he will have to be perfected."[22]

Were not the learned Bacon[23] and the great Washington[24] equally indebted to their mothers, because of the studiousness of the one and broad culture of the other? No one can direct the early training of the child as can the mother herself; she gives a bias to the youthful mind which it is more than likely to retain.

> "Tis education forms the common mind.
> Just as the twig is bent, the tree's incline."[25]

Ought not women to have broad and full and able minds to perform aright the duties of motherhood? Is it not to the interest of society, of the state, of the nation that women be liberally educated? To have the mothers ignorant would be through them to weaken the sons, and finally the commonwealth.

> "The hand that rocks the cradle,
> Is the hand that rocks the world."[26]

Fear not to lend your influence for the higher education of woman. She will be none the less a woman when she has received an education; she will have lost none of that grace and sweetness of character which men admire. Woman asks not of education to make her a man; she asks that herself be given back to her, but herself awakened, strengthened, elevated. Would you open new avenues of employment for her; would you render her a useful[27] and independent member of society? Then give her a higher education.

22. Plato, "The Laws," 4:174. Plato's version reads, "The [sum] of education is right training in the nursery."

23. Francis Bacon (1561–1626), English philosopher, scientist, essayist, and jurist.

24. George Washington (1732–1799), America's first president.

25. Pope, "Epistle to Cobham," 22.

26. Wallace, "The Hand That Rocks the Cradle," stanza 1, lines 7–8. Wallace's line reads, "For the hand that rocks the cradle / Is the hand that [rules] the world."

27. The original reads "an useful."

Would you develop[28] the hidden resources of her mind; would you fit her to raise the tone and character of society? Give her a higher education. Would you have her assist her husband in his vexed problems of thought, would you have her his companion in intellectual and spiritual life, would you have her train her children aright and be a fountain of knowledge to her family? Then give her a higher education!

28. The original reads "develope."

A Plea for the Co-Education
of the Sexes

JOSEPHINE J. TURPIN

No interest is more related to national weal or woe than that of education. It is recognized as one of vital importance, and therefore elicits wide comment and intelligent discussion. The wisest men deem it worthy of their attention. Various theories are expounded, methods proposed and suggestions offered. Perhaps no phrase of the subject receives greater notice and draws forth opinions more varied, though equally sincere, than the co-education of the sexes. This is what we now would consider.

While maintaining the advisability of educating together the youths of both sexes, we do not claim for this, as the preferable system, any virtue of perfection. Wherever human nature operates, flaws may be found. Somewhat of inconvenience or embarrassment is inevitably connected with the most approved methods. We simply hold that the advantages of co-education far outnumber its disadvantages; that whatever may be truthfully said against it, much more, with equal truth, may be said in its favor; and that it is superior, as an educational system, to the separate schooling of the sexes.

Our first argument is that co-education is natural. In the beginning God created them male and female, and gave them equal dominion over all things made. This, the earliest formative state of society, recognized the equal companionship of the sexes. In the words of one, "All the impulses and activities of nature enforce co-existence."[1] Boys and girls are born into one family. They grow up under the same parental roof. As children in the home, they play together, work together, study together. In happy concord they recite their lessons about the mother's knee, and the vexed question of superiority never troubles their infantine brains. When, according to a *régime* unnatural and rapidly becoming unpopular, the Tom Tullivers[2] (as narrated in George Eliot's *Mill on the*

---

* "A Plea for the Co-Education of the Sexes," *A.M.E. Church Review* 3, no. 3 (January 1887): 267–71.

1. Bureau of Education, *Co-Education of the Sexes in the Public Schools of the United States,* 17.

2. The original reads "Tullevers."

Floss) are sent off to school alone, a false system of education, with its artificial environments, inculcates and fosters mistaken ideas of their own and their sister's relative ability. It is then Maggie is told that "girls are unfit to study Latin and Euclid."[3] By placing together in the family circle the two young lives, there to receive in concert the earliest instruction and discipline, the Creator himself seems to favor co-education.

Following out, in the extended educational course, this family plan, man but accords with the teachings of God and Nature. Those who are destined to live together are surely right in thus together learning how to live.

Co-educational is strictly impartial. It provides that young men and maidens may be educated under precisely the same advantages. Opportunities for culture are no greater for one than for the other. It precludes all just ground for complaint on this point. "But," croaks one, "woman is intellectually inferior to man, and therefore unable successfully to compete with him in the higher branches." What proves such inferiority? Certainly not the fact that her brain weighs less than man's. Many great men have had comparatively small brains, and *vice versa*. The London bricklayer whose brain weighed sixty-seven ounces more than that of the famous Cuvier,[4] was unable to read or write, having no remarkable mental force. The Chinese brain is larger than that of the European; yet who thinks of claiming for the average Chinaman a superiority to the average European? The matter of quality is to be considered as well as quantity. Besides, when we notice the relative size of man and woman, we observe that woman's brain is larger in proportion to the size of her body than man's is to his body.

It may be argued that woman does not need the same kind and extent of education as man, and that she should be placed where she can receive the instruction peculiarly suited to her future duties as wife and mother. As replying in part to this, we quote Herbert Spencer where he says, "A college course is designed pre-eminently to give power to acquire and think, rather than to impart special knowledge or special discipline."[5] Woman has need of all that the most ambitious institution can give her. The limitations of her acquirements should be co-incident only with those of her capacity. Who objects to the future lawyer or doctor taking a college course, on the ground that professional life will not bring into active use Greek and the higher mathematics? There can be no mis-

3. Washington's quotation does not appear verbatim in Eliot's *The Mill on the Floss,* but it expresses the home environment to which the rational-thinking Maggie is exposed when she is denied schooling equal to that of her lackluster brother. When Maggie offers to help her brother with his studies, he tells her, "Girls never learn such things. They're so silly" (132).

4. Baron Georges Cuvier (1769–1832), well-known French researcher in natural sciences.

5. Not Spencer but Yale president Noah Porter, "What to Learn," 166.

sion requiring a more thorough development of all the thinking faculties than that of wifehood and motherhood. Simply remarking upon the desirableness of equality in intellectual matters, as in others, between husband and wife, we may well pause to speak at greater length upon the requirements of that even more responsible function of motherhood. Surely she upon whom is largely dependent the formation of another mind, to whose fostering care is entrusted the growing intellect, who is so situated as either thoughtlessly and ignorantly to crush, or wisely and skillfully to encourage, the budding thought, ought to be ably prepared for these noble tasks. What woeful mistakes are hers when "she knows nothing about the nature of the emotions, their order of evolution, their functions, or where *use* ends and *abuse* begins!"[6] Again quoting Spencer, and this time where he deplores the general superficiality of female education: "Ignorant as she is of that with which she has to deal, she is equally ignorant of the effects that will be produced on it by this or that treatment. What can be more inevitable than the disastrous results we see hourly arising? Lacking knowledge of mental phenomena, with their causes and consequences, her interference is frequently more mischievous than absolute passivity would have been."[7] Nor is woman confined to the home, as elevated as is her station there, and as holy as is her influence. The broad and true conception of the feminine sphere is not that bounded by men's prejudices and ideas of propriety, but a sphere appointed by God and bounded by the powers He has bestowed. If woman is to compete with man in the world's great work, which she is surely doing in most of the industries and professions, who can doubt that she should have equal training?

Not only should an equal, but the same educational training be hers. We cannot detect any such disparity in the intellectual powers of the two sexes as to warrant, on that account, fundamental distinctions in the subjects of their study. The text-books, designed to impart knowledge and discipline, contain nothing outside of woman's need. No instruction is given young men in common school, academy, or college that she cannot, to mutual advantage, receive with them. As to the theory that while in school she should be taught the house-wifery arts, the details of domestic life are best learned at home, and the mother is generally the best instructor. Yet a separate training in special industrial pursuits is not inconsistent with what is commonly understood by the theory of co-education.

The claim is sometimes advanced that young women are not physically able to endure the strain incident to study with young men, particularly in the higher departments of learning. We do not admit that, on account of ill-health, girls are more irregular in attendance upon school-duties than boys; but even if this is so, they can afford occasionally to absent themselves without falling behind

6. Spencer, "What Knowledge Is of Most Worth," 12. Washington italicizes "use" and "abuse" for emphasis.
7. Ibid.

their fellow-students; since girls at the same age with boys are acknowledged to be more mature in mind as well as in body, and better able to grasp and retain thought. When we do hear of the break-down of some girl in school, we are nearly always correct if we attribute it to a disregard of the laws of health, and not to over-work of a mental kind. Improper dress, inattention to exercise, late suppers, a superabundance of sweet-meats, and similar indiscretions are generally the real causes of such collapses.

Co-education is preferable as being the more economic system. One school suffices where, under the opposite conditions, two would be needed. This difference of expenditure is not so great in large cities, where educational institutions are many and near together. Under such circumstances, but little extra expense is necessary in order to have separate schools for the sexes. But in the sections where school-houses are few and widely scattered and educational appliances scanty and insufficient, the attempt at separate education becomes most vexing and embarrassing, as viewed even in a monetary light. Here ensues the expense of two schools in a district where otherwise one would be sufficient, or else pupils of either sex are under the necessity of going long and tedious miles to the special school set apart for them, perhaps passing by a school near their home, from which nothing debars them but the fact of their sex. Arguments similar, but even more forcible, apply to the high schools and colleges. Comparatively few of these are needed, and certainly the same locality can be supplied by a very limited number, when the sexes are educated together. On the other hand, separate them, and either colleges must be built to meet the need of a few aspirants for the higher education, or else young women suffer from lack of adequate educational advantages. Of course, the matter of employing different professors and procuring separate class-room apparatus is comprehended in the economic consideration of this question.

No argument adduced in favor of co-education is more potent than that of its benefit to the youths of both sexes. What have been termed the "demoralizing influences of co-education" are not due to the system itself, but to its mismanagement. Negligent teachers and faulty discipline have much to account for in this respect. Under proper restraints, the influence exerted by either sex upon the other is of the most humanizing and refining nature. This favorable influence is not confined to any one channel, and does not promote growth in any one direction alone. The young of both sexes are stimulated to habits of greater neatness, and proper personal pride is encouraged. Meeting in the class-room, moving socially among each other, foolish timidity and bashfulness are removed. Grace and ease of manner are imparted; and a culture, not otherwise obtained, is acquired. A generous rivalry in study is aroused; students are incited to greater industry and perseverance. Minds alike in many respects, yet differing somewhat in special aptitudes and predilections being thus brought together, afford mutual inspiration and assistance. Girls gain by contact with the masculine mind practicality and more deliberate judgment; while boys profit by the delicate and subtle intuitions of the feminine mind. Each throws a particular light upon the subject of study. Not only is there this gain in mind and manners, but also in morals. Boys become more gentle and polite, and refined; girls, braver, more broadened and strengthened. In the one is developed all the chivalry of the manly character; in the other, all the grace and nobility of womanly bearing. In each sex is cultivated that respect and esteem for the other so necessary to the relations of later years. Woman proves herself the equal of man, and a proper recognition is accorded her as such. No longer regarded as a mere pet and plaything, or as but the necessary appendage to a home, she stands forth his peer in every respect, prepared to fight beside him in the battle-field of life and to share with him its trials and triumphs.

The circulars of the Bureau of Education for 1883 contain statements and statistics showing the almost universality of opinion and practice in favor of co-education in the United States. The demand for co-education is becoming more and more potent; and one institution after another is throwing open its doors to woman. Old superstitions are being cast aside, and progress leads the van. What may we not expect of glorious conquest for the cause of education when, instead of separation tending to constant deterioration, the world will universally adopt co-education as the only natural system, ensuring impartiality, encouraging economy and promoting the general benefit?

Washington, D.C.

Teaching as a Profession

JOSEPHINE TURPIN

A glance into the working world reveals the fact that most men give themselves to special employments. This one tills the soil and prepares fruit and grain, not only for his own use, but also for the busy marts of the crowded city. That one erects the dwelling, the church and the school, not simply for his own accommodation, but for that of his neighbor the farmer, and for others not fitted to perform for themselves this needed service. A third devotes himself to the spiritual welfare of a community; a fourth cares for men's bodies; and, in like manner, we might enumerate the whole list of the trades and the professions.

Why is it that, with common consent, we apply ourselves to particular lines of work? The human being is born into the world with especial tendencies and proclivities. Whether these are wholly hereditary or are in part the peculiar gift of the individual, regardless of ancestral characteristics, we do not need here to determine. The fact of their existence remains undisputed. Unless unfavorable circumstances counteract the original inclination, it is strengthened and developed with years; and we find a Watts[1] musing over the steaming kettle, or a Pope[2] "lisping in numbers, for the numbers come."[3] Goethe[4] has beautifully expressed this truth in the following lines, taken from his "Hermann and Dorothea."

"We have no power to fashion our children as suiteth our fancy; as they are given by God we so must have them and love them, teach them as best we can, and let each of them follow his nature. One will have talents of one sort and different talents another. Every one useth his own,

> In his own individual fashion,
> Each must be happy and good."[5]

* "Teaching as a Profession," *A.M.E. Church Review* 5, no. 2 (October 1888): 103–11.

1. Isaac Watts (1674–1748), English hymnist.

2. Alexander Pope (1688–1744), English poet.

3. A variation of Alexander Pope's "I lisp'd in numbers, for the numbers came" (from "Epistle to Arbuthnot," 176).

4. Johann Wolfgang von Goethe (1749–1832), a German writer, physicist, and statesman.

5. From Goethe's epic poem "Hermann and Dorothea."

There is also another reason why men follow particular callings. It is a principle in the economy of labor that special and exclusive application to any pursuit, whether mental or physical, tends to perfection in that pursuit. The youth, acting in accordance with the necessities of his condition and the custom of his time and country, makes choice of a vocation, and, as is natural, chooses that for which he has talent and inclination; or, as is true of rarer cases, he is irresistibly impelled, by the force of genius, in a certain direction.

Preparation follows choice. The aspirant must fit himself, by years of training for his special branch of toil, whether it is one involving mainly the use of the head or hand. This is demanded by the public, that it is to be the patron, and conceded by the applicant for such patronage. He who demurs against this requirement is thought a fool, and should he fail to prepare himself for the practice of his trade or profession, may rest assured that his leisure will be broken by few demands for his services.

We regret to say that teaching is largely an exception to this rule. Though, in the words of Locke, "a vocation calling for the exercise of every virtue"[6] and "the most responsible office in life except that of parent," it is the occupation most frequently sought and secured by those who have no proper conception of its dignity and importance, and is a popular resort for the inexperienced and the unsuccessful in other callings. Seldom amply prepared for, rarely contemplated as a life-work, often made but a means to an end, it is entered by the young lawyer dreaming of his first brief, the doctor who has never had a patient, the preacher whose people fail to support him, and the "sweet girl-graduate," awaiting the prince and matrimony.

Natural aptitude is an essential element in the teacher. Lacking it, all the technical knowledge in the world can accomplish little. In making such requisition the teacher's vocation is not peculiar. It is the presence or absence of this gift which makes the painter's production a living, glowing creation that speaks in intelligible language to the human soul, or a mere mechanical mixture and spread of colors. Not only is the poet "born" and "not made," but the same is true of the artist in every line.

The term "natural aptitude," as here used, has a double meaning. It refers to the affections as well as to the intellect. He who aspires to teach should have a love for humanity. His heart should be filled with devotion for his fellowmen and with yearnings to do them good. He should especially love the young and be able to sympathize with them. He must be

---

6. The quote expresses the sentiment on morality found in Locke's "An Essay Concerning Human Understanding" (1689), but the words to this quotation and the one immediately following it are directly quoted in Virginia Penny's *The Employments of Women*, 36.

"—with the pupils of his school,
Gentle of speech but absolute of rule;"[7]

never giving way to anger; never losing self-control; kind and winning in manner, yet firm in decision and in execution; with a will that subdues and controls, while it does not crush and destroy. He must have tact, or his other good qualities will prove of little value. It is a virtue difficult to define, yet easily recognized. We all have met the man who invariably says the wrong thing at the wrong time, though with the best possible intention, and, in common parlance, is always "treading on people's pet corns." On the other hand, what a pleasing contrast is that smooth, suave personage who has a happy knack of doing and saying just the right thing in just the right way; who causes the wheels of society to turn without friction, and everybody to feel in a good humor with himself and his neighbor, but who, at the same time, does not warrant the accusation of being either flattering or subservient. There must be a love for the work, an actual delight in teaching "the young idea how to shoot," and in watching, under skillful training, the development of the child's mind. The teacher should be

". . . the joy the sculptor knows
When, plastic to his lightest touch,
His clay wrought model slowly grows
To that fine grace desired so much."[8]

Void of life, interest and enthusiasm, labor is indeed arduous and the end must prove unsatisfactory. This is exemplified, on a small scale, where the teacher has a distaste for a certain study. Despite his efforts to conceal the aversion and to obtain good results, the school is almost sure to feel the contagion of his dislike and to have a corresponding deficiency. Children are wonderfully acute in finding us out.

Apropos, it may be well to observe just here, that while the teacher should be of high moral rectitude, and it is even desirable that he be a consistent Christian, he must avoid, as deadly to his aims, anything approaching cant or hypocrisy. Children have great respect for genuine goodness and piety, but they have a keen sense of the ludicrous and are quick to detect shams.

None will hesitate to concede that one must know what he is to teach. Certainly the failure to know comprehends the failure to cause another to know. A somewhat smaller number, perhaps, would require the teacher to know *more* than he is to teach. Such superior information is by no means superfluous, as might at first appear. A higher knowledge is necessary in order fully to comprehend and

7. Longfellow, "The Student's Tale," 466.
8. Whittier, "At School-Close. Bowdoin Street (1877)," stanza 3, p. 416. Whittier's line reads, "[One knew] the joy the sculptor knows."

to be able to simplify and explain the lower. I know an old woman who makes the most delicious bread and cake, and cannot be surpassed in the concoction of the various dainties which tempt the palate; yet it would be a most difficult and uncertain task to try to learn cookery from her. Why? She "sights" and "guesses" at every ingredient, takes a "pinch" of this or that seasoning, and is grossly ignorant of weights, measures and quantities. What she herself can do well, having gained an empirical knowledge by many years' service, she cannot effectively teach another. The teacher must be a person of education and culture. He should be well-rounded and developed, having every faculty trained and disciplined, and familiar with all the popular sciences. Should he be an instructor in the public schools, he is likely to be required to teach any or all of these; and even should he devote himself, in some college or university, to a special subject, his varied learning will prove of benefit. There is no sharp line of division between different classes of knowledge; and information acquired in the pursuit of one science cannot fail to help, either directly or indirectly, in any other. If it does nothing more, none will deny that it broadens the mind, deepens the power of thought and lends clearness to comprehension and to statement. In the language of a famous author: "Strive, while improving your one talent, to enrich your whole capital as a man. It is in this way that you escape from the wretched narrow-mindedness which is the characteristic of every one who cultivates his specialty alone."[9]

Thus far we have considered only the natural gifts of the teacher and those general attainments which he possesses in common with other well-educated persons. He is not to stop here. As yet he is but partly fitted for his vocation and is deficient in a very important respect. Art must perfect what Nature has begun. When the aspirant for church honors has taken his college course, he enters the theological seminary and there makes special preparation for the divine calling. The young man who has decided upon the profession of medicine as his life-work, whatever his knowledge of the classics and the higher mathematics, and even of the practical sciences, some of which bear directly upon his contemplated profession, does not deem himself competent to practice the "healing art" till he has spent years in special training for this work. Indeed, the matter is not left to his conscience and discretion, but precautions are wisely taken, in the various States [*sic*], to protect the community from charlatans. The same is true of other professions and trades. What man who has never had a day's instruction in carpentry attempts to build a house? If you wish your coat to fit will you go to one who is utterly untaught and inexperienced, and who, as the saying is, merely "took up" the tailor's trade of himself? Then why are you content to send your child to a teacher who knows nothing of the grand work of education, who is not acquainted with a single one of its methods and principles

9. Bulwer-Lytton, "Essay X: Hints on Mental Culture," 106–7. Bulwer-Lytton's version reads, "Strive, while improving your one talent, to enrich your whole capital [as Man]."

as such, and who undertakes the task in a thoughtless and frivolous spirit, without any adequate conception of its nature? You have known good teachers who did not have this special preparation? So have I; but they are the exception, and not the rule; besides, who knows how much better they would have been had they made that preparation which in every case, mark you, they appreciate, and in many the lack of which in themselves they have been known to deplore?

This great need among the instructors of our youth has been long recognized by the thoughtful few. The list of efficient normal schools in the country is continually swelling, and every year increases the appreciation of the work they are accomplishing. It cannot be too strenuously insisted upon that all who contemplate being teachers should take a course in one of these schools. I am an advocate of the higher education, for women as well as for men; but if the embryo teacher, after completing a common English course, has to choose between the college and the normal school, by all means let him or her take the latter; for the same reason that the young man who is to practice law, choosing between college and the law school, must needs take the law, when he can have only one, though both are eminently desirable and almost indispensable. In the normal school every subject is studied with the view of its being one day taught by the pupil. Especial care is paid throughout the course to the *how* to teach. It is in no wise made subservient to the *what*. The science of teaching is studied, its methods and principles expounded; and to psychology, than which no branch of knowledge can be more useful to the teacher, particular attention is given.

What Herbert Spencer says of the deficiencies of the average young mother applies with equal force to the average teacher, whose type the normal school is designed to eradicate: "But a few years ago she was at school, where her memory was crammed with words and names and dates, and her reflective faculties scarcely in the slightest degree exercised—where not one idea was given her respecting the methods of dealing with the opening mind of childhood, and where her discipline did not in the least fit her for thinking out methods of her own. * * * And now see her with an unfolding human character committed to her charge; see her profoundly ignorant of the phenomena with which she has to deal, undertaking to do that which can be done but imperfectly even with the aid of the profoundest wisdom. She knows nothing about the nature of the emotions, their order of evolution, their functions, or where use ends and abuse begins. She is under the impression that some of the feelings are wholly bad, which is not true of any one of them; and that others are good, however far they may be carried, which is also not true of any one of them. And then, ignorant as she is of that with which she has to deal, she is equally ignorant of the effects that will be produced by this or that treatment. What can be more inevitable than the disastrous results we see hourly arising?"[10]

10. Unknown quotation.

The teacher should realize the importance of "a sound mind in a sound body;" he should remember that such is the mutual dependence between the dual parts of man's nature, that the condition of one necessarily affects the other. It is a question which has serious discussion, whether a grand physique is not the usual concomitant of high intellectual powers, and is not in some sense productive thereof. In the *North American Review* of May 1888, Dr. Woods Hutchinson ably argues this point in an article headed "Physical Basis of Brain Work." While we do not go so far as to say that our teachers should be chosen for physical strength and beauty, we do claim that more attention should be paid to the care of the body, by educated people generally, and especially by those who mold[11] the minds of the young; for it is to this class that we look for the proper consideration of important matters, and for conduct and lines of thought that the masses can safety follow. The human body is the casket of the soul, the temple of the Holy Ghost, and as such is worthy of reverential care; but it is, besides, the only medium through which our real selves can communicate with the outside world. Let the sentient medium become impaired, and to the same extent is the perfection of percept and concept impaired. A faulty mirror cannot give back a true image. The teacher, then, should understand the rules of health and should conscientiously regard them. He should instruct his pupils in the fundamental laws of hygiene, and should urge their careful observance.

A recent writer gives, as an argument for having a larger proportion of male teachers in the public schools, that they would be to the lads examples of manly strength and prowess, and incentives, by precept as well as by practice, to hardy and vigorous sports. Many of our female teachers do make a great mistake in discouraging exercise among their pupils, especially among the girls—except, perhaps, a half hour or twenty minutes of tame calisthenics; and in character-izing all hearty playing and romping as "so unladylike," "so ungentleman-like." Children grow up with false ideas as to their physical selves, and think their highest merit lies in overtaxing the brain at the expense of the body. It is grat-ifying to know that most of the northern colleges give prominence to physical culture, and it is the general testimony of presidents and professors that ath-letic exercises neither injure nor preclude scholarship. Of course, there exists the possibility of going to the extreme also in this direction, and that is to be avoided.

Teaching is a grave responsibility, and should be so regarded by those who make choice of it as a vocation. Without a feeling of awe in the contemplation of its serious and sacred duties, a prerequisite is wanting. He who has the least abil-ity is likely to have the most assurance. It is Bulwer who says, "Man is arrogant in proportion to his ignorance:"[12] and we all know the adage, "Fools rush in,"

11. The original reads "mould."
12. Bulwer-Lytton's novel *Zanoni: A Rosicrucian Tale*, bk. 4, chap. 4.

etc. A due feeling of accountability and a modest estimate of one's gifts are by no means incompatible with the necessary and commendable self-confidence and self-respect. Instead of which, they induce the humble, earnest, prayerful attitude of mind which usually precedes and accompanies great success in any line.

In the employment of inefficient and untrained teachers a flagrant injustice is done the public. To the shame of those in authority it must be admitted that merit is not always the criterion of appointment. Personal or political favoritism often influences selection.

The colored people are likely to fall into a peculiar error with respect to their schools. It is the choice of men of color as educators without due regard to their fitness. Please do not misunderstand me. *I am most heartily in favor of "colored teachers for colored schools,"*[13] *provided that the colored applicant is as well qualified for the position sought as any available candidate.* Otherwise, let the aforesaid applicant wait till he can be adjudged as a man and a scholar, and not as a *colored* man. We do not wish the standard of excellence lowered for us. To admit the necessity is to insult the Negro. Our youth have a right to the best possible training, and we should not allow a mistaken race pride to cause us to impose upon them inferior teachers. The only way to make this colored applicant for professorial honors the undeniable equal of his white rivals, is in his youth, the training time, to give him equal facilities of education—included among them equally good instructors. We have special need of skilled teachers. Everywhere the duties of the preceptor partake largely of a missionary character, but especially is it so with us. The most of our children come from ignorant homes, from homes lacking in culture and refinement, often lacking decency and morality; and the teacher who has the true interests of the pupil and the race at heart will strive to supplement, as far as in him lies, this deficient and defective home training.

Having studied the science of teaching, its principles must be applied to the art. There is just the difference between the two that there is between the abstract and the concrete; and the talent which readily acquires the one is not necessarily equally proficient in the other. In the well-conducted training school the two processes are carried on conjointly; and the pupil has the opportunity, under the guidance and criticism of able instructors, to apply in practice what he has learned in theory. It is, however, only when he has become a "full-fledged" teacher and has a school of his own that the real test is offered. Then he must "sink or swim, live or die," on his own merits or his lack thereof. The per-

---

13. "Colored Teachers for Colored Schools" was African Americans' urgent plea to the school board of Richmond, Virginia, and state officials to hire black teachers to instruct black students. In 1881, Richmond had 14 black teachers compared to 129 white instructors. One-fourth of the white teachers taught at black schools (Alexander, *Race Man,* 16; H. Green, *Educational Reconstruction,* 167–73).

son best fitted by nature and by discipline for the task will find it no light one. What, then, must be the fate of him who is wanting in both these requirements? The young educator cannot hope to adhere to cast-iron rules and regulations. He cannot expect to follow rigidly even the maxims and wise suggestions he has gained from textbooks and teachers. Occasionally there will be reasons for deviation from all known precedents. He must have within himself resources to which he can turn when all authorities fail. If he is not able to do this, he is nothing better than an educated machine, a talking automaton, and is altogether out of place in a school-room of live children. This power is one gained largely from experience, and young teachers need not wholly despond should they find themselves somewhat deficient therein. To recognize a virtue and to desire its possession is to make a step towards its acquisition.

The teacher should keep himself in the line of progress. No work can be of a stereotyped character which deals so intimately with the human mind. The study is one of infinitude and cannot be exhausted. Investigation and discovery are continually going on. The live teacher keeps abreast of the times. He avails himself of modern methods and appliances, does not scorn the use of teachers' journals and other helpful literature, frequents teachers' institutes and associations, and makes the whole tenor of his life contribute in some way to his efficiency in his chosen profession. He must bear in mind his relation to society and the community at large. He is looked upon as a leader; and, whether he wishes it or not, his conduct and speech are scrutinized and criticized,[14] and, in many instances, imitated. You cannot say to your pupils, "Do as I tell you and not as I do." Teaching and preaching of that style do little good, and often more harm than good, because they make some natures skeptical[15] of all human integrity and sincerity. This thoughtful attitude and proper consideration for a high office may be preserved without doing what is commonly called carrying the "shop" into social intercourse, or assuming a solemn and sanctimonious air. The teacher was a man before he was a teacher, and a man he should never cease to be. (By the frequency of the word "man" you will not be led to think that women are meant to be excluded. They, perhaps even more largely than men, are engaged in the work of education—certainly they are in the majority in the public schools, and many of them are doing a grand and noble work. We use the term in the generic and not the specific sense.) There is nothing in the profession which is inconsistent with a healthy, happy manhood or womanhood. What is proper amusement or recreation for the pupil is proper also for the teacher, provided of course, the difference in age and maturity of taste is considered. It is the office of the teacher, as well as of the preacher, to lead the people to discriminate

14. The original reads "criticised."
15. The original reads "sceptical."

between innocent pleasure and that which is vicious and degrading, and should not, therefore, be pleasure to the pure and high-minded.[16]

What is it that the teacher has not to do for the child? He cares for his physical being by keeping the school-room properly ventilated and well ordered, by regulating the hours of study so as to allow for sufficient exercise, by encouraging the little ones in their games, by exhorting to cleanliness and decency of person and surroundings, and by discarding that pseudo-modesty which finds science indelicate, and instructing the young in the physiology and hygiene of their bodies. He imparts a love for study by ignoring all unnatural methods, by developing the faculties in their order, by going from the known to the unknown, from the concrete to the abstract, from the particular to the general, and by recognizing the right of every child to have its native bent and inclination considered and respected in its education. He teaches his pupils to systematize knowledge, to associate thought; how to study and how to retain what they study. He shows that all acquirements have two ends—that of information and that of discipline. He points out the relation between the knowledge gained and the practical requirements of every-day life. He makes the boy feel that knowledge is indeed power, and he sends him forth from the walls of the schoolroom exultant yet humble, buoyant with the draught he has quaffed from the springs of learning and thirsting for larger drinks of those perennial waters. Nor is this all. The true teacher seeks to imbue his charge with high and noble ideas of living, to make them scorn mean and petty things, and to fit them for the rightful performance of life's duties, then which there can be no better preparation for eternity.

This article is not designed to offer any discouragement to those, who, entering the profession, feel themselves deficient in many respects mentioned. The best men and the ablest workers are generally most humble in their estimate of self. We are all familiar with that much-quoted comparison which Newton[17] made of himself, as picking up shells on the shore while the great ocean of Truth lay undiscovered before him.[18] Our aim is to educate the ignorant and thoughtless as to the nature and dignity of their office, and to call the attention of the already informed to truths which cannot be too frequently reiterated, and with

16. The original reads "highminded."

17. Sir Isaac Newton (1642–1727), English mathematician and developer of the laws of gravity.

18. The quotation to which Washington is referring is as follows: "I do not know what I may appear to the world, but to myself I seem to have been only like a boy playing on the sea-shore and diverting myself in now and then finding a smoother pebble or a prettier shell than ordinary, whilst the great ocean of truth lay all undiscovered before me." Brewster attributes this saying to Sir Isaac Newton (1642–1726) in his *Memoirs of the Life, Writings, and Discoveries of Sir Isaac Newton*, 2:407.

which they cannot be too deeply impressed. To the unprofessional teacher, to him who pursues the work as a temporary avocation, we do not say, "Stay out of it," for a twofold reason. In the first place, you probably would not do so, perhaps could not do so, many being forced by the exigencies of their condition, into pursuits for which they have little taste and less fitness. In the next place, many who do not contemplate teaching as a life-work, entering upon it with some degree of preparation, recognizing their deficiencies and striving humbly and hopefully to make the best use of every opportunity for improvement, yet do much good. None, however, can realize the full dignity and efficiency of the vocation save him who adopts it as a life-work, who makes it his profession. To others it must be but a mistress; to him, a wife.

Let teaching be regarded as a profession, engaged in by those who have for it natural aptitude and who have acquired the necessary training, and the results will be most beneficial. Society then will be composed of a class of men and women who have clearer and better conceptions of the meaning of life. A love of knowledge will be diffused among the people. Graduation will not be the end of systematic study, but in truth the "commencement." Ideas will be definite instead of vague and confused. A higher state of morals will prevail. There will be greater proficiency in the duties of parenthood, and increased ability in all the affairs of life. The teacher's office will gain in dignity and in public esteem. Salaries will be raised, and perhaps a tenure of life system be inaugurated. Whatever other recompense the teacher may or may not receive, he will have the love and veneration of the young lives he has served, and an old age crowned with the blessings of an approving conscience.

Josephine T. Washington Writes of Tuskegee's Commencement Week—A Splendid Occasion

JOSEPHINE T. WASHINGTON

Editor Freeman:

Tuskegee Institute has celebrated its fourteenth commencement. As usual, a vast crowd was present. In the words of Frederick Douglass, descriptive of a similar occasion at Tuskegee, there were "miles of people and acres of mules."[1]

The graduates numbered twenty-seven. The young women were attired in simple, inexpensive white dresses made by their own hands. The orations all had the true Tuskegeean stamp. In every sentence uttered breathed the spirit of putting into practice the things learned, of applying education, of helping others even as these young people have themselves been helped. Among the subjects discussed were such themes as "The Way Out of Poverty," "What the Home Should Be," "The Mission of Educated Negro Women," "Reforms for Southern Farmers," and "Applied Education."

Mr. S. Lang Williams,[2] of Chicago, delivered the annual address, speaking on the "New Education." The Negro was advised to remain in the South where are his best business opportunities, to pin his hopes for the solution of the problem to education in its broadest sense of development of head and heart and hand, and to devote his energies to working out his salvation along this line. Among the visitors of prominence was the State Superintendent, who expressed himself as enjoying the exercises "beyond the power of language to express." All day long the crowd thronged the buildings and grounds of the institution, learning their lessons as surely as did any of the pupils to whose recitations they listened. Especially interesting to most of the visitors was the industrial exhibit where

---

* "Josephine T. Washington Writes of Tuskegee's Commencement Week—A Splendid Occasion," *Freeman*, 15 June 1894, 2.

1. Frederick Douglass delivered the commencement speech at Tuskegee Institute on 12 May 1892.

2. Samuel Lang Williams (1863–1921) received a bachelor of arts degree from the University of Michigan in 1881 and graduated from Howard University's law school.

products of the farm and the shop were ranged in attractive order. The day closed with a reception to the graduates, at which were present the orator of the day, the teachers and the Alumni of the school, and many visitors.

Commencement day proper, though an important feature of commencement week, is not the only one of interest. The exercises really continued through a whole week, beginning with the joint public meeting of the literary societies, followed by the public rhetoricals, the union entertainment of the religious organizations, the closing of the training school, the graduating exercises of the Bible School, the industrial exhibition, and the commencement sermon. Tuskegee had the distinction this year of having the commencement sermon preached by Dr. E. Winchester Donald, the successor of Phillips Brooks as pastor of Trinity Church, Boston.

The graduating class of the Bible School numbered five, four of them men with an average age of forty years and pastors of large churches in town. Members of these congregations come out in large numbers to see their minister[s] receive diplomas. The following subjects among those discussed will give some idea of the practical nature of the themes: The Value of a Well-Informed Ministry, The Duty of the Minister to His Church and to His Community, and Why Colored Young Men Should Enter the Ministry. Of the five graduated there were three Methodists and two Baptists. Other denominations represented in the school are Presbyterian, Congregationalists, and Christian.

The exhibition given by the industrial department was the first of its kind in the history of the school, in previous years the certificates to those who had served a satisfactory apprenticeship having been awarded on commencement day. Samples of industrial work were arranged on the stage. Papers were read on topics connected with the industries and various features of such work were illustrated. Girls showed how to clean a lamp, how to cut and fit a dress, to make bread, to iron a shirt; boys illustrated brick-house-building, wheel-wrighting, brick laying, mattress-making, shoe-making, ironing a buggy, etc. Thirty-nine certificates were awarded to representatives from fourteen trades. Sixteen of the number receiving these certificates have completed also the literary course and will go out into the world to practice some form of the knowledge they have gained here. The others will continue their studies, being greatly helped in their efforts of self-support by what they will be able to earn at their trades, working on Saturdays and on the regular workday which comes once a week for every student in the school.

The growth of Tuskegee Institute has been marvelous. Starting in 1881 with one teacher and thirty pupils in a log church and two shanties loaned for the purpose, without a penny save the $3,000 donated by the state for salaries, it numbers now 1,025 persons, including 809 pupils in the Normal School, 150 in the Model School, 66 in teachers and superintendents. It owns 2,000 acres of land and has about forty buildings, either finished or in course of construction.

Twenty-five industries are taught, and nearly everything used by the school is made or raised on the grounds.

Of course, the expense of such a vast undertaking is enormous. The fixed income of the school amounting to not more than $10,000, a large sum must be secured by private subscription, and every year much time and energy are expended in the effort to raise the needed amount. Students meet their own expenses, save that of tuition which is fifty dollars annually for each individual.

An endowment fund is considered the great need of the institution. Tuskegee believes, however, that as long as she proves true to her mission friends will be found willing to extend their aid. For a long time a pressing want was a new chapel large enough to comfortably seat the whole school. A few days ago our hearts were gladdened by word from over the sea that one who does not wish her name mentioned will give ten or twelve thousand dollars for the construction of such a building.

Tuskegee, Ala., June 1, '94.

A Plea for the Moral Aim in Education

JOSEPHINE T. WASHINGTON

A plea for the moral aim does not imply a sanction of the mere moralist. Religion, "the crown and consummation of morality,"[1] is also its surest foundation. As dogma, its teaching may be prohibited, but as a reverent belief in the Power that makes for righteousness, it encounters no opposition. With this belief there is religion in the school, just as surely as without it there is irreligion. No neutral ground is possible.

The mere moralist is not even a good teacher of morals. He lacks the divine fire which gives warmth to words and kindles a response in the heart of the hearer. Human effort needs divine reinforcement. As Phillip Brooks said: "I do not know how any man can stand and plead with his brethren for the higher life unless he is perpetually conscious that round them with whom he pleads there is the perpetual pleading and the voice of God Himself."[2] Without question of creed, this attitude can inspire the noblest ideals. The fruit of the Spirit is manifest in joy, peace, long-suffering, gentleness, goodness, faith, meekness, temperance.

Whether "Education is for conduct," "is preparation for life," is "for social efficiency," or "for citizenship," as is variously expressed with but slight difference of meaning, the implication is clear: the ethical intent is the golden thread running through all true educational activities. Anything else may be instruction, termed education, it would be misnamed.

Cox[3] says: "Religion, or character, is life, and life is character." Character then, has to do with all of life; is taught by all of life, and cannot be taught a part from life. There is no situation or circumstance which does not leave its stamp. The teacher is to recognize the continuous nature of the educational process, and make every step favorable to the highest order of development. To this end, the moral aim must be held consciously in mind.

While it is true that from the personality of the right sort of teacher helpful

---

* "A Plea for the Moral Aim in Education," *A.M.E. Church Review* 38, no. 2 (October 1921): 67–71.

1. Unknown quotation.

2. Brooks, "February 12," 29–30.

3. The original reads "Coe."

influences will radiate, there should be a definite effort to cultivate in the child the traits deemed desirable. This effort, associated with everything entering into the experience of the child, and continued throughout the period of tutelage, constitutes the moral aim in education. Its realization calls for intelligence, sympathy, tact, philosophy, faith. It is work which demands the best the artist has to offer, no bungler can succeed.

In the public schools of the United States there is no well-defined system of moral training. In this respect we are behind England, France, Japan, and other leading nations. That our country is awakening to this need, is evidenced by recent utterances of the National Education Association,[4] as well as opinions from prominent school men in various parts of the country.

It will take a long pull, a hard pull, and a pull all together, however, to undo the harm wrought by past neglect. We have an alarmingly large class of young people whose only idea seems to be to have what they call "a good time." Life for them has no serious meaning, they are here to get what they want, regardless of the rights of others, religion is a myth, morality a farce, those who would be governed by them "old fogies." The viewpoint of these young people is, if possible, to be changed, others are to be formed in character and ideals, instead of being neglected until they need reforming.

The school cannot relegate this duty to the home and the church. In many homes there is neither the desire nor the ability to undertake moral training. Only fifty-five percent of the families of the nation have even a nominal church affiliation. Were home and school measuring up to their highest possibilities, the school should have a share in this work.

The very fact that so many of the child's waking hours are spent in the schoolroom fixes there a large measure of responsibility. Besides, teachers have the advantage of pedagogical training. They at least, are beginning to comprehend child nature. They realize that the boy who almost drives distracted parents well-meaning but ignorant may have in him the making of a great man. The fact that he "will not keep quiet" and "does not take to books" perhaps merely indicates that he is of the motor-minded type. The same energy that, misused, causes him to be classed as "bad," properly directed, will make him good for something.

The moral aim must concern itself with the question of health. Children should be taught to look upon the care of the body not merely as something desirable in itself, but as a duty which bears an important relation to the right performance of every duty. Those who have noticed their own inclination to be worse than their usual selves when suffering from even a trifling complaint, have had an experience which is in line with scientific testimony.

4. The National Education Association was formed in Philadelphia in 1857 as a professional organization to articulate the needs of America's burgeoning public-school system (Cardinal, "National Education Association," 1771).

Darwin, in his "Descent of Man," says: "That the state of the body, by affecting the brain, has great influence on the moral tendencies is known to most of those who have suffered from chronic derangement of the digestion or liver. The same fact is likewise shown by the perversion or destruction of the moral sense being often one of the earliest symptoms of mental derangement, and insanity is notoriously often inherited."[5]

The school should teach temperance as meaning moderation in things helpful, no less than total abstinence from that which is harmful. Gluttony is to be condemned as well as drunkenness.

Reverence the child should be taught for the wonderful mechanism of the body, and for its more wonderful functioning with spirit in the carrying out of high ends. Reverence, however, does not enjoin silence when the spoken word is needed. The [*sic*] rather does true reverence seek to protect her own. Though subjects to be treated with the utmost delicacy, sex hygiene and sex morality should have a place in the educational scheme. Too long have ignorance and innocence been confounded. Unless boys and girls grow up with correct information and the proper attitude towards such problems, their education will be deficient in an essential respect. If, at the period of adolescence young people are impressed as one writer has put it, with the truth that they are links in the great chain of humanity, bearers of a heritage from the distant past to the limitless future, that this responsibility can be met only by conserving their powers and dedicating them to the ends for which they were given, that dissipation means disease and death fewer would fall victims to vice.

In most cases wrong training is responsible *too* for boys and girls growing up indolent and self-indulgent. So often are they needlessly thwarted in their desire to take part in the activities going on around them, their feelings hurt, and aspirations crushed, that it is small wonder the spirit of service yields to that of selfishness.

There is a saving power in work if we would but wisely use it. The lad who is interested in useful employment is in little danger of going astray. Thos. A. Edison says: "I have never had the time to be tempted to do anything against the moral law."[6]

With industry goes thrift. "Teach economy," said Abraham Lincoln, "it begins with saving money."[7] It does not end there. Children should be taught to avoid waste of time, energy and material. They should be led to see, however, that thrift sometimes means wise expenditure.

This is seen in the results of an investigation recently made by the Department of Agriculture, showing that *poor* roads are very expensive things for

5. Darwin, *The Descent of Man*, 124.
6. "Edison Never Was Tempted," 79.
7. "President Lincoln," 27.

country communities. The cost of hauling farm produce over ordinary country roads is twenty-three cents a ton mile, whereas over hard-surfaced roads it is only thirteen cents.

Closely related to thrift is recreation, for true recreation entails such a spending of leisure as promotes efficiency in work. Educators know, too, that play has a large part in moral development, furnishing as it does, an outlet for pent-up energy, relieving nervous tension, exercising the imagination, strengthening the will, and affording opportunities for harmonious, cooperative activity. It is not enough though, that school authorities make provision for the recreational side of life as a present need of youth. There is need of keeping alive the play instinct even after entrance into the working world. Only by making play universal can its moral value be of permanent social significance.

An interesting article on "The Church and Recreation," published some time[8] ago in *The Churchman,* quoted the following testimony of a prominent physical director in the Young Men's Christian Association:

> "A single game of basketball,[9] properly played, involves practically every fundamental of right human development. Every lesson of the Bible may be carried out within the four walls of the gymnasium, and be made to play its practical part in the building up of human and Christian character."[10]

The teaching of self-mastery, for which there are such excellent opportunities on the playground, should be carried into all activities. Too many adults, admirable in other respects, fly into a fury on the slightest provocation. A certain clever newspaper man is said never to have kept any position more than a few months, because he had the habit of getting into a rage over trivial annoyances and throwing up the job, however desirable, in his saner moments, it seemed to him.

Even children can learn to be tolerant, to differ without losing temper. They should learn to respect the right of the other person to whatever belongs to him—opinions included. The sacredness of property claims should be emphasized. Outside of the grosser forms of misappropriation there are minor offenses of this sort of which children are often guilty. One of these is borrowing and failing to return promptly, or even borrowing without permission.

It is important that we cultivate in the child a sense of honor. If he can be led

8. The original reads "sometime."

9. The original reads "basket ball."

10. Goodnow, "The Church and Recreation," 81. Goodnow's quotation reads: "[For example,] a single game of basketball properly played involves, [these Y.M.C.A. physical directors say,] practically every fundamental of right human [deportment]. Every lesson of the Bible may be carried out within the four walls of the gymnasium and be made to play its particular part in the building up of human and Christian character."

to pride himself upon keeping his word, scorning the scheming which would gain at the expense of another, much will be accomplished in his moral training.

In all these endeavors trust has a place. While exercising due vigilance the teacher, or other grown-up, must show that he believes in the good intentions of the young people for whose care and training he is responsible. This inspires the self-confidence necessary to the realization of the best in human beings.

Doubt is disastrous to growth. The boy who is accustomed to hear that he is "the greatest liar in creation" is likely in time to merit the opprobrium.[11] It must be remembered too, that children's so-called "lies" are not always lies. They may be mere "make-believes." This manifestation of the dramatic instinct, common to childhood, is to be distinguished from the real lies which even young children sometimes tell. Yet patient effort will perhaps show a small child that society is built on our trust in one another, and that the structure would fall should lying become general.

Beginning with those near and dear, the child's regard for the welfare of others should reach out from home and school and familiar friends to take in all human beings. Thus will grow patriotism.

Thus will grow that larger thing—the spirit of inter-nationalism, the spread of which makes for universal peace. So will race hatred and national antipathies with all their baneful and death-dealing influences, be swept out of existence. Interest in one another and, to a great extent, esteem, grow out of acquaintance-ship. To the true educator no human being is alien, but each is a member of a common brotherhood. The child brought under any other influence is perverted in his development.

It is not actions alone with which we need to be concerned. The way we think and feel about things has dynamic as well as ethical importance. When during the Revolutionary War it was advised that the British troops be increased in Boston until they outnumbered the American, Pitt is said to have remarked that "what the British had to fight against was not so much the guns of the Americans as the sentiment of liberty."[12]

It has been pointed out that there are three primary means of moral training: (1) The establishment of correct habits; (2) The development of right, feelings [*sic*], (3) The cultivation of wholesome interests. It goes without saying that these methods are to be used simultaneously.

Every condition or incident, every subject presented, the method of teaching, the school environment, the personality of the teacher—above all, the personality of the teacher—has its influence, and may be made a factor for good in the hands of the teacher who accepts the moral aim. Bare walls will be brightened by at least a copy of a good picture, and otherwise cheerless atmosphere glad-

11. The original reads, "approbrium."
12. Pitt, "Lord Chatham's Speeches on the American Revolution," 455.

dened by a simple bloom. Something there will be to feed the starved soul of the sensitive child, for many, it should be remembered, enter the kingdom of God through the Gate Beautiful.

The moral aim requires an observance of the rules of good breeding, not only as a lubrication of human intercourse but as a form which tends to fashion the spirit desired.

Under the influence of the moral aim all school subjects take on a new significance. Geography is not a collection of meaningless data about rivers and mountains and cities, but a study which arouses pride in our own country and fosters interest in the peoples of other lands.

History appears no longer a mass of dry facts invented for the confusion of the learner, but is invested with a warm, human interest.

"The utility of history," wrote Lord Chesterfield to his son, "consists principally in the examples it gives us of the virtues and vices of those who have gone before us, upon which we ought to make the proper observations. History animates us and excites us to the love and the practice of virtue by showing us the regard and veneration that was always paid to great and virtuous men, in the times in which they lived, and the pride and glory with which their names are perpetuated, and transmitted down to our times. . . . Such are the characters that you should imitate, if you would be a great and good man, which is the only way to be a happy one!"[13]

With the moral aim in mind, nature study is used not only to instill the elements of science, but as Professor John Dewey says, "to cultivate a sympathetic understanding of the place of plants and animals in life and to develop emotion and aesthetic interest."[14]

Literature, no longer merely a specified amount of required reading, contributes to love for beauty, truth and noble living.

Music and art, instead of being formal and lifeless accomplishments, become vital factors in the child's education, refining taste, awakening the higher perceptions, and deepening the affections.

Advocates of the moral aim give manual training an important place because of its dynamic value in character-building.

13. Stanhope, "Letter XLVII," 1:153. Stanhope's version reads, "The utility of history consists principally in the examples it gives us, of the virtues and vices of those who have gone before us; upon which we ought to make proper observations. History animates us and excites us to the love and to the practice of virtue; by showing us the regard and veneration that was always paid to great and virtuous men, in the times in which they lived, and the [praise] and glory with which their names are perpetuated, and transmitted down to our times . . . [such are the rewards that always crown virtue; and such the characters] that you should imitate, if you would be a great and good man, which is the only way to be a happy one!"

14. Dewey, *Schools of To-Morrow,* 98.

Stories are used, not simply to gratify the child's longing for adventure, but to set before him examples of courage, devotion, loyalty—whatever in history and imagination we wish to impress upon the plastic mind. G. Stanley Hall says: "Let me write the stories, and I care not who write the textbooks."[15]

It is impossible to enumerate all the ways in which the moral aim may find expression. On every hand are opportunities for the teacher who, having eyes, will see. As has been said in another connection: "She has only to see the aim clearly to keep it ever before her mind, and she will have little difficulty in finding ways in which to realize her object. Every study furnishes its characteristic opportunity."[16]

To recapitulate: We hold that character-formation is the essential thing in life—therefore, in education, that some sort of development is going on all the time, whether or not willed; that growth in the right direction is fostered by a conscious moral aim, that the real worth of educational processes is conditioned on their ethical significance, that all studies, situations and surroundings may be made to furnish helpful lessons, that, after all, the most powerful agent in the moral training of the child in school is the personality of the teacher. As has been well said, "The teacher is the constant text-book of the child."[17] She is the medium through which all is reflected, her viewpoint colors everything.

This subject has a meaning for all. All are not teachers or parents, but all are citizens. As such, each person bears a measure of responsibility for the character of the institutions under which he lives. When the people demand that the moral aim be made paramount in education, no teacher lacking in this respect will continue to find employment in the schools.

15. Cronk, "Missionary Education through Ear-Gate," 292. Hall's words read: "Let me tell the stories of a nation and I care not who writes the text books."

16. Johnston, "Vocational Guidance thruout the School Course," 648. Johnston's version reads, "She [the teacher] has only to see him clearly."

17. Unknown quotation.

PART II

LITERARY ENHANCEMENT

Holland's "Kathrina"

JOSEPHINE J. TURPIN

Holland's "Kathrina" is before me. "Her life and mine in a poem,"[1] the author tells us. It is a book with an object. The poem is true poetry. In sentiment [it] is noble and inspiring. In expression, graceful and musical. There is no search for quaint figures. Beautiful imagery flows as naturally from the poet's pen as song from the bird's throat. He affects not love of nature, but feels it intensely. His pages hold grand truths, unlike the comet that flashes occasionally[2] across the heavens, but like the brilliant stars that glitter all over the sky. No summer day calm pervades this production, nor are the storms perpetual. Sometimes the peace is like the gentle rippling of a quiet sea. A bit of humor here and there delights the laughter seeker. Ever and anon, we watch the play of passions that possess the wild grandeur of some famed cataract. Through all runs a vein of pathos that invades our own bosom, causing our heart to throb in a sympathy which is half pleasure, half pain.

To Northampton on the "winding and willow-fringed Connecticut,"[3] is due the honor of the hero's birth. A dreamy, sensitive boy whose memory in after years goes vividly back to his mother and an ancient elm (his best beloved friends) he learns a family secret [sic]. The current of his thought is changed; he doubts the loving kindness of a God who allowed his father, a man good and true, his mother said, to take his own life.

With the hidden burden of his knowledge and rebellion, his mother was more than ever his idol. An incident soon made known the powers within him. Having chased an escaped lamb up a mountain steep, he kneels on the summit and a revelation burst upon him. What can be more beautiful than his much-quoted description of the scene?

> "I saw before me, like a jeweled cup,
> The valley hollowed to its heaven-kissed lip

---

* "Holland's 'Kathrina,'" *People's Advocate* (Washington, D.C.), 30 June 1883, 1.

1. Holland, Josiah Gilbert, *Kathrina: Her Life and Mine in a Poem* (Sampson Low, Son & Marston, 1869); hereafter citations to this edition will refer to part and page number.

2. The original reads "occasionly."

3. Holland, *Kathrina*, pt. 1, "Childhood and Youth," 17.

> The serrate green against the serrate blue-
> Brimming with beauty's essence; palpitant
> With a divine elixir-lucent floods
> Poured from the golden chalice of the sun,
> At which my spirit drank with conscious growth,
> And drank again with still expanding scope
> Of comprehension and of faculty."[4]

A little later he says:

> "I bowed my head
> Beneath the chrismal light, and felt my soul
> Baptized and set apart to poetry."[5]

The boy heretofore led by a gentle woman, in the new life dawning within him, becomes her counselor. Heretofore taught by her, he now passes with other youths into the village seminary. He tells us:

> "Victories
> Were won too easily to bring me pride,
> And only bred contempt of the low pitch
> And lower purpose of the power which strove
> So feebly and so clumsily."[6]

Afterwards he seeks the college halls that he had seen "from boyhood's mount of vision." It was his last year there.

> "Spring
> [That ushered in my closing college year]
> Came up the valley on her balmy wings.
> And winter fled away, and left no trace,
> Save here and there a snowy drift to show
> Where his cold feet had rested in their flight."[7]
> A memorable morning brings a messenger:
> "Your mother can not long survive,
> Come home to her today."[8]

Harrowing fact! his loved one is raving; she knows him not. Burning language depicts his condition, as he "gave to grief his strong and stormy nature."[9]

---

4. Ibid., pt. 1, 32.
5. Ibid., pt. 1, 33.
6. This and the following quotation can be found ibid., pt. 1, 45 and 55, respectively.
7. Ibid., pt. 1, 57.
8. Ibid., pt. 1, 58.
9. Ibid., pt. 1, 61.

Night falls; the patient dozes; the nurse sleeps. With the craftiness of one mad, the sick woman had pretended unconsciousness. She arouses and realizes the situation. She commits the deed to which for years she has been impelled. She leaves life as her husband left. "In a common sepulture"[10] the son "laid his mother and his faith in God." In a plaintive complaint he bewails the "indifference of Nature to the fact of human pain," and ends with the sorrowful conclusion that "God is gone and Love is dead and Nature spurns her child."

L'art second holds somewhat of cheer.

> "As from a deep dead sea, by drastic lift
> Of pent volcanic fires, the dripping form
> Of a new island swells to meet the air.
> And, after months of [idle] basking, feels
> The prickly feet of life from countless germs;
> Creeping along its sides, and reaching up
> In fern and flower to the life-giving sun;
> So from my grief I rose, and so at length
> I felt new life returning; so I felt
> The life already wakened stretching forth
> To stronger light and purer atmosphere."[11]

But still our poet mourned the lack of love in a life that needed its inspiration.

Passing a church one Sabbath morn a voice—a woman's or an angel's—impels his entrance.

> "The heart is wiser than the intellect,
> And works with swifter hands and surer fect
> Towards wise conclusions."[12]

That very day, after but one look into bonny blue eyes, he questions:

> "A pious girl! (for such he had learned she was)
> And what could I be to a pious girl?
> What could she be to me?"[13]

His description of "doing good after [the] modern styles,"[14] contains both truth and satire. Happy coincidence! In meeting his mother's friend, he meets the

---

10. This and the following three quotations can be found ibid., pt. 1, "Complaint," 68 and 70, respectively.

11. Ibid., pt. 2, "Love," 73.

12. Ibid., pt. 2, 76.

13. Ibid., pt. 2, 87.

14. Ibid., pt. 2, 88.

pious girl as her niece, Kathrina, a model of womanly excellence; a character without a flaw. Kathrina, who when asked concerning her meetings with
humble Christians, "Can they do you any good!"[15] replied.

> "They can; but were it otherwise,
> I can serve them; and so should seek them still."

With a poet's fervor he told his love, and then follows a strain of exultant joy.
She is his and he is hers, yet he feels no motive stirring him to action. He slum-
bers in the Elysian of domestic happiness; and wraps his talent in a napkin. In
this state he cries out,

> "Of all the dull, dead weights man ever bore,
> Sure none can wear the soul with discontent
> Like consciousness of power unused."[16]

His wife's prophecy that one day he would long for something more, something
higher than love she could give, comes back to him. He thinks to satisfy himself
with fame. He longs for the competition of the crowded city. He burns his ships
behind him, and together they go husband, wife, and child.

The dullards of college, grown to eminence, meet him. He is stung to earnest
endeavor; his efforts are successful; he is the lion of the day, the favorite of the
hour. But the wife's clear brain and Christian heart see through the flattering
caresses. She realizes their instability of structure, their inefficiency to satisfy.
Many a brilliant but good natured repartee on the subject passes between them.
Soon the poet sees the fallacy; he ceases attempting to please the people, he will
write for the sake of art alone. He composes with his mind on fire, his thoughts
soaring even into the infinite. But woe to the creator's spirit! the child of his
imagination lacks the grace and beauty with which it had, in his mental vision,
been invested. In the depths of his despair, Kathrina's words strike him:

> "All gifts of men
> were made for use, and made for highest use."[17]

Increasing his misery tenfold, the wife is taken suddenly ill. He wonders he
had not before noticed the cheeks grown pale and the silver threaded hair. But
his work for fame and art had absorbed him. Now with a clang of wildest grief,
he sees he must lose her. She lies calmly awaiting death; but before she goes she
must be able to cry, "It is finished."[18]

One day the tinkle of her bell called him. She tells him she has been home,

15. This and the following quotation can be found ibid., pt. 2, 88 and 117, respectively.
16. Ibid., pt. 2, 158.
17. Ibid., pt. 3, "Labor," 225.
18. John 19:30.

she paints the glories of the scene, she repeats a message from his mother, she shows him the source of human comfort. In this chapter, the poet reaches the sublime. The dying wife, the celestial spirits, the angel mother, the voice of God in his own soul cry, "Kneel!"[19] and he kneels; "pray!" and he prays. The mission is accomplished; the spirit leaves the body; the bereaved weep in peaceful resignation.

"These words—this tribute—for the sake of truth to God and womankind,"[20] teach a lesson well worth conning. Man may possess the love of one beloved, he may enjoy wide renown in an applauding world, he may revel in appreciation of the beautiful; but unless he holds[21] the glory of his Maker as the chief end of his being, there is still an aching void.

19. This and the subsequent quotation can be found in Holland, *Kathrina*, pt. 4, "Consummation," 280.

20. Holland, "Kathrina: A Tribute," in *Kathrina*, 11.

21. The original reads "hold."

Anglo-African Magazine

JOSEPHINE J. TURPIN

One of the Landmarks of the Past
—Prepared for The *Globe*

"Full many a gem of purest ray serene
The dark unfathomed caves of ocean bear,
Full many a flower is born to blasts unseen
And waste its sweetness on the desert air."[1]

I agree with the poet. Full many an event in the history of the colored man, which, if known, would fire the soul of the youthful with ambition and give fresh impetus to their exertions, is buried in the dust of neglect. Full many an achievement of the despised race glorious and great, and grand, instead of being compiled in the annals of the people, instead of being woven into story and song, instead of being talked on in the family circle and held up before the admiring eyes of our children, sleeps quietly in the grave of oblivion. Such an event, such an achievement is the publication of the "Anglo-African Magazine."

At a time when the curse of slavery blurred the fair fame, of our western world, when "the wealth, the intellect, the legislature, the pulpit and the science of America concentrated on no one point so heartily as in the endeavor to write down the Negro as something less than a man;"[2] at a time when race prejudice was at its greatest development, certain noble men from among us banded themselves together in the enterprise of sending out into the world a publication which should be a revelation of the "horrors of the slave trade, a denunciation of the cruelty and injustice of the institution, and a vindication of the manhood of the race. In the introductory, speaking of the twelve millions of blacks in the United States, it says: "These millions, in order to assert and maintain their rank as men among men, must speak for themselves; no outside tongue, however gifted with eloquence, can tell their story; no outside eye, however penetrating, can see their wants; no outside organization, however benevolently intended, nor however

---

* "Anglo-African Magazine," *New York Globe*, 13 October 1883, 1.

1. Gray, "An Elegy, Written in a Country Churchyard," 5. Gray's version reads, "[unfathom'd]," "[flow'r]," and "[blush] unseen."

2. "Apology: Introductory," *Anglo-African Magazine* 1, no. 1 (January 1859): 1.

cunningly contrived, can develop the energies and aspirations which make up their mission."[3] A little further on it says: "In addition to an expose of the condition of the blacks, this magazine will have the aim to uphold and encourage the now depressed hopes of thinking black men in the United States—the men who for twenty years and more have been active in conventions, in public meetings, in societies, in the pulpit, and through the press, cheering on and laboring on to promote emancipation, affranchisement, and education; some of them in, and some of them past the prime of life, yet see as the apparent result of their work and their sacrifices, only Fugitive Slave laws and compromise bills and the denial of citizenship on the part of the Federal and State governments."[4]

Under such aims and resolves was the "Anglo-African Magazine" sent out upon the sea of journalism. The first number appeared in January, 1859, and succeeding numbers were issued monthly, until the close of the year. The copy with which fortune, in the person of a friend, favored me, is a bound volume of the twelve issues. These four hundred pages between their modest covers contained that which filled me with wonder, roused me to pride and thrilled me with hope. I wondered—that despite the horrors of those dark days of the past, such men had sprung into being; men giants in intellectual strength, warriors in the cause of right and justice, truly men among men. I was proud—that from among this people, so scorned and derided and depressed, have gone out these living assertions of our equal manhood, and these in a time when the Negro's total subjugation to the powers of ignorance was "a consummation most devoutly to be wished,"[5] and a little learning was indeed "a dangerous thing."[6] I hope—in the light of these things, what may we not hope for the race? If men made such development who had so many hindrances; if men grew to such strength who had so little sustenance; if men climbed to such eminence who were so often pushed backward; if men rose to such planes of greatness and goodness opposed by devils—and devils in men's forms, what may we not hope from those who are given education, encouragement, equality before the law? Hope thou, my soul, and sing.

The volume before me teems with able articles. The writers are men well known among the people; some hold high rank today as educators and leaders, others have fought the good fight and finished their course. No. 1 of this "Anglo-African Magazine" contains an engraving of Alexandre Dumas[7] and a sketch of life of this eminent colored novelist. James M'Cune [Smith] discourses logically

3. Ibid.

4. Ibid., 3.

5. Shakespeare, *The Tragedy of Hamlet,* 3.1.63–64.

6. Pope, "An Essay on Criticism," line 215. Pope's line reads, "A little learning is a dangerous thing."

7. Alexandre Dumas (1802–1870), French playwright and novelist.

on "Civilization—Its Dependence on Physical Circumstances." He says: "Not only is the dwelling and assembling together of men an essential condition of civilization, but the more men mingle, the larger the dwelling together, the greater is their advancement; and whatever has prevented men from coming together, whether self-imposed laws, difference of language, climate or geographical position, these have and do constitute barriers against civilization; and in proportion as these barriers have been taken down, mankind have advanced."[8] "Caste is the general term for that feature in human institutions which isolates man from his fellow man. Wherever caste is established civilization is arrested, and either remains stationary as in China, or sinks back into barbarism." "The only drawback in prosperity is the caste which slavery has thrown in our midst, and which is chief minister to the continuance of slavery. The retrograde movement of States in which slavery and caste have greatest influence, compared with the advancement of other States comparatively uncursed with these isolators,[9] is abundantly known."

Mr. Smith writes on the "German Invasion" and other topics of interest.[10] M. R. Delany's papers on astronomical subjects[11] evince profound learning. The few chapters of his serial "Blake, or The Huts of America," contained in the different numbers, possess a thrilling interest.[12] We follow the movements of Henry with admiration and apprehension; we grow indignant over the wrongs of handsome Maggie, and boil with wrath at the infamy of the slaveholder. "Hetrogene" makes us laugh over Mrs. Freshington, the black companion piece of Mrs. Parington [sic].[13] Wm. C. Nell fires our soul with the valor of the "Colored American Patriots."[14] "Ethiop," whose real name I know not but would like so much to know, has my sympathy in his intense feeling of race pride. I roam

8. Smith, "Civilization," 5. The next two quotations are from pages 15 and 16, respectively.

9. The original reads "isolaters."

10. James Smith, "The German Invasion," *Anglo-African Magazine* 1, no. 2 (February 1859): 44–52; and *Anglo-African Magazine* 1, no. 3 (March 1859): 83–86; James Smith, "On the Fourteenth Query of Thomas Jefferson's *Notes on Virginia*," *Anglo-African Magazine* 1, no. 8 (August 1859): 225–38.

11. Martin R. Delany, "The Attraction of Planets," *Anglo-American Magazine* 1, no. 1 (January 1859): 17–20; Martin R. Delany, "Comets," *Anglo-American Magazine* 1, no. 2 (February 1859): 59–60.

12. Martin R. Delany, "Blake, or The Huts of America," *Anglo-African Magazine* 1, no. 1 (January 1859): 20–28. "Blake" was serialized in the following issues of volume 1 of the *Anglo-African Magazine*: no. 2 (February 1859): 37–43; no. 3 (March 1859): 69–79; no. 4 (April 1859): 104–14; no. 5 (May 1859): 129–39; and no. 6 (June 1859): 161–72.

13. Hetrogene, "Mrs. Partington and Mrs. Freshington," *Anglo-African Magazine* 1, no. 3 (March 1859): 129–30.

14. William C. Nell, "Colored American Patriots," *Anglo-African Magazine* 1, no. 1 (January 1859): 30–31.

with delight through the "Afri-American Picture Gallery," where he shows us Attucks,[15] Toussaint L'Ouverture,[16] Aldridge,[17] Phillis Wheatley,[18] together with other pictures as equally interesting and inspiring.

J. Holland Townsend, writing of "American Caste and Common Schools," says, "The Prosperity and Happiness of a nation depends mainly upon the intelligence of the great mass of the people, especially in a country like that of our own where the popular will is the law of the land. It is a well-established fact that an ignorant people must always be a poor people; it matters not how fortune may favor them, for a time, in the accumulation of wealth, sooner or later it will find its way into the hands of the more intelligent."[19] Robert Campbell writes of affairs in Jamaica,[20] and J. T. Holly performs a like office for Hayti.[21] J. W. C. Pennington gives a "Review of Slavery and the Slave Trade,"[22] and grows eloquent over the meanness, the baseness, and the cruelty of the "peculiar institution." M. H. Freeman urges the need of education among the colored people.[23] In the days before Frances[24] Ellen Watkins was merged into Mrs. Harper, her gifted pen contributed to the attractions of the "Anglo African Magazine."[25] Dr. Blyden

15. Crispus Attucks (1723–1770), a front-line participant in the Boston Massacre of 1770 and the first one killed.

16. Toussaint L'Ouverture (1743–1803), an ex-slave leader in the Haitian Revolt (1791–1804) that led to Haiti's independence from French rule.

17. Ira Aldridge (1807–1867), an African American actor.

18. Phillis Wheatley (1753–1784), African American poet.

19. Townsend, "American Caste and Common Schools," 80.

20. Robert Campbell, "Struggles for Freedom in Jamaica," *Anglo-African Magazine* 1, no. 3 (March 1859): 90–92; Robert Campbell, "Effects of Emancipation in Jamaica," *Anglo-African Magazine* 1, no. 5 (May 1859): 151–53.

21. J. T. Holly, "Thoughts on Hayti," *Anglo-African Magazine* 1, no. 6 (June 1859): 185–87; subsequent articles entitled "Thoughts on Hayti" appeared in the following issues of volume 1 of the *Anglo-African Magazine*: no. 6 (June 1859): 185–87; no. 7 (July 1859): 219–22; no. 8 (August 1859): 241–43; no. 9 (September 1859): 298–300; no. 10 (October 1859): 327–29; and no. 11 (November 1859): 363–67.

22. J. W. C. Pennington, "Review of Slavery and the Slave Trade," appeared in the following issues of volume 1 of the *Anglo-African Magazine*, no. 3 (March 1859): 93–96; no. 4 (April 1859): 123–26; and no. 5 (May 1859): 155–59.

23. M. H. Freeman, "The Educated Wants of the Free Colored People," *Anglo-African Magazine* 1, no. 4 (April 1859): 115–19.

24. The original reads "Francis."

25. Frances Ellen Watkins published several poems and a short story in the *Anglo-African Magazine* in the following issues: "Truth," vol. 2, no. 3 (March 1859): 87; "Gone to God," vol. 1, no. 4 (April 1859): 123; "Our Greatest Want," vol. 1, no. 5 (May 1859): 160; "The Dying Fugitive," vol. 1, no. 8 (August 1859): 253–54; and "Two Offers," vol. 1, no. 9 (September 1859): 288–91; and vol. 1, no. 10 (October 1859): 311–13.

wrote from Africa "A Chapter in the History of the African Slave Trade."[26] Prof. John M. Langston gives an interesting account of "The Oberlin-Wellington Rescue."[27] Among other contributors were Robert Gordon,[28] George R. Vashon,[29] James Fields,[30] Sarah Douglass,[31] and Grace A. Mapps.[32]

Such is the "Anglo-African Magazine," a book with which every youth desirous of learning the achievements of the noble colored men of twenty years ago, should acquaint himself. It cannot fail to fill his head with knowledge and wisdom, and to fire his heart with hope and courage.

26. Edward Blyden, "A Chapter in the History of the African Slave Trade," *Anglo-African Magazine* 1, no. 6 (June 1859): 178–84.

27. John M. Langston's "The Oberlin-Wellington Rescue" relates the story of the kidnapping of John Price, a black man from Oberlin, Ohio, on 13 September 1858 and his subsequent rescue in Wellington, Ohio. Details of his seizure and rescue can be found in Langston's "The Oberlin-Wellington Rescue," *Anglo-African Magazine* 1, no. 7 (July 1859): 209–16.

28. Robert Gordon, "Intellectual Culture," *Anglo-African Magazine* 1, no. 6 (June 1859): 187–91; Robert Gordon, "In the Constitution of Man Exists a Religious Element," 1, no. 8 (August 1859): 238–41; and Robert Gordon, "On the Personality of the First Cause," 1, no. 9 (September 1859): 279–82.

29. George R. Vashon, "The Successive Advances of Astronomy," *Anglo-African Magazine* 1, no. 7 (July 1859): 204–8.

30. James Fields, "The Shadows of Intemperance," *Anglo-African Magazine*" 1, no. 7 (July 1859): 221.

31. Sarah M. Douglass, "A Good Habit Recommended," *Anglo-African Magazine* 1, no. 5 (May 1859): 154

32. Grace A. Mapps, "Lines," *Anglo-African Magazine* 1, no. 11 (November 1859): 345–46.

The Province of Poetry

JOSEPHINE TURPIN WASHINGTON

What is poetry? Of what does its essence consist? What is its distinguishing principle?

Perhaps in this instance it is easier to give a negative than a positive definition. The language of Shelley, in his "Hymn to the Spirit of Nature," might appropriately be applied to the genius of poetry:

> "All feel, yet see thee never;"[1]

and two other lines, taken from the same, may fittingly be added:

> "Lamp of Earth, where'er thou movest,
> Its dim shapes are clad with brightness."

It is agreed that all verse is not poetry. We read perchance a newspaper or magazine effusion and throw it down in disgust, exclaiming, "There is no poetry in that." Why? Probably not one in a hundred could tell, and yet the judgment of the whole hundred might be correct. The want is one easily felt, but difficult to express. Of the explanations attempted, some might approach the truth after this wise: "Oh, there is no soul in it," or "It does not make me feel," or "It deals altogether with the trivial and superficial."

Poets and critics have responded to this inquiry with answers variously worded; but, beneath the outer garb of diverse language, we catch the glimpse of a common meaning. Webster defines poetry as "Modes of expressing thought and feeling which are suitable to the imagination when excited or elevated, and characterized usually by a measured form of one sort or another." Emerson says, "Poetry is the perpetual endeavor to express the spirit of the thing; to pass the brute body, and search the life and reason which cause it to exist."[2] Ruskin calls poetry "the suggestion, by the imagination, of noble grounds for the noble emotions."[3] Charles James Fox characterizes it as "The great refreshment of the human mind,

---

* "The Province of Poetry," *A.M.E. Church Review* 6, no. 2 (October 1889): 137–47.

1. Shelley, "Prometheus Unbound," 2.5. The next quotation is taken from the same drama, act, and scene. Shelley's line reads, [I] feel [but] see thee [not].

2. Emerson, "Poetry and Imagination," 731.

3. Ruskin, "Of the Received Opinions Touching the 'Grand' Style," pt. 4, chap. 1, p. 11.

the only thing after all."[4] Aristotle terms it imitation.[5] Bacon says that "It was ever thought to have some participation of divineness, because it doth raise and erect the mind by submitting the show of things to the desires of the mind, whereas reason doth buckle and bow the mind unto the nature of things."[6] Shelley calls it "The best and happiest thoughts of the best and happiest minds,"[7] and Poe declares that "A poem deserves its title only inasmuch as it excites by elevating the soul."[8] Matthew Arnold thinks poetry "Simply the most beautiful, impressive and widely effective mode of saying things,"[9] and Macauley says, "By poetry we mean the art of employing words in such a manner as to produce an illusion on the imagination; the art of doing by means of words what the painter does by means of color."[10]

If we dared to essay a definition, not discarding and yet not wholly accepting any of the above, but combining with the substance of each the popular idea, which generally has its foundation in truth, we might say that poetry is a species of composition, usually metrical in form, addressed especially to the imagination, and tending to please, instruct and inspire.

There are people who pride themselves upon being what they call "practical," and who look with contempt upon anything verging on sentiment. By the term "practical" they mean that which directly contributes to worldly success, business prosperity, the accumulation of wealth—in short, whatever primarily aids in the solution of the problem what we shall eat, what we shall drink, and wherewithal we shall be clothed. The talk of such a character is of stocks and bonds, of the state of the market, of buying and selling, his highest aspiration to be a "good liver," to dress his wife in silks and furs, to be spoken of as a prosperous business man, one who knows how to get along in the world. For him, Nature has no charm, save as a contributor to his physical wants; literature no allurement, unless it teaches him how to turn what he touches to gold. He could see nothing in Niagara but wasted water-power, and would consider Homer to have been better employed casting up accounts in a ledger than writing the

4. Emerson, "Poetry and Imagination," 733. Emerson quotes Charles James Fox on poetry.

5. Aristotle, *The Poetics of Aristotle,* pt. 1, p. 7.

6. Bacon, "Of the Proficience and Advancement of Learning Divine and Human," bk. 2, pt. 4, pp. 343–44. Bacon's version reads, "[And therefore] it was ever thought to have some participation, of divines, because it doth raise and erect the mind, by submitting the [shews] of things to the desires of the mind."

7. Shelley, "A Defence of Poetry," 136. Shelley's quotation reads, "The best and happiest moments of the happiest and best minds."

8. Poe, "The Poetic Principle," 1:227.

9. Arnold, "Heinrich Heine," 235.

10. Macaulay, "Essay on Milton," 12.

Iliad. The deepest and most tender affections are beyond his comprehension, and he goes through life maimed in soul, dwarfed and incomplete.

What thinks such a man of poetry? All bosh, nonsense, as some think of religion, fit food for women and children. What of poets and their devotees? Fools, simpletons, crack brained folks, worthy only of commiseration.

> "A primrose by the river's brim
> A yellow primrose is to him.
> And it is nothing more."[11]

There are Mr. Gradgrinds outside of Dickens' pages, and the young lives of many a Tom and Louise have been sadly wrecked by their blundering stupidity. Only the weak are afraid of being tender; only the fool cultivates one part of his nature at the expense of the other. A great brain and a great heart are usually found conjoined.

Sentiment may be termed the true sense of things. It is the underlying thought of being, the soul of phenomena, the reason for the existence of external manifestations. In the words of Madame De Staël, "What a world, when animated by sentiment, without which the world itself were but a desert!"[12] There is a closer connection between what is entitled sentiment and what is classed in the category of the practical than most people think. What teacher has not had pupils who "couldn't see any use in the study of the classics and the higher mathematics?" I have even known a young man, and one *too* who aspired to pulpit oratory, to say that he "Didn't think he needed to take history and literature—they would be of no practical service to him." There are older and more experienced people in the world quite as narrow in their views as this simple youth. Everybody is familiar with the arguments for the study of sciences of which we do not make direct use in common, everyday life. Similar reasons, though these not the most worthy which can be given, might be advanced for the cultivation of sentiment and its handmaiden, poetry.

Let it be observed here that there is a distinction between sentiment and the weak mawkishness known as sentimentality. The one is genuine coin, the other spurious imitation; the one alive to all honest, active endeavor for humanity; the other, "dabbling in the fount of tears, divorces the feeling from her mate the deed."[13] The one is affected to tears by the woes of the imaginary hero of stage or novel, yet indifferent to the misery of real men and women; the other, while

11. Wordsworth, "Peter Bell," 2:252. Wordsworth's lines read, "A primrose by [a] river's brim/ A yellow primrose [was] to him, / And it [was] nothing more."

12. De Staël, *Corinne; or Italy*, 55–56.

13. Tennyson, "The Brook," 137. Tennyson's quote reads: "[who] dabbling in the fount of [fictive] tears / [And nursed by mealy-mouth'd philanthropies / Divorce] the Feeling from her mate the Deed."

perhaps no less moved by the distresses of fictitious beings, is touched by the actual suffering about him, and labors for its relief.

While sentiment, feeling, the cultivation of an inner, a soul life, does not directly contribute to the bread-winning process, it sweetens and strengthens and ennobles man's whole nature, and so fits him for the better performance of any duty; arms him more effectually for any conflict, whether with difficulty or temptation, and makes him more of a man, abler to do a man's work in the world.

> "Whatever elevates,
> Inspires, refreshes any human soul,
> Is useful to that soul.[14]

Mr. G. J. Goshen, an English banker and political economist, declares that the cultivation of the imagination is essential to the highest success in politics, in learning, and in the commercial business of life. He who lacks a poetic taste lacks imagination, without which are wanting clearness of vision, comprehensiveness of understanding and the subtle tact which is as oil to the machinery of both public and private life. To the cultivation of this faculty all who are deficient therein should assiduously address themselves. How this may be done Pres. Porter states: "The study and reading of poetry exercise and cultivate the imagination, and in this way impart intellectual power. It is impossible to read the products of any poet's imagination without using our own. To reach what he creates is to recreate in our own minds the images and pictures which he first conceived and then expressed in language."[15] One who cannot like poetry may be said to have been born into the world mentally blind and deaf—a misfortune as much greater than the deprivation of the corresponding natural senses as spiritual things are superior to material.

Poets are seers, divining and revealing hidden truths; interpreters of beauty and inspirers to a life of a loftier type. In these choice and gifted spirits the great heart of humanity finds its voice; through them all that is best in man speaks from soul to soul. Sentiments we hold sacred are clothed in worthy language. That we have long thought or felt vaguely is expressed in fitting phrases:

> "As imagination bodies forth
> The forms of things unknown, the poet's pen
> Turns them to shapes, and gives to airy nothing

---

14. Holland, *Kathrina*, 236.

15. The portion of the quotation, "It is impossible to read the products of any poet's imagination without using our own," appears to be from Charles Francis Richardson, "How to Study: Poetry," 335. The rest of the quotation, "To reach [read (in the original)] what he creates is to recreate in our own minds the images and pictures which he first conceived and then expressed in language," comes from "Books and Reading: Poetry and Poets," 507.

A local habitation and a name."[16]

Our most indefinite yearnings for higher things, our half unconscious longings and aspirations are recognized and addressed. Each finds passages that seem meant specially for himself, so fully are the varied needs of the soul understood and supplied. The poet's is

> "The gift, the vision of the unsealed eye,
>   To pierce the mist o'er life's deep meanings spread.
> To reach the hidden fountain urns that lie
>   Far in man's heart."[17]

Poetry has a particular charm for the lover of nature. It knows his favorites, paints them lovingly, descries new beauties, points out hidden relations, unveils the thought behind their creation, and sends him back to the woods more humble and reverent of spirit, and yet filled with new delight in what was before his pleasure. The green of the grass is fresher, the glitter of the dewdrop more brilliant, the carol of the birds a divine paean.[18] It is as if he has had his eyes touched with holy spittle: he no longer sees "men as trees walking," but looks forth with clear and perfect vision. To him who has hitherto been dull to the glories of nature, it may be said to add a sense. The world takes on a new aspect for him. Nothing is any longer commonplace or ordinary. He can find beauty, melody, sweetness everywhere. He rejoices in the scent of new-mown hay, the sheen of leaves, the waving of branches, the smell of damp fresh earth, the coloring and grouping of clouds. Solitude no longer means loneliness, nor leisure ennui. He now hath

> "The child's sight in his breast,
> And sees all *new,*
> What oftenest he has viewed,
> He views with the first glory
>   Fair and good
>   Pall never on him."[19]

The poet

> "Finds tongues in trees, books in the running brooks,
> Sermons in stones, and good in everything."[20]

---

16. Shakespeare, *A Midsummer Night's Dream,* 5.1.14–17.
17. Hemans, "A Poet's Dying Hymn," 392.
18. The original reads "paen."
19. Browning, "The Poet," 28.
20. Shakespeare, *As You Like It,* 2.1.15–16.

"The violet by the mossy stone,
Half hidden from the eye,"[21]

is to him not merely a bit of vegetable beauty, but a symbol of modesty and sweet retirement. He considers "The lilies of the field, how they toil not, neither do they spin,"[22] and from them learns a lesson of quiet trust and restfulness in the sustaining power of a gracious Providence. The great ethical truths which Nature "half reveals and half conceals" are presented by the poet: yet we do not feel that he aims to "point a moral," but rather that his heart is full, and he needs must speak what is. His is the surest fame. He writes for no one time or country. With him anachronisms are impossible. He addresses himself to the heart and by the heart; the same in every age and clime, he will always be understood. He portrays the beauty of Nature, perennial in its charm and constant in its attraction for the sons of men.

Poetry is closely allied to our best affections. Home, wife, mother, country, are themes ever dear to the poet. He recognizes that "The heart has needs above the head,"[23] and seeks to supply it with food fit for its use. By the study of poetry the affections are strengthened, purified and refined, divested of earthly dross and rendered more ethereal in their nature. We are taught to accord the sensibility its proper prominence in life and to keep the heart child-like, tender and susceptible of holy emotions.

The whole aim of poetry, working within her God-given sphere is to spiritualize the nature. Even when perverted and debased, divorced from her rightful function, she yet shows some signs of her original calling. Perhaps no great poet has so misapplied his powers as Byron; yet what lofty and soul-inspiring strains are found in his works. As illustrative of his higher and better self, the following stanza may be quoted:

"There is a pleasure in the pathless woods,
    There is a rapture on the lonely shore,
There is society where none intrudes,
    By the deep sea, and music in its roar;
I love not man the less, but Nature more,
    From these interviews, in which I steal
From all I may be, or have been before.
    To mingle with the Universe, and feel
What I can ne'er express, yet cannot all conceal."[24]

21. Wordsworth, "She Dwelt among the Untrodden Ways," 1:250.

22. Matt. 6:28.

23. Whittier, "To J.T.F.," 246. Whittier's line reads, "The heart has needs [beyond] the head."

24. Byron, "Childe Harold's Pilgrimage," canto 4, stanza 178, vol. 4, p. 299. Byron capitalizes [Sea], [Man], and [Nature]. Another line reads, "From these [our] interviews, in which I steal."

Even Don Juan contains occasional passages of purity and delicacy. What can be finer than this?

> "'Tis sweet to hear the watch-dog's honest bark
>   Bay deep-mouthed welcome as we draw near home;
> 'Tis sweet to know there is an eye will mark
>   Our coming, and look brighter when we come;
> 'Tis sweet to be awakened by the lark,
>   Or lulled by falling waters; sweet the hum
> Of bees, the voice of girls, the songs of birds,
> The lisp of children, and their earliest words."[25]

Poetry takes us out of ourselves; it carries us into a new world, the world presided over by

> "The glorious faculty assigned
> To elevate the more than reasoning mind,
> And color life's dark cloud with orient rays.
>
> . . . .
> Imagination lofty and refined."[26]

What delight to escape for a while from the cares, the vexations and annoyances of the common life and spend an hour with creations of divinely inspired origin. Irving says of Chaucer's "Flower and Leaf:" "It brings into our closets all the freshness and fragrance of the dewy landscape."[27] Poetry rejuvenates the old, imparts to the world-worn a relish for simple pleasures, and converts even the cynic to sympathy with the innocent gladness of childhood, the bright hopefulness of youth, the rapture of first love, the smile of woman, the fond pride of the young mother. It is not true that the poet paints a life which does not exist. He paints the best of the life which is, a life opposed to the worldly and artificial, "hidden from the wise and prudent and revealed unto babes." All children are poets, for in them the believing predominates over the examining state of mind.

Poetry is the divinest of all arts. So thought Milton, who wrote with the conscious dignity of a prophet. In the words of Poe, it produces "An elevating excitement of the soul quite independent of that passion which is the intoxication of the heart, or of that truth which is the satisfaction of the reason."[28] Carlyle,

---

25. Byron, "Don Juan," canto 1, stanza 123, vol. 10, p. 97. Byron's line reads, "Of bees, the voice of girls, the [song] of birds."

26. Wordsworth, "Weak Is the Will of Man," 2:308. Wordsworth's lines read: "[Who wants] the glorious faculty Assigned / To elevate the more-than-reasoning Mind."

27. Irving, "Rural Life in England," 43.

28. Poe, "The Poetic Principle," 254. Poe italicizes *"an elevating excitement of the Soul,"* and he capitalizes "Soul," "Heart," and "Truth."

in his "Life of Burns," calls "A true poet a man in whose heart resides some effluence of wisdom, some tone of the 'eternal melodies,'"[29] and declares that he is "The most precious gift that can be bestowed on a generation." That is not true poetry which cannot lift and inspire. It may be rhythm or verse, but it lacks the divine fire without which the draught is flat and vapid. "The poet is born, not made."[30] He writes because he must, not because he will. Pope says of himself:

> "As yet a child, nor yet a fool to fame,
> I lisped in numbers, for the numbers came."[31]

What is more ludicrous than the pretensions and affectations of would-be poets—jugglers in the divine art? Some of these are poor self-deluded creatures who persist in believing themselves inspired, the verdict of all mankind to the contrary not-withstanding; others, because they think it a "fine thing" to be a poet, turn to poetry with a deliberateness they would carry into watch or cabinet-making, not realizing that they needs must be filled with an inflatus from on high. They ape the style and manner of Apollo's favorites, adopt Byronic collars and flowing locks, assume an air sometimes wild and frenzied, sometimes dreamy and abstracted; disregard the simple things of life, and strain after what is high and mighty. With such individuals, sense is

> "sacrificed to sound,
> And truth cut short to make the period round."[32]

While there is much written for poetry which does not deserve the name, there are poems that are never penned. There are "mute, inglorious Miltons who die with all their music in them."[33] To these has been given the poet-soul, but not the poet's power of expression. They have somewhat of that "divine madness," of that "fine frenzy" which characterizes the poet, and are those who best understand and appreciate him.

All true poets are "touched with a coal from heaven,"[34] but all do not burn with the same intensity; all are not poets of the same order. We would not have it

---

29. Carlyle, "Life of Burns," 16. This and the following quotation can be found on page 16. Carlyle capitalizes "Poet" and "Wisdom."

30. Fletcher, "The Poet—Is He Born, Not Made," 117.

31. Pope, "Epistle to Dr. Arbuthnot," lines 127–28, p. 178.

32. Cowper, "Table Talk," 7. Cowper's line reads, "[If sentiment were] sacrificed to sound /And truth cut short to make a period round."

33. Gray, "An Elegy, Written in a Country Churchyard," 5. Gray's line reads "[some] mute inglorious Milton here may rest."

34. An interpretation of Isa. 6:6. The biblical verse reads, "Then flew one of the seraphims unto me, having a live coal in his hand, which he had taken with the tongs from off the altar."

otherwise. Tennyson is best suited to some minds, Longfellow to others. Today we may enjoy the sublime eloquence of Milton; to-morrow prefer the calm beauty of Wordsworth. The mountains uplift the sensitive soul to an exaltation of delight, but stay too long among them and the feeling of awe becomes oppressive.

The poet is his own benefactor as well as ours. There are many who put on their singing robes when sad and weary, many who strike the lyre when their hearts are torn with grief, and are comforted by the strains they themselves evoke. When the real world was shut out from James the First of Scotland, he consoled himself with the world of imagination. Tasso relieved the gloom of his lonely cell with the splendid scenes of his Jerusalem. A poet, describing the pleasure derived from exercising the imaginative faculty, exclaims, "Oh! to create within the soul is bliss!"[35] Tennyson, in his "Memoriam," a poem which is the product of a great grief, speaks of even "The sad mechanic exercise"[36] of verse-making "like dull narcotics, numbing pain." Many an overtaxed heart or brain, which otherwise might have succumbed to the burden imposed upon it, has found vent for itself in song. Who knows what relief the writing of Samson Agonistes, whose hero was afflicted with the poet's own sad malady, may have been to Milton; or the "Raven" to Poe, with whom poetry was "not a purpose, but a passion?"[37] Even Byron's egotism may be viewed leniently when we consider that probably he wrote for the relief of a life which, however erring, was much wronged and most unfortunate.

In this age, when, with the advancement of civilization and the greater cultivation of the physical sciences, the tendency seems to be toward the material, toward what we are pleased to call the "practical," there is special need of the spiritualizing influence of poetry. Macaulay says that "In the progress of nations towards refinement, the reasoning powers are improved at the expense of the imagination;"[38] and that "As civilization advances, poetry almost necessarily declines." If this is true, we ought the more assiduously cultivate the poetic taste, that so noble a gift may not be wholly lost, and to appreciate the more highly those great bards who have already sung for us, since the probability of having others decrease as the centuries of civilization roll by. The tendency toward Epicureanism, which the modern adaptation of the results of the physical sciences to our bodily wants encourages, must not be allowed to strangle that religion of inner and spiritual things of which poetry is the apostle.

---

35. Goethe, *Faust,* translator's preface, vi. Swanwick's preface to Goethe's *Faust* reads, "A poet, [in] describing the pleasure [attending the exercise of the creative] faculty, exclaims, Oh! To create within the soul is bliss."

36. Tennyson, "In Memoriam." This and the following quotation, "like dull narcotics, numbing pain," can be found in canto 5, p. 106.

37. Poe, *The Raven and Other Poems,* preface, iii.

38. Macaulay, "Essay on Milton," 10; the subsequent quotation is ibid., 8.

Men have at all times yielded to the sway of the seer. Originating as the poem did in the religious instinct, we are peculiarly rich in what may be termed "religious poems," many of them of great power and beauty. Combined with music, as vehicles of appeal they have been most effective. One heart may be open to conviction through the sermon, while another may be influenced more readily by the hymn. This is not due to the music alone: the words sung have also their weight. Who knows the power that has been wielded by "Rock of Ages" or "Nearer, my God to Thee?" Moody would never have had the marvelous success which has attended his efforts as evangelist had it not been for Sankey's services in connection with the work. The Psalms of the Bible and the inspired utterances of the Hebrew prophets take rank in the highest order of religious poetry.

Of songs on secular subjects there are many which have moved the hearts and influenced the lives of mankind. Thomas Moore immortalized Ireland by his patriotic lays, as did Scott his own native land. "Home, Sweet Home," is familiar, yet ever dear. The "Battle Hymn of the Republic" and the "Star Spangled Banner" never fail to evoke the enthusiasm of American citizens. The antislavery poems of Whittier and Longfellow helped to break the chain which bound the slaves. Even the rude rhymes of the oppressed, sung amid the toil of the field, tended to ease the burden of pain at their hearts. Who can read "Evangeline" without being taught a lesson of patient love and resignation? or "Aurora Leigh" without gaining a nobler conception of womanhood? or "The Cotter's Saturday Night" without heightened sympathy with the domestic life of the poor?

Longfellow's fame may be said to rest chiefly upon Hiawatha, a romance of Indian life, but he has many minor pieces unsurpassed for melody and moral sweetness. Can any doubt the influence for good of such poems as the "Psalm of Life, "Excelsior," and "The Builders?" Burns, like the true bard that he is, recognizes that poetry lies in the sentiment, and not in loftiness of theme or pomp of language. He does not disdain such simple subjects as the "mountain daisy" and the "wee, cowering, timorous beastie."[39] What of interest does the poetic mind find in a barefoot boy? Yet to Whittier, with his poet's perception of the nearness between the realms of reality and ideality, he is a source of inspiration:

> Ah! that thou couldst know thy joy
> Ere it passes, barefoot boy!"[40]

We quote from Tennyson lines which seem to us to contain the solution of the vexed question of the relative superiority or inferiority of man and woman:

---

39. Burns, "To a Mouse," line 1, p. 31. Burns's line reads, "Wee, sleekit, cowrin, tim'rous beastie."

40. Whittier, "The Barefoot Boy," stanza 5, p. 196.

"For woman is not undeveloped man,
But diverse; could we make her as a man,
Sweet Love were slain; his dearest bond is this,
Not like to like, but like in difference.
Yet in the long years liker must they grow:
The man be more of woman, she of man.
He gain in sweetness and in moral height,
Nor lose the wrestling thews that throw the world,
Till at the last she set herself to man.
Like perfect music unto noble words;
And so this twain upon the skirts of Time
Sit side by side, full-summed in all their powers,
Dispensing harvest, sowing the To-be,
Self-reverent each, and reverencing each.
. . . either sex alone
Is half itself, and in true marriage lies
Nor equal nor unequal; each fulfils
Defect in each, and always thought in thought,
Purpose in purpose, will in will, they grow,
The single pure and perfect animal.
The two-cell'd heart beating with one full stroke. Life."[41]

Who is so lacking in patriotic feeling that he has not thrilled at these words of Scott?

"Breathes there a man with soul so dead,
Who never to himself hath said,
        This is my own, my native land!
Whose heart hath ne'er within him burned,
As home his footsteps he hath turned
        From wandering on a foreign strand."[42]

What can be greater and more inspiring than this from Holmes?

Build thee more stately mansions,
O my soul.
As the swift seasons toll
Leave thy low-vaulted past!
Let each new temple, nobler than the last,
Shut thee from heaven with a dome more vast,

---

41. Tennyson, "The Princess," canto 7, p. 436. Several lines are missing in Washington's excerpt.
42. Scott, "The Lay of the Last Minstrel," canto 6, stanza 1, p. 35.

Till thou at length art free,
Leaving thine out-grown shell by life's unresting sea.[43]

The following lines are characteristic of Wordsworth:

"Nature never did betray
The heart that loved her. 'Tis her privilege
Through all the years of this, our life, to lead
From joy to joy! for she can so inform
That is within us, so impress
With quietness and beauty, and so feed
With lofty thoughts, that neither evil tongues,
Rash judgments, nor the sneers of selfish men,
Nor greetings where no kindness is, nor all
The dreary intercourse of daily life
Shall e'er prevail against us, to disturb
Our cheerful faith that all which we behold
Is full of blessings."[44]

Does not humanity owe something to the poet, to the high priest of the beautiful, the lofty, the true? It has ever been slow to pay its debt. Living, the world's heroes and benefactors are neglected; dead, their dust is sacredly treasured. Thus it was with the Christian apostles, with Socrates, Galileo, and Roger Bacon. Burns spent his last days friendless and poverty-stricken; but a splendid mausoleum marks his resting-place. Even the immortal Milton was little regarded as a poet by his contemporaries. "The old blind poet," says Waller, "hath published a tedious poem on the 'Fall of Man.' If its length be not considered as a merit, it hath no other."[45] In the words of Carlyle, "Men of genius ask for bread and receive a stone."[46]

There comes, however, a time of posthumous retribution, and he who was unappreciated by his own generation receives honor at the hands of posterity. Then every possible relic, every personal memento, every associated article becomes a priceless possession, and the old house at Stratford-on-Avon the Mecca of many a pilgrimage. Yet there are those who recognize the divine right of

43. Holmes, The Chambered Nautilus," stanza 5, line 1, p. 149.

44. Wordsworth, "Lines, Composed a Few Miles above Tintern Abbey," 2:164. Wordsworth's lines read, "[Knowing that] Nature never did betray" and "[The mind] that is within us so impress."

45. Waller's quotation is originally from a letter he wrote, but this particular wording, "The Old blind poet, says Waller, hath published a tedious poem on the 'Fall of Man'" appears to be from Welsh, *Development of English Literature,* 487.

46. Carlyle, "Life of Burns," 17.

poets, whether living or dead, to the highest meed of honor. It is gratifying to note the widespread and enthusiastic celebration of recent birthdays of our own Whittier. Why not let the great ones of the earth know, while yet among us, the esteem in which they are held?

> "Blessings be with him and undying praise,
> Who gives us higher love and nobler cares."[47]

Milton calls a good book the life-blood of a master spirit. This is especially true of a good poem, for it comes directly from the heart, and is the very essence of being. We have only pity for those old days of Puritan rule when poets were styled the "Caterpillars of the Commonwealth,"[48] and indignation moved Sidney to write "The Defence of Poesy." Wolf[49] had a true conception of the worth and dignity of the poetic art when he declared that he would rather have written the "Elegy" than to capture Quebec.[50]

But if mankind owes much to the poet, does not the poet owe much also to mankind? He is made the instrument of a Divine message to the world. Woe betide him if he utter it not in clear and unmistakable tones. Given as he is a nature sensitive, intense and passionate, "dowered with the hate of hate, the scorn of scorn, the love of love,"[51] he may be peculiarly subject to temptations, but living so near the border-land of the spirit world, having communion with creatures bright and blest, he should be stronger than ordinary mortals to resist the evil. The waywardness characteristic of so many poets should not be attributed to the nature of their calling. On the other hand, probably poetry is a safety-valve for their excess of emotion, and they are the better men for being poets. The greatest punishment the erring seer can undergo is that agony of soul derived from his own clear perception of his deviation from his ideal. Yet there is a general nobleness mingling even with the errors of the true poet. Amid all the excesses of Robert Burns, not one mean or petty action can be found.

The poet is but the mouthpiece of God, and should be modest in his highest flights. Mrs. Browning voices this thought when she says:

> "Learn from hence, weak mortals, all ye poets that pursue
> Your way still onward up to eminence!

47. Unknown quotation.

48. Shakespeare, *The Tragedy of King Richard II*, 2.3.165.

49. This reference is to General James Wolfe (1727–1759).

50. Willson, "General Wolfe and Gray's 'Elegy,'" 865. Wolfe's statement reads, "Gentlemen, I would rather be the author of that poem than take Quebec."

51. Tennyson, "The Poet," stanza 1, p. 16. Tennyson's line reads, "[Dower'd] with the hate of hate, the scored of scorn."

> Ye are not great, because creation drew
> Large revelations round your earliest sense,
> Nor bright, because God's glory shines for you."[52]

Receiving true rays of light from the object, the faulty mirror may so distort them as to give back but an imperfect image. What an awful and yet sublime responsibility is his who is sent into the world to proclaim a message thereto! That grand and austere old poet, Milton, says: "He who would write heroic poems must make his whole life a heroic poem."[53] It is small wonder that Rassalar [*sic*], after listening to an enumeration of the qualities essential to the poetic character, exclaimed: "Who, then, can be a poet?"[54]

---

52. Browning, "Mountaineer and Poet," 2:87. Browning's line reads, "Learn from hence [meek morals], all ye poets that pursue."
53. Carlyle, "Burns," in *Carlyle's Essay on Burns,* 94.
54. S. Johnson, "Rasselas," chap. 10, line 2, p. 12.

PART III

GENDER PROPRIETY

Notes to Girls. No. 1.

"JOYCE"

"How divine a thing a woman may be made."[1] It is for you who are daily maturing [in] character, to emulate the brightest examples, and to strive to show womanhood in its highest nobility. These early girlish days of comparative ease and irresponsibility are given you to fit yourselves for a broader place of action, where

> "Not enjoyment and not sorrow
> Is our destined end or way,
> But to act that each to-morrow,
> Finds us further than to-day."[2]

You should, during this period, become proficient in the performance of each household task. There is nothing disgraceful, nothing unrefined, nothing even unpoetic about work. It is strange, is it not? that some girls shrink from doing these things, and others work with a will because they must, but are ashamed to acknowledge it.

If we associate a domestic character with a figure whose face is blackened by contact with kitchen utensils, whose hair is disordered, whose dress is untidy, whose feet are exposed in slipshod shoes—the idea is repulsive. But this should not be. There is a dress suitable for the sitting-room and another for the kitchen, and each can be neat and tasteful in its way.

Being properly arrayed for culinary employment and wearing the apron badge, be thankful you have a mother whom you may help, and who will instruct you. It is an accomplishment, a domestic accomplishment, to know how to make good bread; to be able to concoct the various delicacies that nourish the body, and have an undeniable influence on mind and temper. 'Tis good to know how to sweep well; to be able to make a bed a smooth expanse of snowy whiteness; to possess the art of rendering a room clean and fresh and sweet, by giving a few quick touches here and there. Moreover, girls should pride them-

---

* "Notes to Girls. No. 1," *People's Advocate* (Washington, D.C.), 20 November 1880, 1.

1. Wordsworth, "To a Young Lady," 2:193. Wordsworth's lines read: "[Shalt show us] how divine a thing / A woman may be made."

2. Longfellow, "A Psalm of Life," 1:6.

selves on their knowledge of needlework, as much as they do on their taste in parlor arrangement.

An ingenious mind and ready hand can form pretty adornments for mantel and wall and corner out of very trifles. Sometimes it is little rustic decorations of leaves and acorns and grasses and vines that cause the most exquisite pleasure. The eye wearies of the costly works of art, and turns with delight to these reminders of Nature's great storehouse. In the season when flowers grow with little cost and care, even the poorest may have a few plants to cheer the sight with their bit of green. The more we move among flowers and music and beauty, if these influences be not perverted, the more refined our nature becomes, and the greater grows our love for "the good, the beautiful, the true."[3]

While our hands are engaged in these outward works, our eyes in these perceptions, heart and mind must undergo the struggles that come with a degree of intensity to all mankind. If you know how grand a thing it is to crush the evil of your inner selves, by mastering selfishness, by returning a kiss for a blow, by conquering anger, by leading peacemaking lives; you will endeavor for all this, and more than this, to be shown in your lives, even in life at home. There, even more than elsewhere, you meet the rugged stones that throw into tumult the stream of your existence. You can make these impediments give fresh vigor to your zeal, and new beauty to your curse; until you

> "Know how sublime a thing it is
> To suffer and be strong."[4]

3. Aiken, *Memorials of Robert Burns*, 7.
4. Longfellow, "The Light of Stars," 1:7, stanza 9.

Notes to Girls. No. 2.

"JOYCE"

"He that attends to his interior self,
That has a heart and keeps it—has a mind
That hungers and supplies it, and who seeks
A social, not a dissipated life,
Has business."[1]

Girls, think not that the poet excludes you. It is a belief long past that women should not seek intellectual pursuits. It is a belief banished with the dark ages, when a learned woman was synonymous with an outcast. These bright days of the present, when you may study what men study, may become versed in arts and sciences, may learn to talk with grace and good sense—should be duly appreciated. The best way to exhibit this appreciation is to strive for mental improvement.

It is a deplorable fact that girls in general leave school too early. It is not always because father gets little work, or mother's health is poor, or family expenses overbalance family earnings; and the daughters must be called from the school room to teach a country school, or to roll somebody's baby carriage, or to rouse the music of the washing board in the back rooms. Sometimes it is the daughters themselves who propose a release from the thralldom of school.

Their reasons may be summed up in the expressions that fall from them and those who entertain a similar opinion: "I know enough," "I am tired of studying," "I am old enough to stop school," and "Girls don't make any use of education," "That is enough for a girl to know." Well, they do know something: they can read and write, and have dabbled in arithmetic, grammar, and geography. A few years later, we hear of one of them as having completed her mission in life; that is, she and some inexperienced youth have agreed to take each other for worse, and to make one another miserable for life.

Oh! girls, who sigh in after times for lost opportunities, I would that I could impress you with a sense of the importance of endeavoring to elevate yourselves—using "Honest work for the day, honest hope for the morrow."[2] Whether

---

* "Notes to Girls. No. 2," *People's Advocate* (Washington, D.C.), 27 November 1880, 1.
1. Cowper, "The Garden," bk. 3, p. 73.
2. Meredith, *Lucile*, pt. 2, canto 6, no. 40, p. 351.

you come home with the honors of graduation, or whether you leave school before this event, let not this period date the close of your intercourse with books. Without neglecting your share in the daily round of housework, you can find leisure to nourish the knowledge already gained, and to learn something more each day. If you have a talent for music or composition or drawing, cultivate it. It will do you good. At the same time, do not neglect the careful perusal of books of history and holography, and commune oft times with the poets; remembering the words of one who says,

> "Who does the best his circumstance allows,
> Does well, acts nobly, angels could no more."[3]

Were some enterprising spirit to organize a ladies' literary club for populous city or country village, it would effect much good. There women who have led pure lives, and who have attained to high intellectual heights, might meet; there slips of school girls, with bright fancies and lofty aspirations, could resort; there would be strengthened the bond of social intercourse, that conduces to the formation of firm friendships; while there would advance reading of good books, clear expression of thought, and quotations from choice works.

> "When e're is spoken a noble thought,
> When e'er a noble deed is wrought,
> Our souls in glad surprise
> To higher levels rise."[4]

Some women, among the gifted few, grow great in fame; others remain in the security and seclusion of a domestic sphere; but education of heart and brain is essential to all. Some brighten the world with the blaze of their genius, and instruct with grand truths many a fellow creature; while others gladden the hearts at home, and bestow a mother's teachings. Some hold court with learned men; others bless with congenial companionship a loving few. Is not each a mission for which one needs earnest preparation? If we soar not into the clouds, we need not grovel in the dust; but

> "Let us be content in work,
> To do the thing we can, and not presume
> To fret because it's little."[5]

---

3. Young, "The Complaint," 1:24–25.
4. Longfellow, "Santa Filomena," 1:347, stanza 1. The first two lines are in reverse order. Longfellow's third line reads, "Our [hearts], in glad surprise." He contracts "[whene'er]."
5. Browning, "Aurora Leigh," 350.

Notes to Girls. No. 3.

"JOYCE"

"Honor and Shame from condition rise;
Act well your part, there all the honor lies."[1]

It was a queer contemporary who remarked, "Poverty ain't no disgrace, but 'tis a grate inconvenience."[2] Blest be he who adopts himself to the inevitable order of things in his own sphere, and lives and moves contentedly in it. Nothing is calculated to do us most miserable, than an envious spirit.

Do you not think your loving parents experience a tinge of pain, when you come home and expatiate on that handsome new outfit of Cathy's; mourn out jealous declarations of how "perfectly charming" she looked in it; how the girls all thought it "just lovely;" and how you wish you had one too, for, grumbling and complaining, you "never do have anything anyhow!" Though, like the Flora McFlimsy[3] of childhood's rhyme, you may have numbers of dresses, neat and nice. Perhaps, to avoid the sigh of your clouded countenance and mopping movements, this overindulgent pair may give you what you desire. Does it satisfy you and make you pleasant and obliging? No; the costly article once secured, the goddess Fashion places another ignis fatuus before your eyes, for which you are widely groping.

She who seeks to whirl the rounds of fashionable life, must needs have a heavy purse and give undivided attention to the accomplishment of the subject. Some girls quietly drop out of society when they find that they shame their lady friends by familiar contact with her whom they term "so shabbily dressed." Some recklessly secure the passports of admittance, and leave only when ignominiously banished. Others, who can afford honesty to dress well, clothe themselves in the finest fabrics, smile on their acquaintances similarly attired—each supremely content to see her associates well-dressed, if their appearance eclipse not her own—and cut the old playmate whose dry goods bill is perceptibly less.

* "Notes to Girls. No. 3," *People's Advocate* (Washington, D.C.), 11 December 1880, 1.

1. Pope, "Essay on Man," Epistle 4, lines 193–94.

2. Variations of this quotation have surfaced throughout the ages.

3. Flora McFlimsy, the heroine in William Allen Butler's satirical poem "Nothing to Wear" (Bauch, *The Complete Compendium,* 415).

Little do these frivolous characters know the strife they are engendering for many another,

> "—in whose breast
> The struggle between right and wrong
> Is raging terrible and strong."[4]

I would not urge you to a Quaker-like simplicity of dress. The aesthetic element within us calls forth admiration of the beautiful, even in shimmering silks, gossamer, laces, and flashing jewels. We love to see you so adorned, with taste and modesty. We can gaze with delight at the pretty pictures many of you form.

But do not, ah! do not allow yourselves to become possessed by the insatiable desire of finery. Do not let the decorations of self be the paramount object of your existence. Do not privately rate your friends according to their ability to dress stylishly. Do not, ah! do not let your actions tell that you appreciate but the external appearance of your associates.

If you are poor and cannot afford to buy fine clothes, without making sacrifices, it is not meritorious to suffer for them; can you not wear your calico or renovated worsted without enduring a pang of envy, which would spoil the pleasure of viewing other girls'[5] pretty things? Surely, you can be brave enough and strong enough for this. If you are tasteful, you can make yourself look well in what you have, and your real friends will not love you any less.

Whatever be the material of your dress, let your hair be that which nature gave you. Nothing appears more ridiculous than a young lady's shoulders covered with long curls and braids, which one can readily detect are hers only because she bought them. Such a sight reminds me of the literary gentleman who lined his walls with skillfully imitated books of wood. One can admire the lovely tresses of hair and the rows of beautiful books, if he can but forget the inappropriateness of each in its particular place.

I would even rather have you wear false hair (which certainly does not injure your own) than to have you plaster your face with the red and white of art, as is the custom with some. Not only do such artificial things impress one with feeling of the wearer's own falseness, but they really harm the complexion. Lastly, do what is a duty, and should be a pleasure, in dressing with neatness and taste; always endeavoring to secure harmony[6] and grace in cut and drapery.

4. Longfellow, "Christus. A Mystery," vol. 2, pt. 3, p. 613.
5. The original reads "girl's."
6. The original reads "harmonious."

Notes to Girls. No. 4.

"JOYCE"

"They are the lovely, they in whom unite
Youth's fleeting charms with virtue's lovely light."[1]

The world is rapidly growing wise. Though we delight in beauty of person, as in a lovely picture; beauty of soul is becoming our beacon. Around one [who] possesses this attraction gather men of sense and worthy, while the parlors of simpering girls hold fashionable fops and uncouth characters. "Indeed, the room is sometimes so crowded we can't find seats for all;" such damsels are heard to remark to each other with charming simplicity.

To meet people of mental attainments and to converse creditably with them, you must—besides a fund of knowledge—possess self-confidence, self-respect, and modesty. I have heard young folks spoken of as being very modest, who were only impressed with a sense of their own awkwardness and were, consequently, restrained and shamefaced. Those same persons sometimes soon after develop[2] alarming symptoms of boldness and recklessness. Often a similar mistake is made in a reversed case.

There is much difference between modesty and bashfulness. One can have respect for one's own self, and confidence in one's own abilities; and still retain the modesty that scorns to flaunt its own accomplishments, and that despises all exhibitions of low and vulgar character. Bashfulness consists in being nervous, weak, uncontrolled, anxious and altogether miserable. The former attribute is as sincerely to be desired, as the latter is to be abhorred.

Your own native good sense should aid in teaching you how to demean yourselves in receiving your friends. Remember there is as much art in acting the good listener by drawing out others, as in unburdening your own mind. When you do talk, let it not be with the boisterous tone and laugh which inform the family across the way that you have company; and do not commit that gross impoliteness of interrupting another's speech. Remember that gossip indicates an ignorant mind. If you interest yourselves in what should engage your attention, you will find enough

---

* Notes to Girls. No. 4," *People's Advocate* (Washington, D.C.), 18 December 1880, 1.

1. Eubank, *Key to Harvey's Practical Grammar*, 162.

2. The original reads "develope."

to talk about in men and things, without descanting on the faults and foibles of your neighbors. Exhibit, however, no pet expressions to prove your knowledge of literature. They might unpleasantly remind a listener of Dickens's Mrs. Blimbers,[3] who constantly reiterated the desire to have seen Cicero in his retirement. He who talks most does not talk best. When you are regaling a dozen people with a choice bit of scandal, or expatiating on some airy nothing, do you reflect that though the tale may be pleasant to you, because it is of your own telling, it may be different with others?

If boys and girls were to grow up together in friendly companionship, there would be more ease and grace and sincerity in their bearings toward each other; and the absurdity of "turning out" would not exist. Do not think there is a certain set of people in the world of fashion with whom you must keep on terms of intimacy. Move with none but the pure and good. Have no friendships but those that will improve you. Learn to care for that which will form for you a world in your own mind, which can brighten solitude and render seclusion cheerful.

> "I have within myself
> All that my heart desires: the ideal beauty
> Which the creative faculty of mind
> Fashions and follows in a thousand shapes
> More lovely than the real. My own thoughts
> Are my companions; my designs and labors
> And aspirations are my only friends."[4]

This is a beautiful thought of the poet[5] with the exception that he excludes *all* companionship and friendship.

It is well to meet and converse with people, at proper intervals. Going out is pleasant, for this reason, and for the additional one that it is an exercise[6] conducive to health. Fine places of social recreation are the picnic and croquet grounds. There one can enjoy the fragrance of a delicious evening, and chat and be gay without the staid stiffness that characterizes some drawing-rooms.

And naturally, with no petty airs and affections of manner. These superficial graces, like soapsuds, often cover unclean depths.

> "O, what a glory doth this world put on
> For him, who with a fervent heart, goes forth
> Under the bright and glorious sky, and looks
> On duties well performed, and days well spent!"[7]

3. Mrs. Blimber, a character in Charles Dickens's *Dombey and Son*.
4. Longfellow, "The Masque of Pandora," vol. 2, pt. 3, p. 793.
5. The original reads "poets."
6. The original reads "excise."
7. Longfellow, "Autumn," 1:13.

Notes to Girls. No. 5.

"JOYCE"

"Needful auxiliaries are our friends, to give
To social man true relish of himself."[1]

Friends are glimpses of blue in a cloudy sky. He who hides himself from men, whether with reverence for a hermit's life or a misanthrope's love of seclusion, fails to do the good he might in the world and to reap the benefit derived from social assembling. Oftimes friendships are formed in youth that emit an elevating influence through life, and help to make the man whatever he is that is great and good.

A pure love never does harm. It always has an exulting tendency; and though it may sometimes bring with it sorrow, this is recompensed in the good it effects. Tennyson says,

"'Tis better to have loved and lost,
Than never to have loved at all;"[2]

and Longfellow explains:

"Talk not of wasted affection, affection never was wasted;
If it enrich not the heart of another, its waters returning
Back to their springs like the rain shall fill them full of refreshment."[3]

The world is a mirror which looks back at us with the face we present to it. Would you make friends?—be courteous, affable, gentle, generous, frank, and sincere. The iron barrier of coldness and arrogance chills the loving hearts that would encircle you. Be ready to yield gracefully to the wishes of another, where the compliance violates no principle of duty. At the same time, be not disinclined to wield your own will with dignity and firmness, when you are advocating the right. No one prides herself on the possession of a friend who invariably copies her associate from the curl of the hair to the weightiest opinion.

* "Notes to Girls. No. 5," *People's Advocate* (Washington, D.C.), 25 December 1880, 1.

1. Young, "The Complaint," 1:41. Young's line reads, "Needful [auxilliars] are our friends to give."

2. Tennyson, "In Memoriam," canto 27, p. 110.

3. Longfellow, "Evangeline," vol. 1, pt. 2, p. 167, stanza 1.

Society is now like a huge flower garden where, in regular rows, the plants are set out according to age and height. It would be a wise reformation to choose the sweetest flowers from each even line and bring them together in one garden plat, placed[4] to grow and bloom in company. If the girls and young ladies and patrons were to meet more often in social gatherings each would improve the entire contact. In viewing the innocent merriment of youth, the tired mothers would forget their cares, and themselves grow cheerful and gay. The maidens would profit by the wisdom and experience of their elders. Sorry am I to say that now little Miss curls her pretty nose, and indiscriminately terms elderly people "old fogies."

Consider yourself fortunate if you feel secure in the possession of one *real* friend. While there may be many, who, in a general sort of way, are interested in your welfare, who are glad to meet you, and regretful to leave you; we find few who are truly sympathetic in joy and sorrow. Such a friend understands you sufficiently to rate you aright; and loves you sufficiently to tell you of your faults that you may gain other friends by their removal. Girls sometimes twine their affections around each other in childhood, and play together in careless joy; who in after life, molded[5] in conventionalism and imbibing a jealous distrust of their girlish friends, pass each other with indifferent nod and "How do you do?"

Many, too, erroneously believe that men and women cannot be friends, fond and true; but still only friends. My dear sisters, this is a belief of which you had best dispossess yourself at once. It is a belief that makes many foolishly vain in the presence of young men; a belief that invests many a one with the idea that every man who pays her kindly attention, wishes her for a life companion; a belief that tends to make men presumptuous. Were youths and maidens to discard the prevailing subject of "courtship" in general meeting, and manifest brotherly and sisterly regard, when a girl strives only to be pleasant and friendly, men would not be so idiotic as to suppose her on the verge of falling in love with them.

Mark not with scornful glance a sinning woman, and then smile blandly on a masculine culprit. Heaven's laws were made for all.

Make not the aim of your life—in terms of the world—to "marry well." Well for you if it be well when it comes; but it is not well, if it comes too soon. With this aspiration in the precocious mind, some doff the paritalettes; with this end in view, some receive select schooling; for this purpose, some are paraded in society's halls; to effect this, some papas give lavish allowances; to gain this, some mothers angle for "best matrimonial catch." "Two years of courtship, five minutes' solemnization of the ceremony, and an eternity in which to repeal," is the sad experience of many a mistaken alliance. Learn to know your own mind; that you may say "no" when that word should be used, and "yes," and regret it not.

4. The original reads "place."
5. The original reads "moulded."

Notes to Girls. No. 6.

"JOYCE"

"Life is real! Life is earnest!"[1]

Because it is prosaic reality, and not an "empty dream;" it is essential that we awake to the fulfillment of our duties, and

"—own man born to live as well as die."[2]

We can render ourselves utterly unfit for earnest work by expending our sympathies and energies on people and things of our fancy's own creation. The lady, reading in the parlor, weeps over the sufferings of the Claude and Isabelle of novel life, while all around her, in this "workaday world," are "duties and dinners and darns" awaiting her touch. It has been truly said that one half of the people of the world know not the life of the other half. Pretty little miss Simplicity, treading on some rose leaves, sipping the dew, raises her hands in horror at the recital of some tale of life in the world's basements. She never did hear of such "disagreeable" things, of poverty and crime and misery; you must be just trying to make her "uncomfortable."

Better, my dear girl, to know if such things be, and to strive to alleviate them; than to seek or fain an ignorance of what so nearly concerns the well-being of your fellow creatures. "Whatever thy hands find to do, do it with thy might"—is the divine injunction. If it is household work, seek to excel in it; if thy working sphere enlarges[3] know

"Better far
Pursue a frivolous but serious means.
Than a sublime art frivolously."[4]

Girls should learn more of independence, more of self-reliance, than they usually possess. However, we may love the timid lady who screams at the sight

---

* "Notes to Girls," No. 6," *People's Advocate* (Washington, D.C.), 8 January 1881, 1.

1. Longfellow, "A Psalm of Life," 1:6, stanza 2.

2. Young, "The Complaint," 1:135. Young's line reads, "[But] own man born to live as well as die."

3. The original reads "enlargen."

4. Browning, "Aurora Leigh," bk. 2, p. 47.

of a mouse, and who must always hide herself behind a masculine presence; it is the noble woman who works her own way with courage and dignity, that calls forth our strongest admiration. You will not let father work himself into the grave, trying to enable the family to live in style and the daughters to dress well. If you exert not yourself to do something, he cannot refrain from watching your suitors with mental anxiety, and inwardly wishing you would consent for one of them to take you off.

Perhaps you will, after a time, discover this state of affairs; and, with the wound of the revelation fresh in your breast, revenge your pride by giving your hand where your heart may not be. In vain you attempt to console yourself with the reflections that after all it was a good chance, you couldn't expect [to] do better, really it was an act of generosity to pa, and you like your husband well enough. You are likely to meet some day him who will touch the strain in your heart, before awakened. Sad for you if you must, for duty sake, turn a deaf ear.

Seek something to do that will give added weight to the family purse, and cease to be a burden to those around you. If your parents are wealthy, of course you do not need to encounter the world as one of the working class. You will do the most pleasant thing of staying home, and learning what home life can teach you. Even then, you will lose the discipline of mind, the expansion of latent powers, that a life of self-dependence does not fail to confer. It is well, too, to grow proficient in some particular direction; for fortune may not always favor you as now.

Whatever be your work, you can be a lady. I would not use this word to mean a delicate shrinking, fastidious creature; but to express the purity and refinement that should halo a woman. A teacher, a shop girl, a writer, a seamstress, a singer, a washer; these, and more than these, need but the one principle or right to actuate them, to produce a level.

A knowledge of some things should be common to you all. The sick room has no more welcome visitor than a woman who knows how to adapt herself to the surroundings. She enters not with screeching boots and all the intricacies of fashionable attire, which weary the feverish [gal?]. Nor does she, in shrill key gossip city talk; nor assume the doleful expression many deem fit for a patient's bedside. In gown of soft folds and soothing tints, she moves with noiseless tread; and does for you just the thing you felt you needed, but knew not how to express. When she addresses you, it is with a cheerful expression and a voice ever "—gentle and low;—an excellent thing in woman."[5] Though you may never be a hospital nurse, you may never go among strangers to risk your life for theirs; at some time, those will be nearer you, for whom it will be your duty to perform these tender offices. Viewing noble acts of self-denial sometimes there comes to us a faint condition of what the poet meant, in saying "We can make our lives sublime."[6]

5. Shakespeare, *The Tragedy of King Lear*, 5.3.275.
6. Longfellow, "A Psalm of Life," vol. 1, p. 6, stanza 7.

On the Street Car

"JOYCE"

"What is your objection to the girl?" I asked, feeling a little resentment against her because of her implied disparagement of the sex.

"Well, you see, my old man, who is right smart learned, has been a-reading in the noosepapers lately how that Ginral Grant is sich a fine man, how that he's been most round the world (though how he could do that being we live *in* the world I can't see) and how that English folks think him sich a grand gentleman, and everybody idilize him—so I just said to my old man 'Jim, we'll name Malinda Ann's boy Genral U. S. Grant and, behold the *boy* was a *gal.*'"

Convulsed with laughter and almost ready to yell in the little woman's face. I was greatly relieved when the car stopped and drew her attention from me. "That driver" we heard a portly, pretentious man growl, "he knows nothing of his business—he ought to be turned out of his place," and the great bear having growled, the cubs took up the cry of complaint. Urged by a touch of the whip, the horses started forward; with an effort pulled the car from the depths of snow, and we were again on our journey.

"Ting, ting, ting," that big cross man is going to get out, and a few satellites are following in his train.

Some men bounded across the street and those inside the car jocosely cry, "Come on, there's plenty of room" though it is still crowded. "Halloo! don't go yet; a big boy, drawing a little girl on a sled and followed by two other small girls, waves his hand to the carman. He lifts the lame child with the patient, pinched face into a seat, while the others sit beside her, and Charlie, as they call him, bids his little schoolmates good by. One, I can easily see, is the pet of parents in easy circumstances; and, with her crimson cap and cape, her round blues eyes and flaxen hair, she appears a modern "Red Riding Hood." The other little one has a look painfully wise and shrewd for one of her years, a look that suggested early acquaintance with want and woe. She is a strong healthy little creature though, and is as careful and tender of Edith's comfort as our sweet Red Riding Hood.

---

* "On the Street Car," *Virginia Star,* 30 April 1881, 4. This essay was to be continued, but no continuation has been located. The next extant issue of the *Virginia Star* is 23 July 1881.

The car moves now at a jolting, irregular rate. The little woman in drab looks out and exclaims, "Why we're off the track!" Sure enough we are; and presently the car stops, and the driver looks in and desperately announces that not another step can he go, unless the passengers all get out and the car is lifted on the track. Each one looks at his neighbor in blank dismay, and then there is a general movement towards the door. The little woman in drab catches up her basket, saying "I must save Malinda Ann's eggs!" and out we plunge into the snow and drizzling rain.

The little lame girl is coming too but a grave dignified gentleman, whom I had not before noticed, interposes. "This little girl must not go out," he says to the driver who nods his snow-flecked head in approval, and then the kind gentleman wraps the dry straw on the floor around the poor little heroine's feet. All is noisy talk and busy confusion outside, until this clear-brained man appears and gives his crisp, concise directions.

> "As when in tumults rise the ignoble crowd,
>   Mad are their motions and their tongues are loud;
> If then some grave and pious man appear,
>   They hush their noise and lend a listening ear."[1]

Strong men's arms lift the car on the track, and again we crowd inside.

---

1. Dryden, Virgil's *Aeneid,* bk. 1, p. 359. The following two lines of Dryden are missing after the first two that Washington quotes: ["And stones and brands in rattling vollies fly, / And all rustic arms that fury can supply;"].

"Joyce" to "Quiz"

"JOYCE"

"Quiz," I confess that I am naturally jealous. That you should get your name twice in public print to my once, I really cannot allow. If, however, you should see fit to again address me, unless you introduce some new subject for discussion I shall be so generous as to retire from the field and leave you the glory of making the last speech. I do think that the question of Joyce's proficiency in duties "and dinners and darns" is about exhausted.

So you think one is necessarily "obscure" because he writes under a *nom de plume*.[1]

> "What's in a name? That which we call a rose
> By any other name would smell as sweet."[2]

The majority of my readers know me as well under the name "Joyce" as they would were I to substitute_____ _____, never mind, I conclude I'll not give it, since it would mean nothing in particular to people outside of my own city and might detract from any fame Joyce may have gained at home. "A prophet is not without honor save in his own country."[3]

You are pleased to style some advice I have given "splendid." I feel it my duty to give you a little pill, though I know not how it may be received. When you see something necessary to be done and you have the ability to do it, don't hold back and wait for somebody else to go forward. Suppose that I had been without due knowledge of housework, as you thought me; I might have married during your long delay. I might have doomed some poor mortal to badly cooked dinners, and pierced somebody's heart through neglected shirts, and rendered some household liable to manifold other ills.[4] Ah! Quiz, when you thought of that unhappy home would not your conscience have reproached you for failing to give the warning you might have given?

I agree that "There is but one lamp by which my feet are guided, and that is

---

* "'Joyce' to 'Quiz,'" *People's Advocate* (Washington, D.C.), 18 June 1881, 2.
1. The original reads "none de plume."
2. Shakespeare, *The Tragedy of Romeo and Juliet,* 2.2.43–44.
3. Matt. 13:57.
4. The original reads "ill."

the lamp of experience"[5]—that experience is, however, not always our own, but the lamp of someone else's experience that sheds its gleams along our pathway. A scanty amount of knowledge would we possess were nothing learned by observation.

I have no unfriendly sentiments towards Quiz. I did not begin the controversy. I have merely endeavored to answer courteously the questions asked me. As you propose, "Let me kiss and be friends;" but I fear kissing through the press is a sensation no more pleasurable than kissing through a veil. You need not say that I must know that from experience, for I don't.

5. Henry, "The 'Liberty or Death' Speech," 76.

A Reply to Quiz's Baptismal Queries

"JOYCE"

One sometime asks questions, not for the sake of receiving information; but that he may more emphatically express his views. Whether this be true of "Quiz," I really do not know; but this I do declare, that so skillfully has my interlocutor showed the foibles that infest the fulfillment of the of the command, "Be baptized" that she leaves little for me to say, but simply to assent to her remarks or to reiterate her sentiments.

Quiz, embalm that compliment in lavender, that you may never tend to the opinion of those cynical creatures who sneeringly affirm that one girl cannot praise another.

No: I do not think we are "obligated to have mothers in the gospel." There is a certain class of people who have great influence during a revival. They are not the people that serve God with meekness and simplicity, but rather those who are ruled of disorder and superstition. Sometimes meaning well but always meting ill, one of these characters entraps "mourners" into confidence. She advises them how to bend the head and disarrange the apparel that they "may be seen of men" to pray. Whether they be willing or unwilling, she drags them to the anxious-seat, patting inspiration through their devoted heads as they kneel. She relates to them mysterious dreams, in which they invariably appear as having something to reveal and that to her. After struggling long to do what they at last find no man can do, God opened their eyes to the knowledge that He, in divine mercy, has forgiven them. But there is that untiring sister of the church who has so flooded the mind with false ideas and so wrought upon the feelings, that through day dreams and night dreams an inquirer is persuaded to believe that she has been "sent" to this person; and then somebody's heart thrills with the pride of having been made a "mother in the gospel."

Aprons, as aprons, are not be despised. Were Fashion's caprices to require us to don them for church wear, they would be worn with greater grace than the ugly bustle now in vogue; and, perhaps, even Quiz might thrust her dainty hands into the jaunty pockets. Old hats, as old hats, I must not deride. Many a season have I worn a head covering till it deserved that appellation, and I know

* "A Reply to Quiz's Baptismal Queries," *People's Advocate* (Washington, D.C.), 2 July 1881, 2.

not what may be the state of my purse by the time I need another. I do, however, object to the desire to being conspicuous, as here manifested. When a worthy object is aided by publicity, then I advocate it. When no good is to be gained and the craving to be noticed is an outbreak of vanity, then I denounce the display.

"Are they obliged to carry the baskets up in church? Could they not leave them in the lower room?" Why, certainly they could. Surely, these energetic sisters, who strive to govern the entire affairs of the church, have discretion sufficient to teach them to refrain from meddling with what belongs to another. This "parade of baskets and long aprons up the aisle during the minister's talk" attracts the attention of the audience, sending their thoughts into the regions of imagination while these interesting folks conjecture as to what the covered baskets contain. It aggravates the preacher to see half a dozen fussy women drawing towards themselves the gaze of the congregation, thus nullifying the impression he has created.

The converts go down in the water quietly and gently; but, once under the liquid current, one might suppose an evil spirit enters them, from the manner in which they come forth, yelling and fighting. Over and over again, they use the stereotyped expressions, "Thang God I was born to die," and "Redeemed, redeemed, and wash clean in Jesus' blood." Declaration these are, proper in season; but, like other things sometimes commendable, to be condemned when out of place.

The presence of the "mothers in gospel" in the pulpit is entirely unnecessary. Those who are commissioned to stand with cloaks ready to shield the dripping forms from general observation are a sufficient force. Young believers of the screaming and splashing order, do not care to have any such hindrance[1] to take their active movements, and prefer to expose their figure in its clinging wet drapery, thinking perhaps, "Men's eyes were made to look and let them gaze."[2]

I wonder if Quiz is a fellow citizen of mine, and if she attended the same church on the third Sunday; for just such a scene as she describes was then and there enacted.

---

1. The original reads "hinderance."
2. Shakespeare, *The Tragedy of Romeo and Juliet*, 3.4.

A Mother's New Year Resolutions

JOSEPHINE T. WASHINGTON

Realizing, as never before, the magnitude of the mother's mission, and feeling my weakness under the weight of its obligations, herewith, at the dawning of the New Year, in humble and prayerful spirit, I subscribe myself to the following Resolutions:

I will remember that my children[1] are not playthings, nor puppets, nor personal possessions of any sort whatever; but immortal beings, loaned by God, to be taught and trained and fitted each to fulfill the purpose of his existence.

I will study my vocation, the sacred vocation of motherhood, striving to make myself more proficient, learning from wise men and from life how best to deal with the little ones entrusted to my care.

I will live *with* my children not merely *for* them; since such companionship is worth more than divergent ways, marked by needless sacrifices on the one side and a growing selfishness on the other.

I will respect the individuality of my children, and not try to change their temperaments, furnish their opinions, nor choose their callings—nor their mates, when the time comes for such selection.

I will do whatever lies in my power to give my children sound bodies, for physical vigor is an asset, the value of which scarcely can be overestimated.

I will provide for my children both work and play, believing as I do that they are equally essential to a full and harmonious development.

I will lead my children not only to love the best in books and art, but, likewise, to rejoice in all the beauty of earth and sea and sky—in the song of the bird, the glitter of the dewdrop upon the grass, the murmur of the wind among the trees, the quiet tints of the greyest day, as well as the glowing colors of the most brilliant sunset.

I will impart to my children the facts of life, that they may look with reverence upon their bodies; thinking God's thoughts after Him as they learn of human relations, and, in the years to come, labor for the enlightenment of those who sit in darkness.

* "A Mother's New Year Resolutions," *Crisis* 15, no. 3 (January 1918): 124–25.

1. At the time this article was written, the "children" referred to are Washington's grandsons, Anthony and Joseph Allen.

I will aim to keep ever before me the great truth that the mother's responsibility begins long before her babe is placed in her arms; and, consecrating
myself anew to the glorious calling of motherhood, I will endeavor so to live
and grow that should other children come to me, they may be dowered with a
richer heredity.

PART IV

CIVIC DUTY

What the Citizen Owes
to the Government

JOSEPHINE J. TURPIN

To the Editor of the Globe:

Every relation has its accompanying duties. Parents and children, bound by the most tender ties, owe, the one parental guidance and protection; the other filial respect and obedience. Employer and worker, connected in business interests, each has a claim upon the other; to the former is due honest performance of labor and faithful care of trusts consigned; to the latter, a reasonable recompensation for toil and a kind consideration of his needs. Between the government and the citizen exists a system of relative duties: and, inasmuch as the American Government differs from other governments, to the same extent do the duties of the American citizen differ from the duties of other citizens.

Submission is a right of the government from the citizen. Divine authority speaks to us from the Hebrews with the command, "Obey them that have the rule over you and submit yourselves."[1]

To obey properly, one must obey understandingly. The citizen should, therefore, learn the laws of his land and acquaint himself with the principles of its government. No personal opinion as to the expediency or inexpediency of a clause in the statute books should cause him to fail in obedience. Where wrong laws are to be righted, they cannot be righted by the petty disobedience of an individual. Our republican government offers a redress both correct and effectual. Let it then be the will of every citizen "to be subject to principalities and powers, to obey magistrates, to be ready to every good work."[2]

The government is entitled to the support of the citizen. It secures his right of property, protects the sanctity of his home, and defends him from violence. "For this cause, pay ye tribute,"[3] and thereby aid in maintaining the powers that are essential to the wellbeing of a people. Taxes are but the demands of the government for services rendered. He who grumbles at their payment or evades

---

* "What the Citizen Owes to the Government," *New York Globe*, 9 June 1883, 2.

1. Heb. 13:7.

2. Tit. 3:1

3. Rom. 13:6. The verse reads, "[For] for this cause pay ye tribute [also]."

them by chicanery, would growl at the servant who asks for his wages, or, cheat him out of his lawful dues.

The citizen should render all necessary and possible service to the government. This he can do in various ways. Since the character of homes decides the character of communities, and the characteristics of children, the characteristics of men, each parent should feel not only the responsibility of training immoral souls, but also of rearing embryo citizens, who are to determine the weal or the woe of the future state. Not only ought each citizen himself to obey the law, but he should use his influence to induce the obedience of others. If he connives at law-breaking, he implicates himself in disobedience; if he exposes not crime, he himself is criminal.

He should vote from principle, rather than from prejudice. In electing rulers, the voters should "provide out of all able men such as fear God, men of truth, hating covetousness, and place such over them."[4]

The true citizen is a patriot, one who loves his country and is willing to give his life for its good. Fighting in a worthy cause, he fears not to fall; protecting his people, he gladly suffers the martyr's fate. "Greater love hath no man than this, that a man lay down his life for his friends."[5]

4. Exod. 18:21.
5. John 15:13.

The Remedy for War

JOSEPHINE J. TURPIN

The evils of war are universally acknowledged. The economist, viewing the subject in a monetary light, regrets the vast expenditure of wealth, the wanton destruction of property, the restrictions laid upon commerce and the diversion of human energies from business pursuits. The philanthropist deplores the almost incalculable loss of life, the unheeded sufferings of wounded and dying men and the desolation of myriad homes all over the land. The moralist laments war's hardening and degrading influences, its lawlessness and debauchery, and the license given to the varied forms of vice. The statesman admits that hostile encounters do not settle disputes, that force is not argument, and that there is no logic in bullets and bombshells. "Is there no balm in Gilead? Is there no physician there?"[1] Surely it behooves mankind to seek an antidote for these great and manifold ills.

In discussing "The Remedy for War," we do not propose entering upon the question as to whether war is, under all circumstances, a moral wrong; nor do we deem it necessary to deny that good is sometimes incident to a contest of arms between nations. The evils of the war system and its inefficiency to accomplish desired ends sufficiently demonstrate the need of a remedy. We shall attempt, therefore, simply to propose the remedy and to prove its desirableness and practicability.

Let us first inquire somewhat into the causes of war. No physician attempts to treat a case until he has made such a diagnosis as acquaints him with the true and original reasons of disease. Wars arise largely from the passions of men. Desire for conquest, ambition for military glory, fancied insult and a mistaken sense of honor—each of these causes has been the little fire from which a great strife has been kindled. We charge the ancients with having fought for extension of territory, but we ourselves are not guiltless in this respect. Whatever the pretext or occasion, the real cause of most wars, for the last one hundred and fifty years, has been the desire to possess colonies with resources to support the conquering country. Hence the rupture of the peace of Amiens by France and the series of Napoleonic wars, closing with the battle of Waterloo; England's succession of wars in India; the

* "The Remedy for War," *A.M.E. Church Review* 4, no. 2 (October 1887): 161–66.
1. Jer. 8:22.

late contest between France and Prussia, and the hostilities of Frederick the Great against Maria Theresa.[2] "Whence come wars and fightings among you?" saith the Apostle James;[3] "come they not [hence, even of] your lusts that war in your members?" Contests of this manner are best combated by the spread of a Christian civilization, which has already done much to lessen their number. The spirit of benevolence is permeating the mass of mankind, and must ultimately leaven the whole. Nations are rapidly learning that extent of territory does not constitute national prosperity, and that the well-being of one State is not only perfectly consistent with that of every other, but is in some measure dependent thereon.

Still, while mutual goodwill and self-interest are vast aids in keeping the peace between nations, there is another restraining power for contests of this kind, as also for wars whose causes are other than those of passion. Nations as well as individuals differ in judgment; and from these differences disputes frequently arise, leading to war.

How are international differences to be adjusted? Is there anything in the nature of men which renders it a moral necessity that they should kill each other *en masse,* because their respective governments chance to disagree in opinion? Individuals settle their disputes without resort to the sword; why not nations? There are two possible ways to choose: first, a peaceful settlement of the difficulty between the disputants themselves, or negotiation; second, a reference of the point at issue to a third party, or arbitration. The first method presents obvious difficulties, and is applicable only to cases of minor importance. The second admits of various modifications. The referee may be a mutual friend offering his services; a commission jointly chosen by the interested parties; or an established international tribunal. In all these cases the principle is the same. Negotiation and arbitration in the two forms first mentioned have been successfully used at various times in the world's history for the settlement of questions threatening hostilities between governments; but a Supreme Court of Nations remains "a consummation devoutly to be wished."[4]

What are the nature and character of such a tribunal? In the first place, a definite and fixed code of international law is a desideratum long felt. No such code at present exists. The most that we have is a set of principles and wise suggestions presented by leading statesmen and publicists. Through courteous deference to the ability of these authorities, and because the need of some degree of regularity in intercourse is recognized, nations have largely incorporated

2. Maria Theresa (1717–1780) inherited the Austrian empire and opposed Frederick II's possession of Silesia, a Hapsburg claim (*The New Encyclopaedia Britannica,*" 15th ed. [2005], s.v. "Maria Theresa.").

3. This quotation and the one that follows it are found in Jas. 4:1.

4. Shakespeare, *The Tragedy of Hamlet,* 3.1.63–64.

many of these principles in treaty form and stipulation. Yet even among friendly and civilized powers has not much discussion been occasioned by the refusal to recognize the validity of certain international practices; and where there is agreement to accept some rule as stated in form, has not each party made its own interpretation of the same?

Hence, the initial step toward the acceptance of the proposed "Remedy for War" is to lay down a definite code of law for nations. The civilized powers of the world choosing to enter into this established relation with one another would each be represented in the Congress assembled for this purpose. It is not necessary here to mention all the details of the plan. We need not specify the manner in which these representatives of government are to be chosen to fix their number. To a people earnestly desirous of inaugurating a measure of reform such perplexities would be but slight hindrances. This Congress of Nations might assemble at any place decided upon—London, or Paris, or Washington—and draw up a code for the conduct of nations in their relations to each other, which code would subsequently be presented to the several powers, and if approved, then ratified.

The next step is to constitute an international tribunal for the interpretation and enforcement of this code. Its members might be selected by the several States, or by their delegates in Congress assembled. Of course the necessity for their being men of the highest integrity and ability is apparent. Such a court of nations would be a most imposing and honorable body, and a seat therein might well be counted the highest possible worldly honor. It would be within the province of this tribunal, vested with both original and appellative power, to adjudicate all international cases presented for hearing, and to give interpretation to all disputed points of international law. The party adjudged guilty of violating the code would pay such indemnity, or suffer such other penalty, except an armed attack, as the court of nations would see fit to impose.

Should this scheme be tried, would it not probably at first prevent forty-nine out of fifty possible wars, and in time entirely supersede the war system? If found unsuccessful, what harm would have been done? On the other hand, if successful, what rich rewards would be ours! All the loss of life and property, the destruction of commerce, the debasing moral influences attending war would be abolished, while international tranquility and an equal administration of justice would be ensured.

If the advocate of war pleads its necessity, we have already sought to show that there are other and better ways of adjusting international difficulties. If his prepossession is founded on the almost universal practice of nations past and present, wither would such argument lead?

Among the Spartans, theft, instead of being condemned and punished as a crime, was dignified into an art and an accomplishment. Yet who of us on this account defends stealing? It may safely be conceded that antiquity is not a stamp of merit.

Is it claimed that wars make heroes, inspire genius and advance civilization? We admit that this is, in some degree, true; but what evil does not incidentally promote some good? The system of slavery in the United States brought a benighted people into contact with civilizing influences; it produced those heroes in the cause of liberty—Phillips[5] and Douglass[6] and Garrison;[7] it moved Mrs. Stowe[8] to write "Uncle Tom's Cabin," and inspired such poets as Whittier[9] and Lowell[10] for some of their loftiest flights. Yet shall we attempt to justify the slaveholders because God overruled crime for good, and made the wrath of man to praise Him?

Besides, we claim that "peace [has] her victories not less renowned than war."[11] In the cause of philanthropy and humanity there is room for the grandest heroism. The noble efforts of Christian missionaries and the friendly intercourse of an unrestricted commerce are the surest means of civilization; while the triumphs of peace are fitter themes for genius than tales of carnage and bloodshed. Who does not see the superiority of this court of nations over the old hostile custom? Some such pacific policy must eventually prevail. All the signs of the times point thereto.

> "Down the dark future, through long generations,
> War's echoing sounds grow fainter and they cease,
> And like a bell, with solemn, sweet vibrations,
> I hear once more the voice of Christ say, 'Peace.'"[12]

"But," the objector may urge, "the world is not ripe for such an innovation." We reply, this is no new principle. There are various eminent examples of its employment throughout the history of nations. It is used in the cases of indi-

---

5. Wendell Phillips (1811–1884), antislavery agitator. He refused to use slave-produced products such as sugarcane and cotton.

6. Frederick Douglass (1818–1895), African American author, orator, social reformer, and founder of the *North Star* newspaper.

7. William Lloyd Garrison (1805–1879), abolitionist and founder of the *Liberator,* an antislavery newspaper.

8. Harriet Beecher Stowe (1811–1896), Connecticut novelist.

9. John Greenleaf Whittier (1805–1879), American poet, abolitionist, and editor of the *Pennsylvania Freeman,* an antislavery newspaper, from 1838 until 1840.

10. James Russell Lowell (1819–1891), American poet associated with the Romantic movement.

11. "Forty-Sixth Congress: First Session—May 19, Senate," *New York Times,* 20 May 1879, 7, col. 2.

12. Longfellow, "The Arsenal at Springfield," 1:123, stanza 11. Longfellow's line reads, "[The] echoing sounds grow fainter and [then] cease."

viduals and communities, and is at the foundation of all our State tribunals. The Amphictyonic Council[13] of ancient Greece was on the same principle. In less than two centuries there have been over fifty congresses in Europe similar to this tribunal proposed. Why not make permanent and regular what has been used temporarily and occasionally with such success, even in our own times? The Treaty of Washington provided for the peaceful settlement, between ourselves and Great Britain, of several disputed questions, each of which was sufficient in itself to have led to war. Nations, after fighting, not seldom resort to the practice of umpireship or arbitration for a solution of difficulties which the sword has failed to adjust. Why not use arbitration at first, and thus avoid war's terrible waste and woe? Victor Hugo[14] prophesied that in the twentieth century war will be dead. Can this seem incredible when we observe that not only the pacific utterances of sages long since departed show the tide of early thought to have been moving in this direction, but many of the wisest men of the present age are lending their influence to the peace policy. The arbitrating movement has had at no time a stauncher advocate than was Charles Sumner.[15] President Garfield[16] and ex-Secretary Blaine[17] proposed the assembling of an American Peace Congress. President Arthur[18] was its friend, and Senator Evarts[19] is numbered among its approvers. In 1884, the Republican Convention unanimously adopted, as a part of their political creed, a comprehensive statement of their and our faith, "International Arbitration for International Differences." As still further illustrating the popular attitude, it may be mentioned that the Bishops of the African Methodist Church, representing a half million members, at their meeting in this city two years ago adopted resolutions approving the National Arbitration League, condemning the war spirit, and invoking united effort and prayer throughout their churches for the abolition of war. That simple shaft, rising in majestic beauty above the city's loftiest heights, commemorates Washington not only as the general, "first in war," but Washington as the patriot and the statesman, "first in peace." Great as was Ulysses S. Grant[20] when he stood at

13. The Amphictyon Council or League was a religious association of Ancient Greek tribes with authority to pronounce punishment on the guilty.

14. Victor Hugo (1802–1885), French poet, novelist, playwright of the Romantic movement.

15. Charles Sumner (1811–1874), United States senator from Massachusetts.

16. James A. Garfield (1831–1881), the twentieth president of the United States.

17. James Gillespie Blaine (1830–1893) served two terms as secretary of state, first under President James A. Garfield and then under President Benjamin Harrison.

18. Chester A. Arthur (1829–1886) became the twenty-first president of the United States after President James A. Garfield was assassinated.

19. William Maxwell Evarts (1818–1901), American attorney.

20. Ulysses S. Grant (1822–1885), eighteenth president of the United States and Union army general in the American Civil War.

the head of a victorious army and received the sword from a vanquished foe, he was far greater when, in the flush of triumph, he turned aside to provide for the comfort of his suffering prisoners. Full worthy to receive the world's undivided homage was the author of that famous message, "Let us have peace."[21]

If a few selfish and ambitious sovereigns are unwilling to lay down arms, is it thus also with the people? They who spill their blood at the behest of government and bear the burden of heavy taxes imposed are becoming more and more averse to the policy which makes such terrible demands upon them, and bestows no commensurate reward. Well has it been explained:

> "War is a game, that, were their subjects wise,
> Kings would not play at."[22]

It requires no great prophetic power to see that as intelligence becomes more generally disseminated among the masses, and independent thought and the spirit of liberty prevail, wars will decrease in popularity and in frequency.

Is it said that nations shrink from the expense of this plan? Such a tribunal would cost scarcely one thousandth part of what the war system does even in time of peace. The war expenses of all Christendom in peace are not less than two or three million dollars daily. A congress of one hundred members, with a salary of twenty-five thousand dollars, would cost only two and a-half millions annually, and one million dollars would support a congress of fifty members at twenty-five thousand dollars yearly each, or nearly sixty dollars apiece per day.

Is it objected that such a tribunal would be dangerous? How and to whom? Its laws would be such as the nations had themselves agreed to; its power would be limited to the settlement of international claims, and it would have no voice in internal affairs.

Someone may say that, after all, such a tribunal would be powerless to enforce its decrees. Why so? Is there no potency save in brute force? The guilty State, rebelling against this lawfully constituted authority, would be arraigned before the bar of public opinion and condemned. To be placed under the ban of civilized countries, and to be severely ignored in an international sense, would entail such humiliating consequences and a situation of so great commercial and political disadvantage as to make it a reasonable presumption that cases of persistent disobedience would be rare.

How shall this desirable state of affairs be brought about? First, agitate; secondly, *agitate;* third, AGITATE. Even now the subject is not confined to philos-

---

21. Grant, "Reconciliation." https://www.virginiahistory.org/collections-and-resources /virginia-history-explorer/lee-and-grant/reconciliation. The words are taken from President Ulysses S. Grant's 1868 campaign slogan.

22. Cowper, "The Winter Morning Walk," 87. Cowper's line reads, "[But war's] a game, [which,] were their subjects wise."

ophers and statesmen, but is publicly discussed as a popular question. Let the interest be made more general. Let the pulpit and the press voice the peace sentiments. Since Congress will move in any reformatory measure only as fast and as far as the people demand, let them acquaint themselves more thoroughly with the bearings of this great problem, that they may act wisely and intelligently in the matter. Let their representatives in legislative bodies send peace memorials to the national governments; and, finally, let us trust that some country will issue an invitation to the other powers asking that delegates plenipotentiary be sent to unite in forming an international code of laws, with the ultimate end in view of establishing a Supreme Court of Nations. All honor to Senator Wilson,[23] of Iowa, who introduced among the first bills of the last session of Congress one containing the proposition to hold an International Peace Congress for the purpose of establishing a tribunal to hear and determine disputes among nations.

Will the United States go down to posterity as the inaugurator in this noble movement? O for a Perseus[24] to slay the Medusa![25] O for the period when the gates of the temple of Janus[26] will close to open no more!

The blood of martyred soldiers calls for a cessation of war's human sacrifice. Commerce proclaims aloud against the disregard of her rights. Poverty points to her rags and then to this reckless expenditure of wealth. Morality is shocked at the debasing influence. Religion shutters over the flagrant violation of the law of love. Education, art and science plead for the removal of the obstruction. Justice demands a surer and safer method of operation. Shall not all these voices eventually prevail? Hasten, O God, the good times coming, when Thou shalt "make wars to cease unto the end of the earth;"[27] when men shall "beat their swords into ploughshares and their spears into pruning-hooks;"[28] when "nation shall not lift up sword against nation, neither shall they learn war anymore."

Vast accumulations of war debts, piled like Ossa upon Pelion,[29] will then melt as snowflakes before the sun. White doves of commerce, bearing the olive-branch of peace, will traverse the wide waters to every clime. Then in Acadia[30] the fields of golden grain will wave undisturbed; with fearless content

---

23. James F. Wilson (1828–1895) served two terms as a Republican senator.

24. Perseus, a winged god who slew the Gorgon Medusa and rescued Andromeda from a sea monster.

25. Medusa, a mythological Greek figure who angered Athena and was turned into a hideous creature with snakes for hair.

26. Janus, the two-headed Roman god who presided over war and peace.

27. Rev. 46:9. The verse reads, "Thou shall maketh wars to cease."

28. This verse and the one that follows can be found in Isa. 2:4.

29. Ossa and Pelion, mountains in northeast Greece. In Greek mythology, the Titans piled Ossa on Pelion and both on Olympus in an attempt to reach and slay the gods.

30. Arcadia, centrally located in the Peloponnese peninsula in Greece.

the husbandman will go to his toil, and with joy return to his tranquil home. No villagers will be forced by sword to flee their native place; no Evangeline[31] sent to roam in lonely exile. Plenty and content will sit at every fireside, industry and cheer abound in every home, learning and culture dwell even with the poor, virtue and religion brood over the land. Then will the world be ruled by the heads of the wise and the hearts of the good, rather than by the hands of the proud, the powerful and the despotic.

31. Evangeline, an Acadian maiden in search of Gabriel, her long-lost love, in Longfellow's epic poem *Evangeline*.

PART V

SOCIETAL RESPONSIBILITY

Unwise Talkers

"JOYCE"

Make speech the servant of reason, the handmaid of virtue. The glorious sun shines in the heavens; but did not the earth turn towards it, some places would never see the day. God distinguished man from beast by giving him mind; but let him make no efforts for its improvement, and he remains uncouth, unlearned, and uncultured. Rocks lie broken and pointed and jagged on the mountain side, but, moving down with the great glacier, their sharp angles are rounded into graceful forms. In spiritual action man gains the beauty of character that lethargy cannot bestow. But to do wrong is more natural than to do right; to say bad things is easier than to say good.

> "The gates of hell are open night and day.
> Smooth the descent and easy is the way.
> But to return and view the cheerful skies
> In this the task and mighty labor lies."[1]

Many of the greatest calamities originate in thoughtlessness. In a meditative mood, King Henry the First[2] would not have uttered the words that caused the murder of Thomas á Becket;[3] through want of consideration. The colonists[4] adopted the hurtful method in their treatment of the Indians; Prince William of England carelessly left his sister in the sinking ship,[5] and lost his life in trying to remedy the neglect. A mental vacuum[6] allows the interspersion in daily talk

---

* "Unwise Talkers," *People's Advocate* (Washington, D.C.), 18 June 1881, 2.

1. Dryden, *Virgil's Aeneid*, bk. 6, p. 399.

2. King Henry I (1069–1135) succeeded his brother King William II to the throne of England and reigned from 1100 to 1135 (Hollister, "Henry I").

3. The original reads "Thomas A. Becket." Becket (1118–1170) was archbishop of Canterbury. He was murdered in Canterbury Cathedral as four of Henry I's knights carried out the murder they thought the king wanted (Knowles, "Saint Thomas Becket").

4. The original reads "colonist."

5. Prince William of Adelin (1103–1120). William Adelinus was son of King Henry I and Matilda of Scotland. At seventeen years of age, he drowned while trying to save his half sister on the sinking *White Ship* (Mason, "William," 37–38).

6. The original reads "vaccuum."

of loose and careless gossip. A breezy body (who honors not the precept, "Mind your own business") attempts to entertain you for an hour with minute details of the affairs of his neighbors. If you are simple and unsophisticated, you gaze into the narrator's face and wonder at the malignity that prompts him to lay bare to the world the private interests of these lives. There may be in that countenance no trace of evil passions, nothing to repel a physiognomist but, perhaps, the idiotic smile that clings habitually to some who are good natured and stupid. He scorns to do low things, he certainly does not lie, for he exercises but a speaker's privilege when he exaggerates facts to give coloring and intensity to a story. Such persons, like broken pitchers, retain nothing poured into them. They seek your confidence one day, and the next your sentences are blurted in the market place. Still, were all actions good which proceed from no wrong intention, we would judge their characters very gently, for they mean nothing bad, they mean nothing good—in fact they mean nothing at all.

Milton describes a fallen angel who attempted to drag others down with him. Today the fallen creatures of the world manifest this tendency in fabricating accusations and insinuating falsehoods. This is the unsatisfactory method they adopt to console conscience and to extenuate general disapprobation, believing that the less honor the world holds, the less censure degradation receives. Sometimes they whisper what they dare not openly affirm, again their meanings are expressed in sly hints and doubtful shakings of the head. Innocent acts are willingly misconstrued, simple speech is given a suspicious significance. You are informed of indiscriminate misdeeds, you are harassed with comments virtuously indignant, but, woe to you, if you utter a word against the absent. Brother B. is informed of your improper defamation, and you have gained an enemy.

It is often the weak who deem themselves strongest. A certain class of "unwise talkers" seize each opportunity to torture an incidental audience with demonstrations of personal wisdom and affirmations of the world's gross ignorance. Some critics pursue a work merely to detect its mistakes, some men pass through life with eyes closed to its good, but with gaze eagerly devouring its follies and mistakes. They contract the brow and curl the lip and drop cutting sarcasms, on every possible occasion, and very often, as Cicero says, "They condemn what they do not understand."[7] No sermon satisfies them: the minister is either dull or conceited, when others praise, they feel called upon to dissent, and meantime they congratulate themselves on their superior intelligence. They hold themselves aloof, and, like Pharisee,[8] they thank God they are what they are while, in their innermost heart, gratitude ascends but to the shrine of Self. They imagine that repetitions of another's wrongdoings throw

7. Quintilian, "Oratory and Virtue," 84.
8. The original reads "pharisee."

their own excellence in stronger relief. They view mankind's faults through the small end of a telescope and the virtue through the large; thus magnifying the defects of performance, and diminishing their view of that which is commendable.

Though these various folks tattle with different motives, their communications bear striking resemblances. One whose mind is more depraved than the heart, tells truth, but truth so spiced and salted[9] and peppered, as to lose its original flavor. Another who is spiritually degenerated, magnifies error and fashions falsehood. Another who lacks both kindliness and common sense, seeks the evil and ignores the good. They all gratify an idle curiosity, demoralize the tone of society, and dry the springs of human sympathy and forbearance. They invade the sanctity of homes, destroy long established friendship, and discourage with disparaging words many a one whom

> "To blame is easier those who him offended
> Than reach the faintest glory round him shed."[10]

Individuals possess concerns, not "secret" but personal, with which the multitude has no right to meddle. Intercourse loses charm when everything is revealed, except between most intimate friends. How much more is mutual esteem endangered where confidence is not bestowed, but where knowledge is obtained by curious inspection or wrenched from one by impertinent questions! If you hear rumors discreditable of an acquaintance, why repeat them? They may be untrue, and you do injustice to a brother. If they be true, does your reiteration remedy the wrong? You are not to be blamed because you see faults in mankind, but you are to [be] blamed if you see not also the virtues, we need "Mutual Admiration Societies" in our communities.

"Avoid the appearance of evil,"[11] but be willing rather to appear wrong than to miss opportunities of doing good. Be not controlled by foolish dread of what "people will say" about you. "Do right, and fear not."[12] One principle is worth a dozen rules, for rules are but the outgrowth of principle. Therefore, follow blind by no conventionalisms. In all questions of duty

> "Think for thyself—one good idea,
> But know to be thine own,[13]
> Is better than a thousand gleaned

9. The original reads "and and salted."

10. Longfellow, "Seven Sonnets and a Canzone," 2:886, stanza 7, "Dante."

11. 1 Thess. 5:22. The verse reads, "Abstain from all appearance of evil."

12. An interpretation of Rom. 13:3, which reads: "For rulers are not a terror to good works, but to the evil. Wilt thou then not be afraid of the power? do that which is good, and thou shalt have praise of the same."

13. The second line reads, "But [known] to be thine own."

From fields by others sown."[14]

And in your relations to your fellow man, remember these lines which hold the maxim of the golden rule:

> "Be to his faults a little blind,
> Be to his virtues very kind."[15]

14. Adams, "Grammar Department," 147.

15. Prior, "An English Padlock," 44. Prior's lines read: "Be to [her] virtues very kind; / Be to [her] faults a little blind."

The Benefits of Trouble

J. J. TURPIN

Life is a school. Here we are to prepare for the great Beyond. God himself is our teacher, and every circumstance is a book from which we can learn some useful lesson. We read with avidity the pages of pleasure, and often satisfied with being entertained, we seek not to be instructed. We comprehend not the benefits to be derived from trouble, and we fain would pass its sober leaves uncut. Happiness has its own teachings of worth to be treasured, sorrow holds its own lessons of wisdom to be conned. Whether privations and disappointments shall injure or elevate us, depends upon ourselves. This one thing is true: that nothing is, but what is best.

> "All is of God that is and is to be,
> And God is good.
> Let this suffice us."[1]

Trouble affects our relations with our fellow-man. He who has suffered, can best sympathize with a sufferer. Happy, careless tender-hearted people may utter exclamations of commiseration on encountering a case of direful distress, and may do what they can to alleviate the pitiful condition; but they cannot feel, as does one who has sounded the depths of a similar woe. The hale and hearty man, who has never known, a day's illness, may pity the invalid confined to his bed week after week; but he cannot sympathize with him. Pity feels for its object as suffering, as weak, as inferior. Sympathy implies a fellow feeling, and it cannot be exercised in the fullest degree without an experience of a similar nature. Man craves sympathy to the same extent that he shrinks from pity. Sympathy cheers, consoles, strengthens and inspires. Sympathy numbs the bitter from memory, sweetens the cup of agony, and nerves for future conflict. Sympathy does all this, and only he who has suffered can give sympathy to the sufferer.

---

* "The Benefits of Trouble," *Virginia Star,* 11 November 1882, 1. Turpin read this essay before the Literary Society of Richmond Institute.

1. Whittier, "Trust," 171. Whittier's line reads, "Let this suffice us [still / Resting in childlike trust upon his will"].

Personal trouble not only teaches us "to feel another's woe," but it shows us how to help that other in his misery. Kind but inexperienced friends, in attempting to condole, may tear open the bleeding wounds afresh. He who has himself been borne down by the same affliction, deftly and tenderly binds up the sores and applies balm to the broken spirit. The heart refuses the consolation of him who knows not whereof he speaks. "He means well," is the inward cry, "but he does not know!" When one comes who, from his own life-experience, understands all the pain and ache, the mourner bends the head and meekly accepts the offered words of advice and suggestion.

Trouble not only creates sympathy for the suffering, it not only gives knowledge of how to assist them, but it serves as an impetus to increased activity for the good of others. He who has no selfish interests to abstract him, who has no personal gratifications to him, who has lost his own great hope of happiness, turns to find his life-work among the suffering of mankind. He who, surrounded by all things essential to human happiness, lives at peace with God and man leads a noble life; but he who, disrobed of all hopes of earthly happiness, lives but to do benefits, leads a nobler life.

Trouble develops character.[2] It has a tendency to induce thought, to promote meditation.

"'Tis held that sorrow makes us wise."[3] It gives an experience that is valuable in every phase of life. This experience sometimes proves its utility by enabling us to bear better the constant ills of existence, sometimes by helping us to help others, and sometimes by aiding in the creation of works of art. Had Tennyson not lost the friend of his youth, "In Memoriam" would never have been given to the world. Milton's "Samson Agonistes" owes its vivid portrayal of the hero's woes, to the fact[4] of the author's own blind and suffering old age. "Hyperion" is the outgrowth of Longfellow's struggle with sorrow.

Trouble secures self-control. He who, in the days of prosperity, yielded to the expression of every emotion, who allowed his face to be the index of his heart, must, when the tides of adversity sweep over him, pursue a different course. He must not overshadow the world with his woe; he must not bury himself in a shell of despondency. He must subdue the elements within; he must say to his soul, "Peace, be still!" and all must be still. Dignity requires it, duty demands it.

Only he has patience who has endured and waited. The germs of patience lie in every nature, but they only take root and spring up in the glow of affliction. He who has availed himself of this discipline, is unmoved amid annoyances, is unirritated under disturbances, is calm even in anguish. Under all circumstances he possesses his soul in patience.

2. The original reads "characters."
3. Tennyson, "In Memoriam," canto 113, p. 125.
4. The original reads "foct."

Strength comes to him who suffers long and who suffers in silence. The God-like part of man rises up in him, and to the cares which assail, he exclaims, with Paul Flemming in "Hyperion," "I will be strong."[5] We are upheld under distresses by the conviction that "it is not all of life to live,"[6] that others have borne bravely burdens as heavy as ours, that a noble character is best formed by the discipline of suffering, that after the cross comes the crown, that the end of life is not happiness, that above us rules a God who doeth all things well.

Trouble trains in courage. He who has known "how sublime a thing it is, to suffer and be strong"[7]—fears not. Is he liable to meet Poverty?—he is well acquainted with her. Is he exposed to physical suffering?—he has become inured to it. Is he in danger of losing one beloved?—this, too, he has learned to bear. A man has gained something when he [has] gone through the fires of affliction, and knows that nowhere in life can await him a trial greater than those he has already borne.

Trouble draws us nearer to God. Man can neither change the circumstances that surround us, nor can he remove the pang they cause. "With God all things are possible."[8] We feel a yearning for a deeper peace not known before; a peace that depends not on the changeful things of time, that rests not upon conditions and possessions of earth, an inward, all-satisfying peace that flows from the great Fountain. We pour out our soul in prayer, and a great[9] calm succeeds the storm. The promises in his Word, of care and comfort and eternal rest assume a new significance. "All things work together for good to them that love the Lord."[10] How many a weary soul has been cheered and strengthened by these words! When a great hope sets, it is like the setting of the sun at even. Darkness surrounds us; our grief seems to shadow the whole world; but as at night the stars, which are invisible by day, appear, so, in the night of pain, we see the lights of heaven shining more brightly upon us. Losing that which bound us to earth, we fix our thoughts more entirely upon heaven and heavenly things. The value of prayer is more sensibly felt, the promises of the Scriptures are more fully appreciated, faith is visibly strengthened and increased.

Have you trouble? Fret not, despond not. "Nothing walks with aimless feet."[11] Gain an ennobling discipline from the cares which harass the soul. Learn a

5. Longfellow, "Hyperion," bk. 4, chap. 8, p. 370.

6. Casey, "Quotes, Wisdom, and Sayings," n.p.

7. Longfellow, "The Light of Stars," 1:7. Longfellow's line reads, "[Know] how sublime a thing it is / To suffer and be strong."

8. Matt. 19:26.

9. The original reads "graet."

10. Rom. 8:26

11. Tennyson, "In Memoriam," canto 54, p. 113. Tennyson's line reads, "[That] nothing walks with aimless feet."

lesson from every circumstance in life, whether pleasant or unpleasant. Sometimes the books we relish least, are those which will benefit us most. Measure not benefit by enjoyment, but by growth in spiritual worthiness.

> "Be resigned,
> Bear up, bear on, the end shall tell
> The dear Lord doeth all things well."[12]

12. Whittier, "The Angel of Patience," 96. Whittier's line reads, "The dear Lord [or-dereth] all things well!"

Paul's Trade and What Use He Made of It

JOSEPHINE J. TURPIN

Somewhere down a busy Corinthian street is a humble tent-maker's shop. There is no mark to distinguish it from any other in this vast city; but, all unconsciously to its inmates, it holds within one in whom is to center an interest that shall outlive ages, one whose residence therein shall give to Corinth[1] an importance which no other event in her history could confer. Who is he with the tender, sweet expression, with the mild look of patient endurance, with the light of thought and meditation upon his face? It is the Apostle Paul; a man learned in the knowledge of the Jews and of the Greeks, having been brought up at the feet of Gamaliel,[2] able to contend with the subtlety and wisdom of the Athenians, and to command the admiration of kings and emperors; it is he whom we find working at a lowly trade.

The fact that Paul had a trade is no evidence that his parents were poor or of an expectation that he would be compelled to earn his livelihood by manual labor. Indeed, we have much greater reason to believe otherwise; for Paul's education was such as could not have been given him by indigent parents and such as would not have been deemed necessary had he been designed for other than a learned profession. It was a custom among the Jews that every boy should be taught a trade. The Rabbis have left on record many maxims relative to the virtue of this usage. They said: "He who does not teach his son a trade, teaches[3] him to steal."[4] To Paul's own master, Gamaliel, is ascribed the saying, "He that hath a trade in his hand to what is he like? He is like a garden that is fenced."[5] Well would it be for the present generation were more attention paid to industrial

---

* "Paul's Trade and What Use He Made of It," *Christian Recorder* 22, no. 7 (14 February 1884): 1.

1. Corinth, a large city in south-central Greece.

2. Gamaliel, a Jewish rabbi.

3. The original reads "teachers."

4. 2 Thess. 3:10. The verse reads, "For even when we were with you, this we commanded you, that if any would not work, neither should he eat."

5. Kitto, "Saul of Tarsus," 96.

education. The prevalence of a contrary idea on this subject is greatly to be deplored; both because it is false and because of the evil results which its acceptance ensures. We might, with wisdom, adopt in great measure the views of the Jewish Rabbis. That Paul was taught this particular trade of tent-making is no doubt due to his being brought up at Tarsus,[6] where a kind of hair cloth called Cilicium, wrought from the goats' hair obtained from the wild goats in the province of Cilicia,[7] was a chief manufacture. Probably his father, too, before him had learned this handicraft; and, as was often the case, the son was instructed in the same. It matters little why this in particular was selected; it is most interesting to notice the uses he made of his trade.

During his labors as a missionary, Paul supported himself by tent-making. Little did the father think when, according to ancient custom, his son was taught a trade, that he would in after years be so situated as to resort to it for earning his daily bread. Man has slight knowledge of what future events will befall him here. He is wisest who, treading his undeniable path of duty, neglects not the present, dreads not the future and as much as in him lies provides for all possible contingencies. If Paul had possessed any means of sustenance, they were his no longer. He began his mission as a poor man. No constraint save that of his own conscience, no influence save that of divine origin, sent Paul into his chosen career. It was one beset by dangers, difficulties, hardships, privations, offering no inducements of wealth, ease, emoluments; yet, he swerved not therefrom. With his wonderful gifts and splendid acquirements he might, in other walks, have risen to a position of worldly power and eminence. Paul counted "all things but loss for the excellency of the knowledge of Christ Jesus,"[8] for whom he "suffered the loss of all things."[9] Instead of basking in luxury, we find him at Ephesus,[10] at Thessalonica,[11] and at Corinth, toiling in a tent-maker's shop. Paul realized a grand truth, which he embodied in a glorious sacrifice. The end of living is the advancement of right principles, of which righteous causes are but the outgrowth. Having, then, embraced the cause the principles of which we feel bound to promote, no consideration of personal comfort or pleasure should prevent the most strenuous efforts for its progression.

Paul used his trade as a means to disarm suspicion and invite confidence. Corinth was a city of most dissolute and depraved character. Farrar calls it "the Vanity Fair of the Roman Empire, at once the London and the Paris of the first

6. Tarsus, the capital city of Cilicia and St. Paul's birthplace.

7. Cilicia, a Roman province located in what is now southern Turkey.

8. Phil. 3:8.

9. Ibid.

10. Ephesus, an ancient Greek city located near what is now modern Izmir, Turkey.

11. Thessalonica, the ancient name for Salonika, a port city in Greece in which Paul worked and preached.

century after Christ."[12] Paul entered it an entire stranger. He had first to seek some place in which to stay and to obtain some employment by which to sustain himself. We are told that he "found a certain Jew named Aquila, born in Pontius, lately come from Italy, with his wife Priscilla (because that Claudius had commanded all Jews to depart from Rome), and came unto them. And because he was of the same craft he abode with them, and wrought (for by their occupation they were tent-makers). And he reasoned in the synagogue every Sabbath, and persuaded the Jews and the Greeks."[13] No one teaches with greater clearness and force than does this apostle the doctrine that "the laborer is worthy of his hire,"[14] and that "they which preach the gospel should live by the gospel;"[15] but he recognized his position as a peculiar one, demanding a peculiar policy, and he determined to accept nothing from those for whom he labored. People flocked to this busy commercial center for the purpose of making money; it was filled with greedy, grasping traders and shop-keepers; what wonder that they were inclined to look upon all others through the lens of their own avarice and selfishness? Besides, the truth that our missionary tent-maker had come to proclaim was by no means popular, nor of the nature to meet the ready acceptance of a wicked and licentious people. With these things against him, therefore, for the sake of the cause to which he has consecrated himself, he must be particularly circumspect. The judgment accorded to the faith for which a man contends is likely to be in some wise limited by the judgment passed upon the man's personal self. Paul, with a wisdom of action equal to the magnitude of his sacrifice, joined himself with these humble workmen, laboring daily for his own maintenance; and on the Sabbath expounded the word. A man's true character will reveal itself nowhere more decidedly than in his business relations. If he is a Christian his Christianity will there appear; if he is a hypocrite, his hypocrisy will not long remain concealed. Paul's method of winning trust and respect to himself is one to be admired and imitated.

Paul's trade enabled him to identify himself more closely with the common people, for whose spiritual good he was exercised. He went in among them and became, in all outward appearances, one of them. He gained greater knowledge of their manner of living, of their habits of thinking; he acquired an insight into their national traits and individual characteristics; he witnessed their condition and understood their situation. His Sunday teachings were not merely of theories and general notions; he knew whereof he spoke, and to whom he spoke. He was able to assail the very sins which governed them, to present the very truths

---

12. Farrar's statement is based on various biblical books including Corinthians and Acts (see "The First Epistle to the Corinthians—Christian Classics Ethereal Library").

13. Acts 18:2–4.

14. 1 Tim. 5:18.

15. 1 Cor. 9:14.

for which they famished. Possessing the advantage of knowing his audience, he could use that style of language, that method of presentation, that kind of illustration best adapted to win their attention and consideration.

Paul's opportunities for doing good were increased by this daily contact which the pursuance of his avocation afforded. Most men are more easily touched by direct personal appeals in private than by the common warnings and exhortations of the pulpit. In the ordinary occurrences of business and of duty, many an opportune moment arises when a word may be spoken "fitly and in season." The elevating, refining, spiritualizing influence, which Paul had over those workmen in Aquila's shop,[16] cannot be estimated. Even the presence of such a man among them would have a most salutary effect. Probably Aquila and Priscilla[17] were not Christians when they came to Corinth; we have no reason to believe that they were. Paul did not attach himself to them because they were fellow-Christians, but because they were fellow-craftsmen. That they were subsequently professed Christians we do know, for we read of their spiritual efforts in behalf of others. No doubt to this apostle abiding in their house, working in their shop, is due, under God, their conversion.

Paul's experience as a common working man deepened and broadened his sympathy. Sympathy is a fellow-feeling. It implies experiences of a similar nature, and is essential to the most effective work among men. We listen more readily to the advice and counsel of him who has himself realized our cares and borne burdens like our own. When Paul addressed those Corinthians in the synagogue, he did not stand afar off and speak to them of things he knew not, but, among them as a brother, as one sharing with them a common fate, from the depths of a full heart he talked to them of the life which was his as well as theirs, of its joys and sorrows, of its blessings and privations, of the all-saving gospel which would lift the shadows and heighten the sunshine.

Paul set an example of inestimable value. He taught industry no less by practice than by precept. Day by day, and even far into the night, he toiled steadily for two years in the little shop at Corinth. His advice to his converts to "work with your own hands, as we command you,"[18] gained additional weight by the fact that he could recall their remembrance to his own "labor and travail; for laboring night and day, because we would not be chargeable unto any of you, we preached unto you the gospel of God."[19] "Not because we have not power, but to make ourselves an example unto you to follow us, for even when we were

---

16. Aquila, the Jew, owned a tent-making shop.

17. Aquila and Priscilla, a Jewish couple with whom Paul reside in Corinth (see Acts 18:3).

18. 1 Thess. 4:11. The verse reads, "[and to] work with your hands, as we [commanded] you."

19. 2 Thess. 3:8. The verse reads, "[that] we [might] not be chargeable [to] any of you."

with you this we commanded you, that if any would not work, neither should he eat."[20]

Physical labor is not incompatible with mental culture and a high degree of spirituality. Paul, as a man possessing a powerful intellect and endowed with wondrous graces of soul, scorned not to work with his own hands. He rather gloried in the fact, and boasted that, "coveting no man's silver or gold,"[21] he had with his own hands ministered unto his necessities. How often do we complain of the lowliness of our service, and pine for higher planes and broader fields of action, forgetful that there is lofty dignity in the proper performance of lowly duties. While the busy fingers wrought with the needle, the mind spun its own fine web of thought. At this time those beautiful epistles were written, which have come down to us as models of literary excellence. A humble occupation does not necessarily confine the mind to the contemplation of material and common-place objects. The blacksmith smiting his anvil, the carpenter fashioning his boards, the housewife engaged in domestic toil, may each, like the humble tent-maker of Corinth, feel his soul thrilled within him by divine fire; may each, in his own individual fashion, give such expression to these thoughts as will bless and benefit others.

Lowly circumstances do not detract necessarily from true greatness. Paul, bending over his work in the tent-maker's shop, was as truly a great man as when addressing the Athenians from Mars Hill,[22] or expounding the Scripture before King Agrippa.[23] Nothing external is a real possession. Intrinsic worth lies only within and constitutes a part of oneself. Surroundings may draw out and present it with more prominence, but they can neither make nor mar. The germs of development lie in the human soul; only the growth there engendered is her own. A tendency leading likely to incorrect impressions and false judgment is to estimate individuals according to the phases of their outward life. From this grow fawnings over the wealthy and aristocratic, the ascribing undue importance to office and position, the scorning of certain employments,[24] the prejudice against classes and races.

Behold, what good Paul did with so humble an instrumentality! Yet did he do anything in his larger and more able way that we in our smaller and weaker way may not do? Paul maintained himself and labored for the Lord. May not we, as opportunity presents itself, do a small missionary work among those about us, and a greater missionary work by giving of our means for the support of those

20. 2 Thess. 3:9–10.

21. Acts 20:33.

22. Mars Hill is located in Athens, Greece; it is also known as the Areopagus (Acts 17:19, 22).

23. King Agrippa is also King Herod Agrippa in Acts.

24. The original reads "employment's."

whose lives are dedicated to this cause? Paul disarmed suspicion, and gained confidence by his disinterested ministry and by his orderly and diligent application to the work in which he engaged. May not we, by our unselfish efforts in behalf of others, and by our conscientious attention to even the most ordinary details of everyday life,[25] win from the world a more pronounced acknowledgement of the beauty and efficacy of the Christian religion? Paul, in consideration of the good that he might do, hesitated not to take a position among the most lowly. Should not we put aside all false pride, and go forth with greater willingness and zeal to teach the ignorant and elevate the fallen? Paul endeavored so to demean himself as to set an example which others might safely follow. So ought we to live that men may see our good works, and glorify our Father which is in heaven.

Washington, D.C.

25. The original reads "every day life."

Needs of Our Newspapers: Some Reasons for Their Existence

JOSEPHINE TURPIN WASHINGTON

Results of an Accomplished Woman Writer's Study of the Negro Press of the Country—Its Intrinsic and Extrinsic Requirements —Written for The New York Age

That the Negro requires a press of his own, few will be found to deny. Were it simply that he desires news in general, this requirement would be much less urgent: for the long established and wealthy journals of other races are much better fitted to meet this demand than we can hope for a long time to be. But he wants besides general news, which any reliable and well-conducted organ can furnish, news of a special type, of such a kind as publications owned and controlled by white men will not give. He needs information of race doings: he needs to know how events appear seen through the eyes of leading colored men. He needs to conduct journalistic enterprises, that he may show to the world his ability in this direction.

You may say that this is drawing the color-line. Why not merge our interests in those of the community, subscribe to[1] the best newspapers only and refuse support to those poor and struggling, irrespective of race or nationality? But why speak of our drawing the color-line? It is drawn and most persistently by the whites. For us to attempt to ignore the fact, would be like trying to walk through a stone wall by simply making up your mind it is not there. The wall stands and you have only a broken head for your pains. The best way to obliterate this color-line, which is contrary to both reason and Christianity, is not foolishly to ignore it, but to act in accordance with the existing facts, while at the same time protesting against the injustice of the situation, and to develop[2]

---

* "Needs of Our Newspapers: Some Reasons for Their Existence," *New York Age*, 19 October 1889, 1.

1. The original reads "subscribe for."
2. The original reads "develope."

to the uttermost the powers within us, to prove ourselves worthy of equality of every sort, to "make by force our merit known."[3]

Studying the Negro newspapers of the country, as any member of the race interested in its welfare must do, I have been struck with certain needs, both intrinsic and extrinsic, in drawing attention to which I hope I shall be understood. I had almost said "pardoned," but that would imply a fault in making criticism, which I do not admit.

In the first place the journalistic field is often entered with the wrong motive. Where motive is low and altogether lacking, there can be no high standard for the paper. Some become editors merely for the sake of notoriety, for the delight of being in print; some are simply political tools, hired to profess the principles they avow; others hope to make a fortune, a hope I hardly need add which has never been realized by a colored editor. Every paper should have an aim, and a high and lofty one, should devote itself to principles of right, and should be brave and outspoken in their advocacy.

A good motive is, however, not all sufficient. Journalistic ability is essential. It is true that not everyone who can write a good magazine article or even a book, has the peculiar gift necessary to successfully conduct a newspaper. There are Negro editors, however, who cannot write a decent article of any kind, who cannot even speak good English. Such men have no business in the editorial chair. I have sometimes thought that were some of them to read an essay entitled "Writing for the Press," in Matthews' *Hours with Men and Books,* they might lose some of that audacity which, after all, is but in accordance with the familiar quotation, "Fools rush in, where angels fear to tread."[4]

The colored newspaper is too indifferent to the quality of its material. Editors seem to accept contributions through fear of losing subscribers or making enemies. Now, if people think that because they take a certain paper that paper ought to print any and all of their senseless effusions, the sooner they are disabused of this idea, the better for them individually and for the race collectively. Those who have control of newspaper columns should put forth efforts to secure the best writers and when able to do so should pay them for their services.

Many of our papers give too much space and prominence to letters containing the local and personal news of insignificant towns, which cannot be of any interest to the public at large.

We ought to have more original and less patent matter. There are few colored papers without a page or two of patent matter. It would be better to have a smaller sheet and that original than one larger mostly patent. It would exact

3. Tennyson, "In Memoriam," canto 64, p. 115. Tennyson's line reads, "[who makes] by force [his] merit known."

4. Pope, "An Essay on Criticism," p. 372, line 625. Pope's line reads, "[For] fools rush in where angels fear to tread."

more time and money and brains, but it would accomplish more for the race; and being more acceptable to the public would in the end be more profitable to its proprietors.

The original matter need not, however, as is often the case, be personal abuse of a journalistic brother or some other disputant. If an opponent's reasoning cannot be confuted, it does not help the argument to impugn his motives or seek to destroy his reputation. Nor should the opposite error of giving fulsome and extravagant praise and bestowing titles where they do not belong be indulged. Our newspaper encomiums are so generally in the superlative degree that one wonders if the authors of such meaningless panegyrics do not experience acute chagrin when something really great is achieved and they can find for its description no language more exalted than that in daily use. Every public man of any ability is a leader, every scribbler of verses a poet, every teacher a professor, every minister a doctor of divinity. All is splendid, grand, magnificent; by criticism praise is understood; and nothing which we do can be surpassed.

Another need is the improvement of the mechanical make-up of the paper. Many of our most talented writers are shy of the Negro press, because of the way in which they are unwittingly misrepresented. Articles appear with misspelt words, mistakes in grammar, sentences and parts of sentences omitted or inserted in the wrong place. Greater care in the selection and superintendence of workmen would remedy this evil.

The editors and managers of our newspapers should also manifest more interest in obtaining subscriptions and advertisements, and in securing active agents throughout the country. Mr. I. Garland Penn, in an able letter published in a recent issue of *The Age,* gives some pertinent suggestions on this point.

Among what I term the extrinsic needs of the Negro newspaper, one very conspicuous is need of support. This is why they "come to stay" and yet disappear after a fitful existence of a few weeks or months. Of course, one reason why many lack support is because they are unworthy of support. The law of the "survival of the fittest" may be usually depended upon, yet there are reasons outside of the press itself why so many of our papers languish and die. Many colored people have a way of sneering at race enterprises. They are not colored men, they say; they are simply men. If the Negro newspaper ranks below white journals which can be bought for the same or a price even lower, they query why should they subscribe to the former. If they subscribe, they openly deride, and do the paper more harm with their tongue than they do good with their purse.

Those who are able ought to help the race by contributions to its literature; but the being able should mean not merely time and taste for writing, but also something to say and a knowledge of how to say it. Too much sameness of subject is a fault to be deplored in our publications. Being Negroes does not prevent us from being also men and women, endowed with powers and inclinations similar to those of others. The race question is a very important question, but it is not the only one for us; nor are church affairs all that concern even church organs. There are political, social, moral, scientific, educational and economic problems which affect us as individuals and as a people. Why not show ourselves capable of aiding in their solution?

This is but one phase of an important subject, and our silence at this time as to the other is no indication that we are either blind or unappreciative. "The Achievements of Negro Newspapers" is a theme worthy of discussion and prolific of material. My preference for this topic which I have chosen is due to the fact that we are already the recipients of too much praise from our friends and too little honest criticism. That vile vituperation of which the race is every day the victim, comes from enemies and, in no sense, can be considered criticism.

The path of the editor, and especially the Negro editor, is thorny and far from being a path of pleasantness and peace. The ideal newspaper can never be realized, but he who works in steady contemplation and pursuit thereof, works more worthily and achieves greater results than those without an ideal. It is encouraging to note that we have newspapers that are striving for dignity and elevation of tone and general excellence of character. Prominent among these are *The Age*,[5] *Detroit Plaindealer*[6] and the *Cleveland Gazette*,[7] while several others might be mentioned. Let the Negro editor who feels himself in his proper sphere grow not discouraged because of imperfections, but persevere in his efforts to work out the salvation of his people.

5. *New York Age* (1887–1953).
6. *Detroit Plaindealer* (1883–1895).
7. *Cleveland Gazette* (1883–1892).

The Problem of the Fallen

JOSEPHINE T. WASHINGTON

The problem of the fallen is coeval with the history of mankind. It had its beginning in the Garden of Eden, when Adam and Eve broke the law and forfeited the privileges of innocence.[1] Like the poor, it is "ever with us;" and as individuals living in a state of society, we are bound to give it consideration.

We cannot solve our problems by simply deciding that we will do what Jesus did. What Jesus did, as man, was determined, in part, by the customs and the civilization of his time. What Jesus would do were he living on earth, as man, under present day conditions, must, of necessity, be conjectural. The only safe rule is to adopt the teachings of Christ and make His spirit ours.

Love, then, will direct our every thought and permeate our lives; for, "God is love."[2] Not only will the righteous call forth affection, but the sin-stricken and diseased.

Love, however, does not necessarily mean complacency. It does mean benevolence. It may deepen into a God-like tenderness for the erring. But love is the need of every human being, not merely of the fallen. We do not sanction those who shower flowers upon the notorious criminal and pass by with indifference to the sufferings of the humble and honest. Love for the wrong-doer in no case means disregard for the welfare of the upright. Measures looking to pardon must not be allowed to mar the interests of those whose feet have not wandered into forbidden paths. Love should envelop all and should labor for the good of all; but, if there must be a sacrifice, the greatest good to the greatest number must be secured.

But love has not always the same aspect. Sometimes she comes laden with gifts and wearing a smiling face. Again, she is stern and forbidding of countenance. A loving parent must punish the disobedient child. God so loved the world that He gave His only begotten Son for its redemption; yet, it is written, "Whatsoever a man soweth that shall he also reap."[3] When nature makes pain

---

* "The Problem of the Fallen," *Colored Alabamian* 3, no. 14 (15 May 1909): 1+.

1. The original reads "innocency."

2. 1 John 4:8.

3. Gal. 6:7

the inevitable consequence of broken law, it is not purposeless pain, but pain given to further wise ends.

Punishment is designed to check the criminal in his lawless course, to bring him to a realization of his wrong, and, if possible, to reform him; to put authority on record as opposed to evil; and to serve as a warning and a deterrent to others.

If error is to be corrected, however, and punishment administered, it must be by those who are themselves trying to lead right lives. Otherwise, the desired effect is wanting. Besides, one who is himself leading the wrong life would not be likely to be actuated by right motives in taking a stand against the wrong. If he persisted in wrong doing, in time he would not even see clearly distinctions between right and wrong.

Just what should be done to express disapproval of violations of the moral code, cannot be formulated in hard and fast rules. If the spirit of love, love in the broadest and truest sense, pervade every act, serious mistakes are not likely.

Love of this kind justifies the withdrawal of social privileges from those persons who defy social laws. The culprit must be made to realize the seriousness of his offense, and society must express disapproval of wrongdoing; but, above all, the young and inexperienced must be protected from the contamination of evil examples. Honor must be given where honor is due. Recognition and encouragement belong where worthy effort is made. Only those entitled to trust should be elevated to responsible positions. These are considerations which should guide us in determining our attitude towards the fallen.

It should go without saying that no consideration of social status, learning, wealth, race, or sex, should move us in our dealing with the problem of the fallen—unless it is the principle enunciated[4] by our Lord that of him to whom much has been given, much is required.

Alas! that the well-to-do may pile wealth upon wealth by corrupt means, and not even incur criticism; though the same methods, in the poor, are seen in their true light. Playing for a prize in the parlor is not recognized as involving the same principle as putting up stakes in the saloon. Men may do with impunity what brings life-long disgrace upon a woman.

Such conditions indicate that moral education is neglected. In the scramble for the dollar, and the zeal for mere book learning, in the anxiety to imitate the white man in glitter and show and the outward symbols of social life, we have overlooked, in too large a degree, the cultivation of sturdy, basic moral principles.

We fail to realize that the welfare, both of the individual and of society, demands that the infraction of law be followed by the infliction of penalty. Too often judgment is obscured and actions influenced by personal motives. Sym-

---

4. The original reads "ennunciated."

pathy for the wrong-doer, because he is of our race, our lodge, our social circle, our family, makes us over indulgent. Or, someone belonging to us has gone wrong, and we hesitate to condemn crime in others lest we be twitted with the unpleasant fact in our family history. Or, someone belonging to us may some-day go wrong: we have children, young brothers and sisters, their characters are unformed; who knows into what error they may fall?

Perhaps we ourselves have been weak; our past is not altogether blameless, and we dare not face the unkind comments which may follow our effort to show that now, at least, we are on the right side. Perhaps none of these considerations move us, but we are concerned about our business interests, and are unwilling to risk giving offense.

Where punishment happily has effected its ends—placing authority on re-cord as opposed to wrong-doing, warning possible offenders against violations of law, and reforming the culprit, it does not need to continue—nay, it should not continue. God forgives the sinner; how can the Christian, following in the footsteps of his Master, refuse to do the same?

There must be repentance—evidenced by confessing sin, humility, sorrow for wrong done, restitution as far as may be practicable, a resolute turning away from the old life of sin and an entrance upon a new life of virtue and of aspira-tion. What circumstances shall be accepted as evidences of sincerity, and how long should be the period of punishment and of probation, must be determined in each particular case by each individual for himself.

It is certain, though, that it is better to err on the side of leniency than to dishearten some timid soul that has begun to reach after better things. Encour-agement, however, must not be understood to mean the rapid pushing into prominence of those who but recently forfeited their claims to leadership. True repentance is modest, even to shrinking. It has nothing in harmony with the conduct of the man who outrages the moral code, and yet, as soon as he has es-caped the clutches of the law or other direct consequences of his guilt, clamors for recognition; or even accepts the too-ready proffers of place by friends more zealous than wise.

That the highest sainthood and service may be attained by characters once diametrically opposed to the right, is strikingly illustrated in a life like that of Bunyan.[5] Even Saint Paul fought against the faith, for which he was afterwards ready to give his life.

It should never be said that any person is lost, as long as time is left for re-pentance. Yet, neither man nor woman need expect to sow "wild oats," and then be the same as though the commandments had been kept from early youth.

5. John Bunyan (1628–1688), Baptist preacher and author of *The Pilgrim's Progress* (1678).

Nature, an inexorable Shylock,[6] exacts the flesh, pound for pound. The remembered lusts of the parents have a sad and startling way of creeping out in the physical and moral weakness of the children.

Certain restrictions, therefore, should be thrown about the marriage relation and the close companionship which may lead to special attachments. It remains, however, the sacred duty of Christian men and women to seek out those persons who have gone astray and to lead them, if possible, to repentance and to reformation.

Moreover, having abandoned the life of sin, they should be helped and encouraged in the struggle, for a life of purity. This, surely, is the Biblical view; else, what is the meaning of the parable of the lost sheep? the acceptance into the vineyard of the tardy laborers? and the advice to the guilty woman to "Go and sin no more?"[7]

But is the greatest effort to be expended along reformatory lines? The highest type of civilization points a better way. Pity moves to the relief of suffering when the sufferer is at our doors, under our very eyes; but it is evidence of a higher order of mind and a finer type of character to sight danger afar off, to be able to follow out a train of course and consequences, and by wise planning and skillful execution to avert probable disaster, by present action. Shall we not be of the latter class?

Shall we not build "a fence about the cliff,"[8] rather than be content with placing an "ambulance in the valley?"[9] Shall not one measure in solving the problem of the fallen be to do more to prevent the fall?

This, then, is the conclusion of the matter: The problem of the fallen belongs to no particular time, nor country, nor people. Each in his age and in his place is called upon to bear a part in its solution. The solution includes punishment, because of the ends which punishment is meant to accomplish. It includes, also, efforts looking to the reformation of the erring, and forgiveness when sin has been repented of and abandoned.

And, yet, after all—and let this last word have greatest weight—formative are more to be desired than reformatory measures—and the best way to solve the problem of the fallen is *to seek to prevent the fall.*

State Normal School
Montgomery, Alabama

6. Shylock, a character in William Shakespeare's *The Merchant of Venice.*

7. John 8:11.

8. Malins, "A Fence or an Ambulance," pt. 1, stanza 2, line 3. Malins's line reads, "Put a fence 'round the edge of the cliff."

9. Ibid., line 4. Malins's line reads, "an ambulance down in the valley."

PART VI

PERSONAL TRIBUTES

Wendell Phillips' Memorial Exercises at Howard University

J. J. TURPIN

Services in memory of the late Wendell Phillips[1] were held in the University Chapel, by the Alpha Phi society, on the evening of February 29, at 8:30 pm. The meeting was called to order by the acting president, W. R. A. Palmer. Palmer was offered by Rev. S. R. Lamkins.[2] The Glee club, composed of the musical talent among the young men of Howard University, rendered a song after which, the president delivered his address.

Mr. Palmer's speech was in itself a most fitting one, and the ease and grace of his delivery added much to the effectiveness. In touching terms he alluded to the sacrifice Phillips made for the sake of the cause to which he gave himself; and in glowing language he rehearsed the mighty work wrought by this mighty man, "more bent to raise the wretched than to rise."[3]

Resolutions of a suitable character were read by Mr. S. D. Fowler.[4] The president then introduced the orator of the evening, Mr. Kelly Miller.[5]

Mr. Miller's deservedly high reputation as a thinker and a speaker warranted his audience in expecting much of him, nor were these expectations disappointed.

* "Wendell Phillips' Memorial Exercises at Howard University," *People's Advocate* (Washington, D.C.), 8 March 1884, 2.

1. Wendell Phillips (1811–1884), Boston attorney, orator, and advocate for antislavery and women's rights.

2. "S. R. Lamkins" refers to Stephen Geriah Lamkins (1857–?), journalist and minister. He received a theology diploma from Howard College in 1885 and edited the *Christian Banner* (Burkett, *Black Biographical Dictionaries,* 80).

3. Goldsmith, "The Deserted Village," 29.

4. Stuart D. Fowler (1865–1934), an Alpha Psi member who received a bachelor of arts degree from Howard College in 1887 (Wilkinson, *Directory of Graduates, Howard University,* 129).

5. Kelly Miller Sr. (1863–1939), a native of Winnsboro, South Carolina, and born to a slave mother and a free Negro father who fought in the Confederate army. He received a bachelor of arts degree from Howard College in 1886. Miller is noted as the first African American student admitted to Johns Hopkins University to study mathematics. In 1890, he accepted a professorship at Howard College (Woodson, "Kelly Miller," 137–38).

His beautiful exordium of liberty at once captivated his hearers and won for him the closest attention. He graphically described the circumstances attending Phillips' entrance upon his public career; and showed the grandeur of a character which turned from all allurements to the help of a despised people which [he] chose "because right is right, to follow right." In burning language he exposed the inconsistency of the church which countenanced the gale of brother by brother, of the government which offered one man protection and refused another, of those who fought bravely for their own independence and enslaved others. The speaker grew eloquent as he depicted the labors of Mr. Phillips in the anti-slavery struggle, the magnitude of the gifts he brought to his work, the greatness of soul he manifested in his devotion thereto. Universal applause followed the conclusion of the oration.

A quartette of the Glee club members sang a piece entitled "Galilee," which by beauty and a sweetness of expression charmed the whole assemblage. This club was organized not long since; and from what it is and seems likely to be, it promises to contribute much to the enjoyment of those who visit Howard and acquire considerable popularity.

The appointed exercises of the evening being over, the privilege of speaking was accorded anyone who chose to accept. Mr. E. P. Corbett[6] followed in a carefully prepared paper, which was listened to with attention. Mr. W. V. L. Tunnell[7] then spoke in his characteristic, vigorous style. Messrs. Fowler and Lawson[8] made speeches which reflected credit upon themselves and upon the institution. Others were ready to lay their tributes of praise upon the grave of the dead hero; but the hour for adjournment had arrived.

After a chorus from the club, Rev. Mr. Moore of the Lincoln Memorial church dismissed the audience.

Many favorable comments have been passed upon the exercises, and the students of Howard University, particularly the members of the Alpha Psi society, have reason to feel proud of the success of the occasion.

March 3, 1884

6. The original reads "Corbet." Edward P. Corbett (1862–1885) received a pharmacy certificate from Howard College in 1882 (Wilkinson, *Directory of Graduates, Howard University*, 86).

7. Reverend William Victor L. Tunnell (1860–1943) pastored at St. Augustine's Episcopal Church in Brooklyn, New York, and chaired the History Department at Howard University from 1891 to 1928 (Bragg, *History of the Afro-American Group*, 178–79).

8. Jesse Lawson (1857–?) received a preparatory certificate (1877), bachelor of arts degree (1881) and master of arts degree (1886) from Howard College (Wilkinson, *Directory of Graduates, Howard University*, 232).

Frederick Douglass

JOSEPHINE J. TURPIN

A Woman of Talent Pays a Glowing Tribute to a Man of Talent

To the Editor of the Globe:

Nearly seventy years ago, on a plantation in East Maryland, was born a remarkable slave child. No trump of joy was sounded at his coming, no proud father bent over the cradle of his son, no congratulations were received by fond parents, no rich gifts were sent this infant of low estate. Ushered thus into the world without pomp and splendor, his advent was scarcely less humble than that of our Saviour. He was unwelcomed into life, for slave mothers rejoiced not to bear children for misery and a fate worse than death. Successor to no noble line of ancestry, his was a patrimony that sought only to bind both body and soul. He was a thing, a chattel, a beast of burden, property to be bought and sold. What today is the once slave boy of Maryland? A man mighty in the land, an acknowledged leader among the people of his race, the admired of ten thousands, the courted of dignitaries. Men hang entranced upon his words; they are impressed with his power, pleased with his wit, charmed with his brilliance and spell-bound by his eloquence. All the world unites to do homage to Frederick Douglass.[1]

Such a man is an example of marvelous usefulness. What may not youth hopefully attempt, in the light of such achievement? Is there injustice, oppression or tyranny? Strike for your liberty, fight for your position, contend for your rights. Douglass himself proved his belief in the truth of Byron's line, "Who would be free, themselves must strike the blow."[2] Are you in lowly station, struggling to make the most of God-given talents; by daily study and self-discipline, strengthening your mind and purifying your heart? Are you filled with the noble ambition to do something for the elevation of your race and of humanity at large? Fear not, faint not, despond not. Struggle on. True worth will reveal

---

* "Frederick Douglass," *New York Globe,* 24 May 1884, 2.

1. Frederick Douglass, born Frederick Augustus Washington Bailey (1818–1895), abolitionist, orator, writer, and statesman.

2. Byron, "Childe Harold's Pilgrimage," vol. 4, canto 2, stanza 76, p. 111. Byron's line reads, "[Know ye not] who would be free themselves must strike the blow?"

itself despite adverse circumstances. Such is the teaching of Douglass' life. He who does nothing, hopes in vain to become something. If you want knowledge, influence and prominence, then industry and perseverance are as essential prerequisites as is native ability. Few men go to sleep and wake up the next day to find themselves famous. Great efforts are necessary to [obtain] great results. This is the lesson the life of Douglass teaches. Are you impressed with the idea that there is something in you worth the recognition of the world? Prove it. Expect not to be honored for what you merely feel yourself capable of doing. The world's test of merit is practical. Seek not to win appreciation by vauntings and boastings. Ability quietly gains a respect which clamor demands in vain. Such is Douglass' example.

A wise God saw fit to place this great mind under a dark skin. The race has reason to be grateful. Frederick Douglass is a more perfect vindication of the colored man's ability than a hundred learned treatises demonstrative of the fact. Races are composed of individuals; hence individual character determines racial character; and the greater the prominence of any particular person, the greater influence has he in forming public judgment. We are proud of Frederick Douglass; as a people, we thank God for the "grand old man." He who is truly great does not derive his greatness altogether from the fact that he is of a certain class, sect, or race. Frederick Douglass is great not only as a colored man, but as a man. The elements of greatness are the same, whatever the color of the individual or the condition of his forefathers. Frederick Douglass is honored not only by his own people, but by all classes and conditions of the intelligent and unprejudiced. His has been service not alone for the colored man, as his fellow-sufferer, but for man as man. When he raised his voice and pen against the giant slavery, he not only sought to destroy a system the aim of which was to debase his brother in bonds, but he sought to free the country from a curse and a disgrace. Everywhere his strength has been used against wrong, oppression and injustice; everywhere his influence has been on the side of right, equity and liberty. America well may be proud of such a citizen. The world well may honor him as one of its great men. Douglass has devoted himself to the cause of humanity; we have nothing to render him but our reverent regard. The exchange is an unequal one, but all great men give more than the world has to offer in return. As long, then, as shall exist in the human heart a tendency to admire self-earned success, to honor fearless advocacy of the right, to be moved by eloquence of speech and to be impressed by grandeur of character, so long will Douglass be lovingly remembered.

Howard University

Charles Dickens

JOSEPHINE J. TURPIN

The most dissimilar events are often simultaneous. The same year which marked Napoleon's invasion of Russia and the second war between England and America, ushered into being one who would be pre-eminently a lover of his kind and a promoter of peace on earth and good-will to men.

At Landport, a village near Portsmouth, on the 7th of February, 1812, was born the great English novelist, Charles Dickens. Like many another who has afterwards risen to fame and favor, he sprang from the common people and passed his early youth amid lowly surroundings. His father was, however, a man of considerable intellectual ability, and was, to some extent, characterized by those keen powers of observation and delineation, and that love of literature which rendered the son eminent in the world of letters. At the earliest period of the boy's existence, his father was an officer in the navy service, from which, a few years later, he retired to enter upon a reportorial career. The elder Dickens was like the Micawber of David Copperfield, constantly immersed in pecuniary embarrassments and as constantly rising serene above his misfortunes; indeed, in the development of this trait, so greatly does he resemble the character that he is thought to be its original. Alike disregarding the ebb and flow of fortune, Charles, a shrinking, sensitive child, debarred from the common sports of his age by a nervous and delicate temperament, lived in the creations of his own fanciful brain and in the few books that bore him company. In David Copperfield, which contains much autobiography in disguise, he writes, no doubt, of this period: "My father had left a small collection of books in a little room upstairs, to which I had access, and which nobody else ever troubled. From that blessed little room 'Roderick Random,' 'Peregrine Pickle,' 'Humphrey Clinker,' 'Tom Jones,' and 'Vicar of Wakefield,' 'Don Quixote,' 'Gil Blas' and 'Robinson Crusoe' came out—a glorious host, to keep me company. They kept alive my fantasy and my hope of something beyond that place and time."[2] Living now in London, and having reached the age of nine, in consequence of various family liabilities and disabilities—culminating in the imprisonment of his father for debt, and the pawning of the furniture including the library—he is put to work

---

* "Charles Dickens," *A.M.E. Church Review* 2 (July 1885): 34–40.
1. Dickens, *David Copperfield,* chap. 4.

in a blacking-house at six shillings a week, his task being to cover the boxes with paper. How his soul revolted from such service and surroundings is by himself described: "No words can express the secret agony of my soul as I sunk into this companionship, compared these every-day associates with those of my happier childhood, and felt my early hopes of growing up to be a distinguished man crushed in my breast. The deep remembrance of the sense I had of being utterly neglected and hopeless, of the shame I felt in my position, of the misery it was to my young heart to believe that, day by day, what I had learned, and thought and delighted in, and raised my fancy and my emulation up by, was passing away from me never to be brought back any more, cannot be written."[1]

The family resources improving, he is sent to a common school, a few years' instruction of which constitutes the whole of his educational advantages. Dickens' father once being asked where his son received his education, replied, with a laugh, that he might be said to have educated himself. A similar remark is made by Weller, in Pickwick, concerning his hopeful Sam: "I took a good deal o' pains with his eddication, sir; let him run in the streets when he was very young, and shift for hisself."[2] At fifteen he was taken from school and put into an attorney's office, the paternal authority designing him for the profession of law. Here, performing the duties of his position, gaining a knowledge of legal environments which he utilized in his after descriptions, frequenting the British museum, reading voraciously, and, amid all this, persistently studying shorthand in his leisure moments, he remained for about four years. At nineteen we find him engaged in a more congenial pursuit and one foreshadowing his future profession, being at this time a reporter for the House of Commons, and reckoned the best among eighty or ninety others.

Three years later, he ventured to send an article to one of the magazines of the day, and what was his joy at seeing himself for the first time in print! His feelings, as depicted by himself, will draw forth the sympathy of all aspirants for literary honors, and will be recognized by each as an individual experience. Alluding to the event, he recalls: "the magazine in which my first effusion—dropped stealthily one evening at twilight, with fear and trembling, into a dark letter-box, in a dark office, up a dark court in Fleet Street—appeared in all the glory of print; on which memorable occasion—how well I recollect it! I walked down to Westminster Hall, and walked into it for half-an-hour, because my eyes were so dimmed with joy and pride that they could not bear the street, and were not fit to be seen there."[3]

Soon afterwards he gave to the public a series of papers termed "Sketches by

2. Ibid., chap. 11.
3. Dickens, *Posthumous Papers of the Pickwick Club,* 296.
4. Ibid., preface, xiv.

Boz." These at once became highly popular, and great was the interest and curiosity as to the identity of the new writer. When the fact became known some wit produced the following:

> "Who the Dickens Boz could be
> Puzzled many a learned elf;
> But time unveiled the mystery,
> And Boz appeared as Dickens' self."[4]

It may be interesting to mention the origin of Dickens' *nom de plume*. A little brother was named "Moses," which a little sister attempting to repeat, was corrupted into "Boz," afterwards a house-hold word with the family. Such was the success of the young author that he was engaged by Messrs. Hall and Chapman to write a series of articles to be published in connection with comic illustrations executed by a talented draughtsman. The result of this arrangement was the appearance of the Pickwick Papers. At once they made their writer famous. Pickwick was the rage. People thought Pickwick, talked Pickwick, laughed Pickwick, lived Pickwick.

During the issue of these papers, Dickens married a Miss Hogarth. It is to be regretted that, despite all his bright pictures of domestic life, the author's own was clouded. The ill-mated pair lived together for twenty years, reared a large family of children, and finally separated on account of increasing unhappiness due to incompatibility of temper. With the production of Pickwick, Dickens began a strictly literary career. Oliver Twist next appeared; and this novel, differing so widely in theme and in treatment from his previous writings, had the effect to open the eyes of the public to powers hitherto unsuspected. Dickens reigned not only in the realms of laughter, but was king in the world of sympathy and of horror. After remarkably short intervals of time, "Nicholas Nickleby," "Old Curiosity Shop," and "Barnaby Rudge" followed.

At this period, even Dickens' strength of endurance began to fail, in consequence of which he took a respite from labor, and, in January, 1842, sailed for America. The literary result of his visit was "American Notes for General Circulation," an expression of his opinion concerning the press, politics, principles and people of the New World. These views, while mainly correct, so decried some American faults and follies, and so attached its pet institution of slavery as to lash the country into a fury. Indifferent to the storm he had raised, Charles Dickens, believing himself right, had the courage to reiterate, in "Martin Chuzzlewit," the obnoxious sentiments.

A residence abroad gave rise to "Pictures of Italy." "Dombey and Son" was commenced by the side of Lake Geneva and continued in France. "David Copperfield" was his next great work. In 1850, having already tried the editing of

5. Mackenzie, *Life of Charles Dickens*, 57.

a daily paper, and having found his powers unfitted for such a work, he began the publication of a weekly literary magazine. In this he was not unsuccessful. "Household Words," and afterwards "All the Year Round," took high rank among the leading periodicals of the day and were widely popular. "Hard Times," "A Tale of Two Cities," "Great Expectations," "The Child's History of England," and the sketches called "The Uncommercial Traveller"[5] were printed first as serial stories in these magazines. "Our Mutual Friend," the last of Mr. Dickens' completed novels, was finished in November 1865. The "Christmas Stories" were published at successive Christmas times. Following the bent of a natural dramatic talent, about this period of his life, Dickens appeared on several occasions as an amateur actor. He also made a tour of readings in England and on the Continent, and in 1867, with this purpose, he embarked a second time for America. His reception was enthusiastic. The people themselves were older and wiser; they had a deeper insight into their own foibles; they had made what reparation they could for their country's greatest crime; and Dickens himself, though as truthful and frank, was no doubt less cutting and severe. This trip was eminently successful in every respect. Mr. Dickens left after a stay of nearly a year carrying with him two hundred thousand dollars in gold, the personal friendship of our greatest men and the loving admiration of the whole people.

"The Mystery of Edwin Drood," Dickens' last work, began to appear in April, 1870. It was never finished. On the 9th of June, in the same year, at the age of fifty-eight, Mr. Dickens gently breathed his last. According to his request, he was buried quietly, without pomp and ceremony; but the nation claimed him for her own, and he was interred in Westminster Abbey, that honorable sepulcher[6] of illustrious men.

Dickens was one of the most prolific and voluminous of writers. His literary productions, besides extensive editorial work, consist of about sixty volumes, comprising novels, sketches, essays, tales, his "History of England," and "Memoirs of Joseph Grimaldi." The number of his distinct characters has been estimated to be one thousand four hundred and twenty-five. "Pickwick Papers" make no pretensions to a plot, and cannot rightly be called a novel. It is a humorous recital of the sayings and doings of a rollicking club, and occupies a unique place in literature as a genus with but one species. Mr. Pickwick, immediately after his introduction, became a great favorite in the reading world, and the Wellers, despite the peculiarity of their pronunciation, were scarcely less welcome. In "Oliver Twist," we have the story of a boy born in a work-house, reared by the parish, thrown among vicious surroundings and depraved associates, yet preserving, by innate purity of nature, a certain delicacy and refinement of sentiment. The representation of Sykes' mental condition, after he had

6. The original reads "Uncommercial Traveller."
7. The original reads "sepulchre."

murdered the girl who betrayed him, and that of Fagin the Jew upon hearing his death warrant, are startlingly vivid.

Had Dickens written nothing but the "Old Curiosity Shop," he would have had fame, admiration and love. The character of little Nell, patient, gentle Nell, went home to the hearts of the people. Her tender care of a weak and aged grandfather, her goodness and innocence and suffering, her childish simplicity, her womanly endurance, her angelic nature, together with her early death, told in Dickens' simple and touching style, make her one of the immortal children of literature. "Barnaby Rudge" is an historic novel, and, while it shows Dickens' ability in this direction, here as in all his writings, the faithful delineation of character is seen to be his real aim. In his presentation of Barnaby himself, the author shows a wonderful acquaintance with the crazed and disordered mind. The principal theme of "Dombey and Son" is pride, appearing in the persons of Mr. Dombey and his young wife, Edith. Paul, a delicate and thoughtful child, who, musing by the sea-shore, wonders what the wild waves are saying, and arouses his elders by his grave and profound queries, is a fit companion-piece for little Nell. "Hard Times" is a plea for the oppressed against the oppressor. "Nicholas Nickleby" exposed the evils and general worthlessness of a system of parish schools then prevalent in some parts of England, and was largely influential in effecting an educational reform. "Martin Chuzzlewit" takes its text upon selfishness and hypocrisy.

The author's own favorite, and the one considered best by many critics, is "David Copperfield." These latter authorities have long since decided, that in the person of the principal character the author has frequently given us glimpses of his own life. This decision appears to be corroborated by the fact that the air of realism so perceptible in all of Dickens' writings is even more apparent here than elsewhere. The hero David, Dora the child-wife, Agnes the angel-wife, little Emily, devoted Pegotty, eccentric Aunt Trotwood, unfortunate Mr. Micawber, Steerforth the polished villain, and Heep and Latimer, scoundrels of the deepest dye, become living and breathing people. We laugh as heartily at the funny points as though we were present in person; we are as grieved at the mishaps of these fancied personages as though they were really in distress. We pass out of ourselves and enter into their life and identity. The "Christmas Stories" are charming contributions to that class of writings. They are bright, cheery, benevolent,—a true index of the author's mind. Several of Mr. Dickens' works are of an aggressive and reformatory nature; they are all of a charitable and benevolent kind, and are to be valued for the practical benefit resulting therefrom as well as for literary excellence.

Dickens is a painter. He has a wonderfully patient, attentive and careful eye for detail. He searches out the minor points which by another would be overlooked in a survey of the general effect. He delights in minute investigation; with loving touch he turns about, examines, and re-examines the object of his contemplation. The bewildering accumulation of an old curiosity shop has for him its attraction; the retrospect of a homely kitchen, with its ample stores and the long, dim passage leading thereto, move him to a description; reading the school-boys' names cut by their penknives, he observes and comments upon each characteristic dash and curve. With scarcely less clearness than he himself sees, does he make his readers to perceive. His scenes move like panoramic pictures before us, his figures stand out in bold relief, his incidents are little less than actualities.

Dickens' imagination is poet-like in kind and power. He loses his own personality and becomes one in identity with his subject. With remarkable success he is able to sustain, at length, a character embodying sentiments and principles at utter variance with his own sympathies. There is no cropping out of the author at unexpected points; no untimely and unnecessary intrusion of personal feeling and opinion. Thieves, drunkards, murderers, maniacs, all phases of criminal and depraved existence, are portrayed with equal naturalness as the more respectable members of society. His imagination invests even inanimate objects with life. The sky, the winds, the waters, trees, flowers and stones, are impressed with the feelings of his individuals; they are glad, sorry, tearful or joyous; they so appeared to Dickens, and so they appear to his readers.

His characters are drawn mainly from low life. He loves to paint the poor in their humble homes, to show their sterling virtues, to awaken sympathy for their sufferings, to expose their wrongs, to influence the philanthropic-minded to their assistance. One of the greatest charms of this writer is, that he invests commonplace people and scenes with interest. We read him, and things take on a new light. We find ourselves looking with curious attention upon the most ordinary surroundings; we study anew the people whom we have daily passed with little scrutiny; we are surprised that there is so much in everybody and everything which we had not before seen. Every-day life assumes a new and highly entertaining aspect.

The number of his distinct characters is truly marvelous.[7] Perhaps no artist ever studied human nature with greater zest or greater result. The individuality of his personages is striking. Once introduced to them you can never mistake their identity or shake off their acquaintance. A notable peculiarity of Dickens' creatures of the brain—and this is particularly true of the comic characters—is, that they each possess some oddity of person or manner, some trick of speech or gesture, which is ever present throughout the fancied career. So manifest, at times, appears the exaggeration of the individual characteristic, that the picture may almost be considered a caricature. Nor should the fact of the author's queer-sounding names be omitted. Probably to this selection of names according with their natures, is partly due the effect produced by the grotesque

8. The original reads "marvellous."

characters. Dickens' style combines simplicity, perspicuity and energy; and each thought is appropriately clothed in the dress suitable to its kind.

Dickens' strength was not only that of mind, but also of body. The weakly child had become the finely-developed and well-proportioned man. He is described as having a firmly-set nose, with the wide nostrils which physiognomists claim are found in men of genius; a rather large mouth, with full and sensitive lips, eyes remarkably bright and searching, and a rare, sweet smile. His disposition well accorded with his appearance. He was frank, genial, generous. Children loved him, men were instinctively drawn to him; he was a personal favorite throughout the neighborhood in which he lived. He had no petty jealousies in his nature to spoil his relations with his contemporary writers. He was the intimate friend of Thackeray, and also of our own Irving. Honored by queenly regard, and even offered a title, he retained his original modesty and preferred to remain simply Mr. Dickens.

Nor was he the friend alone of the famous and wealthy. Many were his acts of kindness and of charity to the poor and humble. While he never openly professed Christianity, or joined himself with any body of worshippers, he had a profound reverence for all things sacred. His was the creed of a noble life, the religion of Abou Ben Adhem[8] and the golden rule. One great shadow overhung his life. It was the unhappy disagreement and final separation of his wife and himself. He may have been much to blame—the best men have their faults— but even this unfortunate fact has not the power to counterbalance the good we know to have been in him. Outside of this, his domestic and social life were of the most charming description. Plain, simple, unaffected in manner, of a jovial and sportive disposition, with a keen sense of the ludicrous and yet a kindly humor that never hurt, fond of society and possessed of an easy, fluent, conversational style, he was the delight of the young and the old who gathered about him.

By no means, however, was he given over to pleasure. He was eminently industrious and methodical in his habits. The program[9] of his day is thus told by one who visited at his home. He arose at seven, devoted an hour to his mail, breakfasted at eight, wrote until one or two o'clock, denying all admission; then was off for his usual tramp of fifteen miles before dinner. He never used, during his working hours, a stimulant of any kind; and, what is still more remarkable, he never employed an amanuensis. Every word of his vast productions was written by himself.

Dickens ranks among the first writers of his kind. Others may excel him in the possession of some one element of literary power, but none are superior in the combination of those qualities which form a great delineator of human

---

9. Abou Ben Adhem, a Christian character in Leigh Hunt's poem "Abou Ben Adhem."
10. The original reads "programme."

nature. No other has been the inmate of so many homes, the companion of so many minds, the brightener of so many hearts. The extent of his influence is incalculable. There is, in this fact, no occasion for regret, since his teachings have always [been] on the side of right. He might have done much evil, but he chose rather to do much good. His writings have effected important reforms; they have invested common life with a greater interest, they have drawn forth sympathy for the lowly, and they have pressed upon human kind the recognition of the man's brotherhood to man. He has taught us to "live, love, laugh, be good, be happy."[10] Such a man dies not, but lives eternally in the unspeakable gratitude of a great literature-loving people.

Washington, D.C.

11. Unknown author of inspirational quotation.

Josephine Turpin Washington Nominates T. Thomas Fortune

JOSEPHINE TURPIN WASHINGTON

William E. Matthews, the Washington, D.C. Money Lender, Often Erroneously Termed a Banker, and His Nomination of Hon. John M. Langston — The Originator

Editor Gazette:

The race has reason to congratulate itself on the prospect of a speedy organization of a National League.

The open letter from Mr. W. E. Matthews[1] to the lion, John M. Langston[2] has had at least one good effect. It has attracted renewed attention to the idea conceived and promulgated by Mr. Fortune[3] more than two years ago and has elicited

---

* "Josephine Turpin Washington Nominates T. Thomas Fortune," *Cleveland Gazette*, 9 November 1889, 1.

1. William E. Matthews (1845–1895), native of Baltimore, Maryland, and 1873 graduate of Howard University's law school. He was a well-known attorney specializing in real estate, banking, mortgages, and loans in Washington, D.C. (Simmons and Turner, *Men of Mark*, 246–51).

2. John M. Langston (1829–1897), a distinguished politician, attorney, educator, and antislavery agitator. A Louisa, Virginia, native, he was educated in Ohio and became the first African American attorney in Ohio (1854). He consorted with President Andrew Jackson (1865); became Howard University's first black law professor (1869); served as president of Virginia Normal and Collegiate Institute (1885–1887), now Virginia State University; and served as Virginia's first African American congressman (1890) (Blume, "John Mercer Langston," 2:459–61).

3. Thomas Fortune (1856–1928), known for his fiery editorials, became one of the most effective and outspoken African American journalists in the nineteenth century. In July 1881, he launched the *New York Globe* newspaper, originally named the *Rumor*, a weekly tabloid he edited with George Parker. Without full ownership of the *New York Globe*, Fortune suffered a reversal when Parker mortgaged the paper without his knowledge. He recovered from his financial setbacks and obtained full ownership of the *New York Globe*. Fortune changed its name to the *Freeman* in 1884. The name was subsequently altered to the *New York Age* in 1887. Fortune sold the newspaper in 1907 (Thornbrough, *T. Thomas Fortune*, 37–38, 58–61, 78–81, and 95–96).

a varied and wide spread discussion. Constant agitation is what the question now demands. Place it before the people and set them to thinking. Their verdict can but be favorable, and action will follow. Already local organizations are springing up in various parts of the country, and we may expect daily to hear from others.

The importance and desirability of a National League is being rapidly recognized. We have reason to believe that an organization like that proposed by Mr. Fortune will have the countenance and support of the best minds among us. Properly sustained and conducted, it must be a great power for good. Its aims and methods are such as to win the approval of all law-abiding and patriotic citizens. It encourages no disorder, incites no riot, opposes violence, and seeks by peaceful and accepted means to secure to the race the protection of the law and the enjoyment of equal rights and privileges. It makes no distinction as to sex, politics, or religion, and is open alike to the humblest or the proudest for entrance or redress.

The time is ripe for the meeting of representatives from the local leagues already in existence, for the purpose of organizing a National League. "Who shall be president?" "Who is to head this vast movement?" are questions that naturally suggest themselves. The hour is with us, and the man Is not wanting. He is T. Thomas Fortune, the originator and disseminator of the great idea.

My dissension from the choice made by Mr. Matthews is not due to any lack of appreciation of Mr. Langston. He is an able man, one of whom the race is proud, one whose services it needs and hopes to have for many a day. Because I prefer a certain person and think him best suited to a particular position, I do not deem it necessary to disparage others, also worthy, though perhaps less eligible to the place in question.

I am ready to give my support to the choice of the people, whoever he may be. They are not likely to go very far wrong in a matter of this kind. I am anxious to see the movement progress, undeterred by factional disputes, and ready to sacrifice any personal preference to the will of the majority. This I believe to be the attitude of every true friend of the League. I do not believe, however, that Mr. Matthews' voice is the voice of the people when he names Mr. Langston for President.

It does not seem to me necessary to point out any unfitness of Mr. Langston for the leadership suggested. It is sufficient that Mr. Fortune is in no way unfit.[4] Our thoughts turn to him as the natural and appropriate leader of the movement which is the product of his own fertile brain. The honor is due him alone, though he would be the last man to seek it. Nothing could justify our preference for another but some incapacity in the man who is the author of the thought we seek to incarnate. Otherwise, our ingratitude will be as patent as is that of the namers of America to every school boy who reads the story of Columbus.

4. The original reads "unfit."

T. Thos. Fortune is eminently fitted for the presidency of the League. Regardless of the fact that the honor is peculiarly due him, he is the possessor of qualities especially needful in such leadership! He is young, progressive, bold, independent, keen of insight, varied in experience, and of wide acquaintanceship. He is, besides, essentially a race man, subordinating personal interests, party allegiance, everything, to what he conceives to be the good of the race. Can we do better than to make him the President of the National League?

Lessons from the Life of McKinley

JOSEPHINE T. WASHINGTON

Perhaps this article cannot be more fittingly introduced than with words taken from the opening paragraph of Carlyle's "Heroes and Hero-Worship."[1]

"Too clearly," this great author modestly writes, "it is a topic we shall do no justice to in this place. One comfort is, that great men, taken up in any way, are profitable company. We cannot look, however, imperfectly upon a great man without gaining something by him. He is the living light–fountain, which it is good and pleasant to be near."[2]

Our late President was one of the century's great men. Whether viewed from the standpoint of the direct results he achieved, or from the standpoint of intrinsic worth, and personal character, Mr. McKinley[3] was great.

In the broader and better sense he would have been as great a man, because as good a man, had he never stood under the flash-light of fame. In the well-known lines of Grey,[4]

> "Full many a gem of purest ray serene,
>   The dark, unfathomed caves of ocean bear,
> Full many a flower is born to blush unseen,
>   And waste its sweetness on the desert air."[5]

But because our hero-President held an honored and conspicuous position in the public eye, his example of great and good and wise living is worth far more to the world than that of any humble, though equally praiseworthy, citi-

---

* "Lessons from the Life of McKinley," *A.M.E. Church Review* 18, no. 3 (January 1902): 210–15.

1. Thomas Carlyle (1795–1881), Scottish essayist, historian, and philosopher. In "On Heroes and Hero Worship" (1840), Carlyle claims that the actions of "Great Men" determine the role of history.

2. Carlyle, *On Heroes, Hero-Worship, and the Heroic in History,* 2. Carlyle capitalizes "Great Men."

3. William McKinley (1843–1901), twenty-fifth president of the United States.

4. "Grey" is a reference to Thomas Gray (1716–1771), English poet.

5. Gray, "An Elegy, Written in a Country Churchyard," 5. Gray's version reads, "[unfathom'd], [flow'r], and [blush] unseen."

zens could be. In this case, "he who runs may read."[6] "A city that is set upon a hill cannot be hid."

What are the lessons which the career of William McKinley, student, post-office clerk, army private, Union officer, lawyer, Congressman, Governor, United States President, holds for us?

Prominent among these lessons is that of diligent application. McKinley was a self-made man. He worked his way from the lower rounds of the ladder to the highest rung. He was not born great; he had not greatness thrust upon him, but he did achieve greatness. It was not in his stars, but in himself, that he distanced his fellows. He was

> "As some divinely gifted man,
> Whose life in low estate began,
> And on a simple village green;
>
> Who breaks his birth's invidious bar.
> And grasps the skirts of happy chance,
> And breasts[7] the blows of circumstance,
> And grapples with his evil star;
>
> Who makes by force his merit known,
> And lives to clutch the golden keys,
>
> To mould a mighty state's decrees,
> And shape the whisper of the throne;
>
> And moving up from high to higher,
> Becomes on Fortune's crowning slope
> The pillar of a people's hope.
> The centre of a world's desire."[8]

A simple, direct, unswerving honesty was characteristic of our dead President. His was not eye-service. Whether he applied himself, as an individual, to the affairs of his private business, or, as a servant of the nation, conducted affairs of state, he was actuated by a simple and noble sincerity. Such was our faith in the uprightness of the man, that many of us felt, even when we longed most for a direct and vigorous denunciation of the horrors being perpetrated upon the Negro in the South, that, somehow, the President must be acting from conscientious

---

6. Hab. 2:2. The verse reads, "[Write the vision, and make *it* plain upon tables, that he may run that readeth it.]" The following quotation comes from Matt. 5:14; the verse reads, "Ye are the light of the world. A city that is set upon [an] hill can not be hid."

7. Tennyson, "In Memoriam," canto 64, p. 115. Washington's original line reads, "And [breaks] the blows of circumstance."

8. Tennyson, "In Memoriam," canto 64, p. 115.

motives. His character and past record held us to the belief that principle, and not policy, dictated his course.

Years ago, when business entanglements arose, and, according to the views of most men, he might with honor have saved something to himself, he gave up everything to satisfy creditors, his wife's little fortune going, at her wish, with the rest, and together they began life over again, with nothing—save an honest and an honored name. And that after an active political life, after long years spent in public service, in positions of power and responsibility, he died comparatively poor, is surely something of a tribute to the rugged honesty of the man.

The strength and fortitude of McKinley's character are traits that have won our admiration, especially in these latter trying days. Bravely he took his stand as soldier in defense of his country; calmly and patiently, he bore the burdens and discharged the duties of the Chief Executive during one of the most critical periods of our nation's history, self-controlled and masterful, he put aside personal anxiety and disquietude, and filled with dignity and graciousness his place as the guest of honor of an admiring people, while the shadow of a great domestic calamity overhung him; with superb courage, he received the shock of the assassin's bullet[9] and bore himself during all the gloom, and doubtful days of that last illness.

Perhaps benevolence, in the broadest sense of that word, was the most beautiful trait of Mr. McKinley's character. "Faith, hope, and charity; these three, but the greatest of these is charity." Who could look upon his countenance, without reading their[10] benevolence, kindliness, love? It was the keynote of his life—love, love to God, love to man. Elected by the Republican Party, he was yet the President of the whole people. As is generally conceded, he was easily the most popular President we have ever had. And this, not because he tried to be popular, not because he resorted to any wiles or tricks to attract. These things usually defeat their own object. He loved, and, therefore he was beloved. "He who would have friends must show himself friendly."[11] "Love begets love."

When, on the occasion of that memorable visit to Atlanta, he donned the badge of the grey, there were those who criticized[12] the act, but none questioned the motive. Sympathy, tenderness, trustfulness beamed from his eye and breathed from every tone. Trustful even to his undoing, alas, he scouted the idea of the necessity of a guard for the person of the President, and relied upon the loyalty and the devotion of the American people.

9. Leon Czolgosz assassinated President McKinley on September 6, 1901 ("McKinley Assassinated," 297).

10. The original reads "there."

11. An interpretation of Prov. 18:24, which reads, "A man *that hath* friends must shew himself friendly: and there is a friend *that* sticketh closer than a brother."

12. The original reads "criticised."

What more pathetic picture is there in history than that of our President, leaning forward with outreached hand, smiling, and yet looking with sympathy upon the cowardly wretch, who, under pretense of being wounded, conceals the murderous weapon which is to end the life of the nation's chief?

His first thought for his wife,[13] his next is for the miserable assassin, whom he requests the officers not to hurt. "Father, forgive them; they know not what they do."[14] Afterwards, in quiet, courteous phrases, he expresses sorrow that through him the pleasure of the Exposition has been marred.[15]

With feelings of reverence we approach the subject of Mr. McKinley's family relations. The beauty and the purity of his domestic life have appealed peculiarly to the American nation—a home-loving nation—and have done more, perhaps, than any other trait of his character, to endear him to the people.

"All the world loves a lover."[16]

Mr. McKinley was always his wife's lover—always the same gallant, courtly, courteous gentleman, the tender, thoughtful husband; the faithful friend and helper. All the world knows of his tender care of the invalid wife with whom we yet mourn, and all the world loves him for it. Scarcely less touching was his devotion to the aged mother[17] whose pride and prop he was.

When several years ago, he forsook the scenes of his official labors and hurried to the bedside of that dying parent, the heart of the nation went with him.

His was a strong nature, yet a tender nature. Oh, rare and happy combination!

Among the lessons to be learned from the life of this great man, let us not forget that of Christian living, of faith in God and submission to His will. "It is God's way. His will be done, not ours."[18] These were his words in the hour of death, and in these may be found the golden thread which ran through all his course. "God's way." He walked "God's way" with diligence, in honestly and singleness of purpose, with fortitude, and in the spirit of love, and then he was not—for God took him.

---

13. Ida Saxton McKinley (1847–1907) suffered from a number of illnesses including epilepsy (Wertheimer, *Inventing a Voice*, 33).

14. Luke 23:34.

15. President McKinley was assassinated prior to the Pan-America Exposition held in Buffalo, New York. Before his death, he expressed concern that his suffering would mar the event.

16. Emerson, "Essay V: Love," 128. Emerson's line reads, "All [mankind love] a lover."

17. Nancy Campbell McKinley (1809–1897) suffered a series of strokes until her death ("Mrs. M' Kinley in Eternal Sleep," *Canton [Ohio] Sunday Repository*, 12 December 1897, 1).

18. Unknown quotation.

William McKinley is not dead.
"To live in hearts we leave behind
Is not to die."[19]

Through all historic time the impress of his life will be for good upon the lives of succeeding generations of Americans—and not upon Americans alone.

"Alike are life and death.
     When life in death survives,
And the uninterrupted breath
     Inspires a thousand lives.
Were a star quenched on high,
     For ages would its light,
Still travelling downward from the sky,
     Shine on our mortal sight.
So when a great man dies,
     For years beyond our ken,
The light he leaves behind him lies
     Upon the paths of men."[20]

19. Campbell, "Hallowed Ground," 167. Campbell capitalizes "Hearts."
20. Longfellow, "Birds of Passage: Flight the Fourth, Charles Sumner," 1:365.

Lessons from the Life of President Paterson

MRS. J. T. WASHINGTON

Some writer has well said that one of the uses of great men is to teach by example. It is fitting, then, that while honoring our President,[1] at the conclusion of three-score useful and eventful years, we seek to make this occasion "point a moral" for the young people who have been committed to our care.

One thing strikingly illustrated in Prof. Paterson is the value of simple living. Plain food, early hours, hard work, clean sport, freedom from luxury and self-indulgence, a boyhood spent largely in the open air, gave the strong body, the wide-awake, observant mind, and a heart attuned to nature's moods. There are some among us who have been born to simple village or country homes. These are fortunate. The rest cannot be born anew into rural surroundings; but, in many ways, we can pattern after the simplicity and the sameness of country living. So shall we lead more wholesome and, therefore, holier and happier lives. To us, then, who, in the love of nature hold communion with her visible forms, she will "speak a various language."

Always usefully employed, Prof. Paterson teaches by example the lesson of industry. As a boy he had no time for lounging on street corners, or standing around stores. He had to work; and labour brought its own reward—not only in added skill and in compensation for toil, but in greater zest for the rare hours of play. He did not wait for a job to come to him; he went after it. If he could not find what he wanted to do, he wanted what he could find. He scorned no kind of honest work. Whatever his hands found to do he did it with his might. To

---

* "Lessons from the Life of President Paterson," *Alumni Reporter* 1, no. 7 (February 1909): 1–2.

1. President William Burns Paterson (1849–1915), a Scotsman who became president of the State Normal School in Marion, Alabama, in 1878. The college was relocated to Montgomery in 1887 and named the Alabama Colored People's University with promised state support. In opposition to local whites who refused state financial support of black education, Paterson worked with blacks who donated money and buildings to open the school at Beulah Baptist Church (see "History of Alabama State University," www.lib .alasu.edu/archives/research/history/presidents.html).

him, "All labour is holy."[2] He did not feel that digging ditches, working on the railroad, or even proving himself an entertaining tramp and thereby repaying a good housewife for the shelter and food of a night, in any wise detracted from his worth as a man. With his beloved Burns,[3] he believes that "a man is a man for a' that and a' that."

Well may we copy his courage—we, a race far too timid with a timidity born of long submission to the will of others. Fearlessly he left his sea-girt Scotland home and traversed the great waters, to make a place and a name for himself in the new world. Fearlessly he entered upon his career without the help or the prestige which fortune and a family name may confer.

With a courage, no less bold than that with which he braved privation, he faced the problems of his varied positions.

Was it delving in the earth and coaxing it to yield a bounteous produce, or was it cultivating the more fruitful soil of a child's undeveloped mind[,] he would study the secret of the process and master the best ways of accomplishing results. Did men attempt to destroy his school, scatter his pupils, and wreck the work of his hands and his brains? He would resist where resistance was effectual, and when defeated at one point sturdily plant his flag-staff on another hill-top. What though he taught a people maligned and misunderstood, and his views of their possibilities aroused the antagonism of many about him. He would bravely pronounce the truth as God had given him to see the truth, and labor[4] by its light while he trusted Providence for vindication.

Another lesson we may learn from the life of Prof. Paterson is that of perseverance. In this he resembles his native hero, Robert Bruce.[5] Decided upon a course of action, he is not to be discouraged by obstacles. A notable exhibition of this quality is seen in the successful effort to establish the school in its present location, despite hostile endeavors on the part of a determined citizenry. Hardly less notable is the gallant though losing fight made for an increased school appropriation from the last Legislature.

That cheeriness which marks most great characters belongs to this subject. It is a kind of compensation which nature gives for the large efforts she exacts of them and the blows of opposition they are to encounter.

Prof. Paterson is optimistic, and in this trait possesses at once a qualification

---

2. An interpretation of Prov. 14:23.

3. Robert Burns (1759–1796), a Scottish poet, writing mostly in dialect.

4. The original reads "labour." Hereafter, the American spelling will be given.

5. Robert Bruce (1275–1329), crowned King of Scots at Scone in 1306. He had to flee his country when England, under the reign of King Edward, the First, dominated southern Scotland. After hiding in a cave for a year, he returned to his home and fought a successful guerilla battle against England (see Cavendish, "Robert Bruce and the Scottish Church," 9).

and a reason for success as an educator. He not only teaches us to look upon the bright side, but he would have us see something of the humorous side of life. What, though, as the poet says, after the laugh, "the moan comes double?"[6] The merry word or the cheery smile will help us[7] to bear the moan when it comes, and perhaps may even so fortify us that we shall not moan, but bear our pain without complaint.

Surely from this life aspiring youth, struggling and hard beset, may learn to despise not the day of small things. Do you deem your lowly origin a bar to future greatness? Here is one who, born of a humble parentage, achieved a worthy prominence. Are you entering life handicapped by a delicate constitution? Here is one who made a fight for health and developed from a weakly boyhood into a strong and vigorous manhood. Are you doubtful of being able to secure that higher training which you crave? He has shown that scholarship is not dependent upon the schools. Does any young man bewail his lack of means to start in business? Here is one who, beginning with nothing, has established a lucrative business and won a competence. Do you complain that you have no influential friends to push your interests and aid you in securing recognition? This man was a stranger in a strange land, yet he worked his way up from the lowest round of the ladder.

And, after all, which has wrought better?—he who succeeds as the happy heir of heredity and the favored offspring of fortune, or he who is like Tennyson's "divinely gifted man."

> "Whose life is low estate began,
> And on a simple village green;
> Who breaks his birth's invidious bar,
> And grasps the skirts of happy chance,
> And breasts the blows of circumstance,
> And grapples with his evil star,"
> and "makes by force his merit known?"[8]

---

6. Dunbar, "Life," 8. Dunbar's lines read, "A pint of joy to a peck of trouble / And never a laugh but the [moans come] double."

7. The original reads "help up."

8. Tennyson, "In Memoriam," canto 64, p. 115. Tennyson's line reads, "[who] makes by force his merit known."

PART VII

RACIAL DEFENSE

The Good Old Times

J. J. TURPIN

Who has not heard depicted the glories of the "good old times"? Who has not listened to vehement disparagements of the present? Who has not witnessed the longings of some mistaken wight for the "good old times" of the past?

Does an accident occur, are lives lost—"ah, well such things didn't happen so often in the olden days; the Lord must be visiting a judgment upon this people." Do we read of a murder, an embezzlement, a seduction—"deary me! what is the world coming to? people didn't used[1] to be so wicked." Do we go into ecstasies over some hero of today—"oh! but those great men of the past times have[2] since produced none like to them."[3]

Blame not these dear old people, these mourners after a past that is forever vanished. They are looking back into the days of their youth; what wonder that they call them the "good old times"!

What we see without is often but a reflection of something within; so they, with the twilight of many years gathering about them, see somber and gloomy colors everywhere. Age has dimmed their mental as well as their natural vision, and the advantages of the present are but faintly revealed. They are gazing backward through a vista which stretches far into distance, the defects of the landscape sink out of sight, a misty veil over hangs the scene, and

"Distance lends enchantment to the view."[4]

So, throughout the ages, have there been men who longed for the days of their youth, as the "good old times." Nor is this all; occasionally we meet young people, in the fullness of their strength, in the light of advanced civilization,

---

* "The Good Old Times," *People's Advocate* (Washington, D.C.), 8 September and 15 September 1883, 1. Turpin read this essay at the closing exercises of the academic year at the Richmond Institute.

1. The original reads "use."

2. The original reads "has."

3. Unknown quotation.

4. Campbell, "The Pleasures of Hope," 3. Campbell's line reads, "['Tis] distance lends enchantment to the view."

who paint the superiority of times they knew not, who decry the achievements of later days, who lean to the theory that the world is growing worse. Shame on them that they appreciate not the advantage they enjoy; shame on them that they recognize not the grand order of progression; shame on them that they are not thankful for being born in the nineteenth century.

As we contemplate the subject, some of the principal features of the "good old times" arise before us.

There were the "good old times" when the useful arts were little known and science was poorly appreciated. In those days people worked harder and accomplished less. The agriculturist had then to perform with tedious hand labor which now his machinery does for him. The mechanic with illy constructed tools and but little experience to aid him, knew not the beauty of finish and quickness of execution that belong to his brother of today. The ancient housewife enjoyed not the conveniences to which we are so accustomed that we forget they once were not. The broom, that well-known implement of industry and warfare, has not always had existence. Had Eve possessed a sewing machine, those aprons could have been made with greater neatness and dispatch. Once upon a time there were no umbrellas to be advertised as "lost, strayed, or stolen"; and books were so rare that the borrower found it difficult to collect a library after the approved method. Doctors were not such adepts in the art of killing and lawyers had not learned to lie skillfully. Travelers endured the crowding, the jolting, and the tedium of the stage-coach; and a trip to Europe was regarded almost as a visit to another world. Those whose memory we delight to honor, were once mocked and derided. Fulton[5] was thought a fool, Columbus[6] a fanatic and Galileo[7] a madman. Faces were upturned to the beautiful sky, but they read not the language of the stars; men watched with fear the lightning's flash, and knew not the power there enchained; the genial sun warmed and cheered, but it revealed not its wonderful secret of picture-making.

Do we long for the "good old times" of ancient schooling? The school houses lacked the modern improvements in heating and lighting and ventilating. There were the backless benches where little ones grew weary, and drooped the shoulders

---

5. Robert Fulton (1765–1815), an American inventor of the steamboat. His first vessel was called "The Steamboat," and its voyage transported passengers on 17 August 1807 from New York City to Albany (Lindsey, "Robert Fulton," 177–78).

6. Christopher Columbus (1451–1506), an Italian explorer, made four voyages to the Americas under the sponsorship of King Ferdinand and Queen Isabella of Spain. His explorations were intended to set the stage for Europe's colonization of the Americas (*The New Encyclopedia Britannica*, 15th ed. [2005], s.v. "Columbus").

7. Galilei Galileo (1564–1642), an Italian astronomer and physicist, validated the truth of the Copernican theory that the planets revolve around the sun (*The New Encyclopedia Britannica*, 15th ed. [2005], s.v. "Galileo").

forward in an unsightly and unhealthy manner. There were the high seats from which little feet could not touch the floor and hung in a tired, strained condition throughout the long hours. There was the old primer in which beginners droned over a, b, c, while more advanced students recited from Webster's spelling book. There was an absence of those appliances which make study easy and interesting. There was the stiff old master who made the brick the administrator of an iron law. System to him meant a strict adherence to a set of rigid rules; discipline implied hard tasks and a frequent application of the rod. It is not strange that "the feet that went creeping into school went storming out to play."[8]

Have you forgotten the "good old times" of superstition, the times which made so vivid an impression that we ourselves bear faint marks? Men sought to find in the heavens a revelation of human destiny, astrologers were consulted concerning important issues, armies hung upon the lips of the oracle. The ordeal, with all its awful torture, was used as a test of guilt. Honest citizens were accused of witch-craft,[9] innocent lives were taken, frenzied crowds

> "—mocked the palsied limbs of age,
> That flattered on the fateful stairs,
> And wan lips trembling with its prayers."[10]

Fortune tellers have been revered as being favored with peculiar prophetic vision. Through this belief, many imposters have triumphed; many credulous have been robbed; and many a one has been delivered by vain and foolish expectations. Sighs that bear no reasonable relation to the thing signified, tokens that have no philosophical connection with the event typified, are but remnants[11] of this barbarism.

The "good old times" of religious persecution, cast a blur upon the past. Men were imprisoned, exiled, tortured for their religious beliefs. Latimers[12] and Cranmers[13]

---

8. Whittier, "In School-Days," stanza 3, p. 407. Whittier's lines read, "The feet that creeping slow to school / Went storming out to playing."

9. The original reads "witch-chalt."

10. Whittier, "Mabel Martin," pt. 3, stanza 5, p. 518.

11. The original reads "remmants."

12. "Latimers" refers to those burned at the stake with Hugh Latimer (1485–1555), bishop of the Church of England. He was persecuted as an Anglican during the rule of Queen Mary, a Catholic (Wabuda, "Hugh Latimer," 632–39).

13. "Cranmers" refers to those burned at the stake with Thomas Cranmer (1489–1556), archbishop of Canterbury, during the reigns of Henry VIII and Edward VI. When Mary I, a Roman Catholic, became queen of England, she ordered Cranmer burnt at the stake for the compulsory enlistment of troops to raise Northumberland's army against her (MacCulloch, "Thomas Cranmer," 15–31).

yield up their lives at the stake, and Lady Jane Greys[14] laid down life upon the block. Bloody Mary[15] lighted the bonfires of England, and a cruel queen ordered the massacre of Bartholomew.[16] William Penn[17] left England on account of religious persecution, and the Pilgrim Fathers crossed to secure religious liberty. Under such a regime, all Christians were martyrs; and denominations feigned to serve God, by persecuting each other.

Our hearts boil with indignation at the remembrance of the "good old times" of slavery. Men whose forefathers wrote the Declaration of Independence, deprived their fellow being of "life, liberty, and the pursuit of happiness." Christians who professed to follow in the footsteps of Him who went about doing good, tortured His creatures with merciless hand. Ministers called of God to preach the gospel as it is in Jesus Christ, were content to expatiate to the slave on the passage, "Servants, obey in all things your masters."[18] Men and women were torn from the attractions of their native homes; they were packed into dark and filthy holes for passage; families were cruelly parted and sold; men with God given talents and great capabilities, were treated as brutes; they were exposed to privations and diseases; they were left in grossest ignorance, they were tempted to vice and immorality, they were required to make "bricks without straw," and they received in return curses and blows and horrors untold. Let us draw the curtain, we thank God those "good old times" are past.

In the "good old times" when woman's true position was unrecognized, she was regarded as a necessary evil. She waited upon him and relieved him of every care, but she was not even allowed to take her meals with *him*. The hardest work and the coarsest fare were hers. Men rejoiced over the birth of a son, but scorned the baby girl. For a woman to interest herself in anything outside of the dreary round of her allotted tasks, was considered unwomanly; and a learned woman was synonymous with an outcast. Womanhood was not then

14. Lady Jane Grey (1536–1554), great granddaughter of King Henry VII and England's ruler for nine days following the death of Edward VI. She was imprisoned and beheaded under the command of Mary Tudor, half sister of Edward VI, who succeeded to the throne (Plowden, "Grey" [Lady Jane], 856–59).

15. Bloody Mary, a name given to Mary I (1516–1558), England's Catholic queen known for her religious persecutions and beheadings of Protestants (Goodare, "Mary" [Mary Stewart], 77–93).

16. "Massacre of Bartholomew" refers to the St. Bartholomew's Day Massacre of 24 August 1572. In a religious uprising against Huguenots, Catholics murdered thousands of French Huguenot Protestants (*The New Encyclopedia Britannica*, 15th ed. [2005], s.v. "Saint Bartholomew's Day, Massacre of").

17. William Penn (1644–1718), a Quaker jailed in London, England, for his religious beliefs. He came to America and founded the colony of Pennsylvania and advocated religious freedom (Geiter, "William Penn," 557–66).

18. Col. 4:18.

reverenced[19] in the varied offices of mother, wife, sister, friend. She was shut out from literature, excluded from science, debarred from the fine arts, driven from the temple, denied admittance to the schools, and welcomed only in the harem.

We shrink in revulsion from the "good old times" of war. Men delighted in slaughter. The great warriors went forth to battle for glory—what glory? the glory of becoming murderers, of devastating cities and towns, of rending the hearts of women and children; for conquest—what conquest? they gained bloody and seared consciences, they gained loads of sin that no human effort could remove, they gained names that call forth shudders of abhorrence from those who live after them; for vengeance—why vengeance? when, "Vengeance is mine, saith the Lord."[20]

The "good old times" are a myth,[21] a fantasy, a delusion, and a snare. The present is superior to all times past. We of to-day possess a peculiar legacy. The intellectual powers of our ancestors have been transmitted to us, their moral virtues have descended to us; their inventions are all ours. We have all that they had, and also our own particular endowments. How can our advantage but be better than theirs? We would not be worthy of being their children, were we not better and wiser than they. The world is progressing. Discovery and invention lighten toil, and secure results more nearly perfect. Education spreads, and men grow in mental stature. Superstition is becoming a relic of by-gone days. Men are tolerant of religious beliefs, and unite in Christianizing the heathen. The people once held in bondage, are now rising in all the dignity of manhood and womanhood to the plane of true and rightful living. Woman, once despised as man's slave, is now honored as his helpmeet. War, once sought is now avoided. Man has more, knows more, does more. Hurrah for the good *new* things.

[There were so many typographical errors in this article last week, that we concluded to republish it.—ED]

---

19. The original reads "reverence."
20. Rom. 12:19. The King James Version reads, "Vengeance *is* mine, [I will repay,] saith the Lord."
21. The original reads "myrth."

"A Great Danger": Annie
Porter Excoriated

JOSEPHINE J. TURPIN

A Vehement Onslaught against the Negro Replied to by a Female Representative of the Race.

To the Editor of the Globe:

In the *Independent* of December 27, appeared an article bearing the title quoted above and written by one who signed herself Annie Porter. The communication is a vehement onslaught against the Negro, who is held up and denounced as "a great danger" to Louisiana in particular and the United States in general. The falsity of some of the statements is apparent from the very nature of things, and the contradictions running through many of the others attest their untruthfulness.

The writer opens with a bitter bewailing of the "extraordinary relapse into barbarism which is going on among the Negroes in Louisiana at this moment;" and shows how dangerous it is to the country that a "large and increasing population of savages should be established in its borders." What does Annie Porter mean by the Negro's relapse into barbarism? A relapse is a falling back into a former state. The use of this term then implies that the Negro was at some subsequent period in a state of barbarism, that he rose above it into some degree of civilization and that he is now falling back or "relapsing" into this former degradation. Is this true? That the Negro in the United States has been in an ignorant and debased condition bordering on barbarism, he, together with his friends and his enemies, is ready to admit. That he has during any time in this country been more advanced in civilization than now, is not conceded. When was this period of pristine wisdom and goodness? Annie Porter cannot mean that it was in the "good old times of slavery;" for, in her own words, she "never approved of slavery" but "always considered it a curse to the people and the country." If then she does think the race a "large and increasing population of savages," she certainly uses the wrong word when she speaks of their "relapse into barbarism." Without saying anything in regard to the improvement that has been

* "'A Great Danger': Annie Porter Excoriated," *New York Globe,* 2 February 1884, 1.

made—an improvement which thousands of honest men and women are ready and glad to declare, these past twenty years have[1] undoubtedly witnessed no relapse.

Speaking of the majority of Negroes in the village in which she resides, it is remarked that the "Negroes' tendency to leave country homes and drift together in centers either of towns or hamlets is inveterate." Is this social inclination peculiar to the Negro, so that it is worthy of being the subject of special comment? And even if it were, would the fact be in any wise discreditable? Why, Annie Porter herself, in applying the remedies for manifold Negro ills, descants on the advantages of having them together in "industrial centers."

We are entertained (?) with a graphic and extended description of a Negro applicant for the situation of cook. Is Annie Porter as deeply impressed by the dress and manners and conversation of all the unlettered and uncultured characters with whom she comes into contact? Can she not find hundreds of women who differ materially in no respect, save perhaps in color, from the one depicted? Would like ignorance of an Irish woman be attributed to the fact that she is Irish, or of a Dutch that she is Dutch, or of any Anglo-Saxon to the fact of her race? Is it just to judge the Negro by a standard altogether different from that according to which other people are judged?

That "Negro men are sunk in sloth," is information as unique as it is startling. It seems rather strange, to say the least, that the men who for, lo, these many years have worked the great plantations of the South, have hoed the corn, picked the cotton, cultivated the rice; the men who have dug the canals, laid the railroads, supplied the factories; the men who are the very bone and sinew of the South, should be spoken of as "sunk in sloth."

How one [who] believes in the power and efficacy of the gospel can think a people possessing any knowledge whatever of it "worse off than if they had never heard of Christianity," I cannot divine. Yet, this is what Annie Porter says of the Negroes, concerning whom she further asserts: "Their idea of God is of the most material and at the same time the most superstitious description. Of Jesus they only know as a sort of charm, though common belief prevails among them that he was a black man." They are, in the language of the writer, "given up to wildest religious excitements," being "full of the wildest, most extraordinary ideas and superstitions." Superstition exists to a greater or less degree among any ignorant people. The proud Anglo-Saxon will find this exemplified in tracing back the history of his race to the early days of their barbarous and savage state. There are ignorant classes of colored people, as there are ignorant classes of white people, and as a natural consequence of their ignorance there is superstition among them; but that their idea of God is of the kind declared and their knowledge of Christ as limited as is affirmed, I most emphatically deny. I am of

---

1. The original reads "has."

these people; and I know them better than one who stands afar off, and fears to have her dainty robes touch their rough and toil-stained garments.

An account is given of a young man "born and brought up a mule driver," who wanted to become a minister. (Rather strange idea, that of being "born a mule-driver!") A better plan of action than to deride his desire because of his unfitness, would have been to attempt to impress him with the importance of due preparation for the accomplishment of his mission. The fact that she had "tried faithfully to teach him," but that he still had "no knowledge of anything except his trade," signifies nothing. Annie Porter shows her lack of faith in the Negro's capacity, when she declares him "entirely unable to take in geographical and political distinctions." That teacher who has no belief in the existence of the very powers which it is her office to draw out, is calculated to do harm rather than good. Had the young man preferred[2] to study[3] this trade under this fair instructress he would probably have known nothing of that.

And now I quote the foulest aspersion against the women of the race: "I firmly believe that no Negro woman brought up in a former slave State and among those who have been slaves knows the meaning of the word *chastity,* or grasps the idea of physical morality in the slightest degree." Is a Negress less than a woman, that any condition could rob her of all natural modesty and delicacy? It is false; I repeat it; it is false. Slavery has much for which to render an account; it invaded the sanctity of homes, it nullified the marriage bond, it exposed to temptation and[4] reduced to immorality, it prostrated virtue at the feet of vice; it did all this and more; it was a huge blot upon the face of society, a great ulcer upon the body politic, a burning shame to the American people; but it did not, because it could not, take from the women of the oppressed race that innate regard for purity and chastity which remained theirs by right of their woman-hood. The instance of a well-taught and well-trained girl falling from virtue and then making excuses for her wrong-doing, is not an uncommon one and is by no means restricted to the Negro race.

If Annie Porter is to write next of murder and bloodshed in the South, she might gain some information by conning matter relative to the late Danville massacre.[5] She might, too, study the art of lynching, prevalent among her white brethren of the South; and might, also, with profit examine into the history of the Ku-Klux. For a Negro to appear as midnight assassin and cut-throat, would be an entirely new role. When he had ample opportunities for gratifying any

2. The original reads "referred."
3. The original reads "studied."
4. The original reads "and and."
5. The Danville Massacre refers to a bloody Democratic victory on 3 November 1883 in Danville, Virginia, and is better known as the "Danville Riot." The riot was precip-itated when a black man accidently bumped into a white man on a street in Danville,

such propensity it did not disclose itself. When the strong and brave among his enemies were away fighting to keep him in bondage and those near and dear to them were at his mercy, instead of rising up to kill and to slay he watched over, worked for, cared for, and harmed not a hair in their heads. Was this the manifestation of a violent and vindictive spirit?

Annie Porter thinks schools and churches, though "excellent things," do the Negro "little or no good;" but recommends industrial centers and a separate system of local government as their salvation. Industrial pursuits do more than has been accredited to them, if they train head and heart as well as hand, and churches and schools do less than they are intended to do, if they cannot spread the gospel and diffuse knowledge among any people. How the inhabitants of the ideal Negro village painted are to profit by that "higher and better civic training," if they are—as the writer maintains—"entirely unable to take in political and geographical distinctions," and unable to learn the teachings of school or church, I cannot determine. This but another instance of contradictory views and statements.

Annie Porter observes that a marked feature of the race is their distrust of white people. If this be true, can it not be easily accounted for? Trust or distrust originates from some knowledge of past action. The black man's terrible experience in the hands of white men may, in many cases, have embittered his mind against them, not because they are white but because they have so wronged him. Every such article as Annie Porter's serves to strengthen this feeling. We have, however, too many friends among the white people for this distrust to be general. We can discriminate between our friends and enemies; between those who would do us justice and those who themselves neither regard us aright, nor would have others do so; between those who, actuated by broad and noble principles, would help and encourage struggling humanity and those who, controlled by blind and ignoble prejudices, would use their strength and influence against the Negro's elevation.

Howard University
Washington, D.C.

Virginia, several days before a political election between the pro-black Readjuster Republican Party and the pro-white Democratic Party. Riled by promises the Readjusters had made to blacks, whites killed four blacks and wounded about seven, although the number of blacks killed and wounded varies depending on who tells the story. Two whites were wounded. For several days after the riot, whites roamed city streets with guns and kept blacks from the polls. Democrats scored a victory and marked the end of the Readjuster movement (*Danville Riot, Nov. 3, 1883, Report of the Committee of Forty*, 5; Riddick, *The Danville Riot*, 5; Wynes, *Race Relations in Virginia*, 31).

Anglo Saxon Supremacy

JOSEPHINE TURPIN WASHINGTON

The Afro Americans attending the National Teacher's Association, at St. Paul, Minn., heard at least one very unpalatable address on the race problem.

Had it been that the simple truth was told, however unpleasant, it could have been received with a certain degree of equanimity. It could have been swallowed as one takes bitter medicine from the physician, who is not mistaken as an enemy because his dose happens to be nauseous. From beginning to end, the address was one mass of misrepresentation, distorted facts and unjust assumptions with regard to the Negro. This is all the more dangerous because the speaker, Mrs. Helen K. Ingram[1] of Jacksonville, Fla., assumed the guise of friendliness.

Our northern friends are not likely to be imposed upon by the utterances of the avowed Negro hater, who expresses himself with violence and frequently makes no other attempt towards argument than the shotgun. His assertions are disregarded or treated as the ravings of a rabid maniac. It is the man or woman of acknowledged respectability, of high moral and social standing, of expressed goodwill to the Negro, and of apparent fairness to him, who can do us real harm with those who are truly our friends, but who are not so situated as to have an opportunity of knowing us well.

Such an enemy, in the garb of a friend, is evidently Mrs. Helen K. Ingram. The fact that she was "born, brought up and educated in New York State" and that for years her "nearest neighbors were the intimate friends of Gerritt Smith[2] and William Lloyd Garrison [3] and active, earnest officials in that mysterious transit line—the underground railway," proves nothing. Does she mention these facts in her personal history because she thinks we must believe that one who

---

* "Anglo Saxon Supremacy," *New York Age,* 23 August 1890, 2–3.

1. Helen K. Ingram (1838–1898), a native of Florida, wrote popular travel and tourists' books: *Florida* (1893*)*, *Florida: Beauties of the East Coast* (1893), *Snowball and Oranges* (1894), *Three on a Tour* (1895), and *Tours and Settlers' Guide to Florida* (1895).

2. Gerritt Smith (1797–1874), founded the Liberty Party. A white abolitionist, he held antislavery meetings at his family's farm in Peterboro, New York.

3. William Lloyd Garrison (1805–1897), a white abolitionist from Massachusetts who founded the *Liberator* newspaper on 1 January 1831, in which he disseminated antislavery views (Currie, *The Liberator*, 30).

lived so near to the friends of the Negro must be necessarily herself his friend? Or that one born and reared in a Northern State must perforce inspire confidence on this question? Mrs. Ingram is not the only Northerner with Southern principles and ideas. The South teems, in some sections, with Northern men who came South and out Herod. Herod[4] himself in injustice to the Negro. The fear of being ostracized[5] in social and injured in business circles, acts as a potent influence. Perhaps the most prejudiced town in the state of Alabama—certainly the only one I know which has separate coaches on its dummy line for white and colored passengers—is the Magic City of Birmingham, built up almost altogether by Northern capitalists. Nor is unfairness to the Negro confined to Northern men who come South to live. We have a prominent example of this in the recent assault, in New York City, on T. Thos. Fortune[6] of *The Age*. On the other hand Cable[7] of Louisiana and Blair[8] of Virginia are Southerners, and yet just and fair in their views on this race question. We cannot with surety classify either our friends or our enemies by sections, but we recognize them when we find them.

According to Mrs. Ingram, even the system of slavery itself cannot be deplored. The slave was happy, care-free, satisfied, "a slave in little but a name." He "was a picturesque feature in our country," "a favorite theme for poet romancers and song makers," a being invested with imaginary ills by soft-hearted romantic folks who were too far off from him to know his real delightful condition. It does seem to me that listening to such a representation of the barbarous[9] system that reduced men to the level of brutes, that maltreated and mangled and killed when it would the body, that warped and distorted and degraded the soul, that disregarded the family relation and set a premium upon vice, that tore husbands from wives and mothers from children, that perpetuated all the evil which can be conceived when one human being is placed entirely within the power of

4. Herod the Great (73–74 BC), ruled Judea as a madman. He murdered his family and Jewish rabbis in order to accomplish his desires.

5. The original reads "ostracised."

6. For information on T. Thomas Fortune, see note 3 in Josephine Turpin Washington, "Josephine Turpin Washington Nominates T. Thomas Fortune," in this volume, p. 133.

7. George Washington Cable (1844–1925), a well-known writer from New Orleans, Louisiana. He rendered realistic portrayals of mixed-race characters in his short stories and novels. In his nonfiction essays, such as "The Silent South" (1885), he opposed Jim Crow discrimination and racial injustice (*Dictionary of Literary Biography*, ed. Donald Pizer and Earl N. Harbert [1982], s.v. "George Washington Cable").

8. Lewis Harvie Blair (1834–1916), a Richmond, Virginia, businessman who opposed racial segregation and advocated benefits to the economy via racial integration. He crystallized his integrationist views in his controversial book, *The Prosperity of the South Dependent upon the Elevation of the Negro* (1889) (Blair, *Encyclopedia Virginia*).

9. The original reads "barbarcus."

another—it does seem to me that we should feel justified in distrusting any statement coming from one who could so seek to palliate the crimes of slavery.

Nor is Mrs. Ingram's representation of the Negro's condition in freedom more reliable. She declares that "every avenue of trade is open to him;" that the South has given him "careful training in equal schools with her white population and she has given him equal opportunities for using that education;" that "not an occupation, trade, profession, or business of any kind is barred to him." She cites as if they were common occurrence, two isolated instances of his employment in Jacksonville, in one case as a clerk in a shoe-store where "a white man and a colored man stand side by side behind the counter" and in the other where "the young man whose hair kinks to the skin and whose eyes and teeth shine like stars in a midnight sky" will fill your prescription in one of the oldest and wealthiest drug stores in the city. "In groceries, hardware stores, anywhere you choose, the same equal chance is given." Can anything be further from the truth? There was not one of those colored teachers who sat within hearing of this assertion that did not in his heart utter a denial; not one of the white people in the audience but knew it was false. There is no one so ignorant of the status of the Negro in this country as not to be aware that neither North nor South are all employments open to him. A few remarkable exceptions only prove the rule of his general exclusion. Were his admission to all grades of employment for which he is fitted a matter of course, it would not excite such comment when it does occur.

The Negro is not given an equal chance, Mrs. Ingram and others of her class to the contrary notwithstanding. A colored photographer may be so fortunate as to have "a conspicuous gallery in a central location on the principal[10] street in Jacksonville," but who does not know that colored professional men in the South, and to some extent in the North also, are daily refused offices in certain localities because neighboring white tenants would be offended? Who does not know that colored men of education, of refinement, of unimpeachable character, cannot rent or buy homes where they will? That colored photographer "cares not which race comes up his winding stair," but I venture to say his work lies principally among his own people. The colored dentist was admitted to practice, but how many white patients will he have? Jacksonville is indeed an exception if "the finest schoolhouses in the city are those built for the use of the colored race." Never having visited the city, I am not prepared to deny this. I must say, however, that I cannot believe in the statement that 52.8 per cent. of Florida's school fund goes to the colored pupils. If this is so, how is it that the colored schools are inferior to the white schools in number, in buildings, in educational appliances, and in the amount expended for teacher's salaries? This is undeniably true of Pensacola, with which I am well acquainted.

What has Mrs. Ingram to say of the refusal to the Negro of equal accommo-

10. The original reads "principle."

dations in hotels, theatres, and railway cars; of the race prejudice shown even in so-called Christian churches; of denials at soda water fountains, and proscriptions on the ocean beach? Then made the objects of such invidious distinctions, shown in these and a hundred other ways, are we given an "equal chance?"

"Ninety-five per cent. of our criminals are Negroes!" This may be a startling statement, but it is not altogether discouraging to one who knows anything of what goes on behind the scenes. How many of these alleged criminals are really guilty, can never be known. In most cases they are tried, without adequate counsel, by judge and jury alike prejudiced. The trial is opened with the assumption that the fellow is an abandoned wretch because he is a "nigger." The predominance of the accused's own color on the jury is, in the case of the Negro, a very unusual occurrence. In some parts of the South colored men are never put on the jury. Their names happen never to be reached. The colored judge is a phenomenon—too rare a genus to be considered. Negroes are arrested for offenses which white men commit with impunity. When the white man is brought before the bar of justice (?) money and influence frequently secure him an acquittal, regardless of his guilt. I do not believe that an impartial administration of the law would give ninety-five per cent of Negro criminals even if under present circumstances it is true; but were we to grant for the sake[11] of arguments, that this is the correct proportion of Negro to white criminals, could we not find another explanation than natural and incurable depravity of the Negro? What of heredity, of the transmission of traits acquired under unfavorable environment, of the influence of two hundred and fifty years of slavery? In this there is nothing to warrant despair. There is no reason to believe that the stain of a deplorable past is not eradicable.

It matters little that Mrs. Ingram characterizes the Negro as "without dignity, sly, deceitful, improvident, simply imitative in small matters, self-sufficient and important," while the Anglo-Saxons have always been "dignified, spirited, valiant, truthful, fearless, enterprising;" that she compares the one to the mule and the other to the horse in their respective capacities for improvement. Simple affirmations, from such a source and in such a cause are not convincing. We could speak of the Negro's patient and forgiving spirit, of his faithfulness and devotion even to the owners who oppressed him, of his loyalty to the union, of his remarkable progress since the acquisition of freedom, in education, in culture, in wealth, in mortality, in all that go to make the man. We could contrast these virtues with the selfish and grasping natures of those who held him in bondage, with the cruelty and brutality with which they exercised their power, with the unjust and barbaric treatment they now accord him; but we will not say, "Behold, these men are Anglo Saxons: such must be the character of all Anglo Saxons." Some Negroes are certainly what Mrs. Ingram says of "the Negro," but the description fits some white men as well.

11. The original reads "sakes."

Apropos of this, soon after the late fruitless conference of able and learned white men who met to discuss the future of the Negro without having extended to any member of that race the courtesy of an invitation to be present and to participate in the discussion, the *New York World* published a short editorial in which it very pertinently remarks: "Negroes there are, but not 'the Negro,' a term which means, if it means anything, a certain type of persons, similarly circumstanced, with identical characters and aspirations, whose case is to be dealt with by formulae, as is done with chemicals in the laboratory;" and adds further on, "The Negro race contains a great variety of individuals so unlike each other as to make generalization concerning them utterly absurd and misleading."

Mrs. Ingram says, furthermore, "All who have risen to any distinction among them (the Negroes) are nearly white." This was clearly and emphatically refuted in the person of the well-known Negro orator, J. C. Price,[12] in attendance on that very convention and one of the invited speakers of the occasion. It is further refuted in the persons of New York's able counselor, T. McCants Stewart;[13] Detroit's eminent lawyer, D. Augustus Straker;[14] Dr. Alexander Crummel,[15] a renowned scholar and theologian; Dr. Edward Wilmot Blyden,[16] a celebrated linguist and

12. Joseph Charles Price (1854–1893), an African American educator and advocate of racial uplift. He founded Zion Wesley College in 1881, which later became Livingstone College, a historically black university (Meier, *Negro Thought in America,* 80).

13. Thomas McCants Stewart (1853–1923), a South Carolina native. He attended the University of South Carolina and graduated with a law degree. He practiced law in New York, became an educator, and served as judge on the Supreme Court in Liberia, West Africa. He died in the Virgin Islands, where he had set up a legal practice (Broussard, *African American Odyssey,* 16–24, 89–99).

14. D. Augustus Straker (1824–1908) was born in Barbados. He received his law degree from Howard University and became a prominent lawyer in Detroit, Michigan. The first black lawyer to appear before the Michigan Supreme Court, Straker argued that the separate but equal law in Michigan was unconstitutional (Simmons and Turner, *Men of Mark,* 4).

15. Dr. Alexander Crummell (1819–1898) founded the American Academy, validating advocacy for higher education and scholarship for African Americans in opposition to Booker T. Washington's call for industrial education. He was educated at Queen's College in Cambridge, England, after Yale University refused him admittance based on his race (Moss, *The American Negro Academy,* 1–2, 19).

16. Edward Wilmot Blyden (1832–1912), born free to literate parents in Saint Thomas, West Indies. He traveled to Liberia, West Africa, after he was denied entry into Rutgers' Theological College in New Jersey because of his race. He was ordained as a Presbyterian minister, edited the *Liberian Herald,* published four books, became Liberia's secretary of state, and taught classics at Liberia College. Considered the father of Black Nationalism, he utilized science to justify and advocate for blacks' equality (Lynch, *Edward Wilmot Blyden,* 3–6, 172–73).

scientist; Kelly Miller,[17] Howard University's brilliant young professor of mathematics, and many others. Suppose we were to admit that the majority who have risen to distinction among us are of mixed blood. It would not prove the natural superiority of the Anglo Saxon. It could be explained very simply on the ground that blood relationship to the Anglo-Saxon race, as the race which has had the hundreds of years of training, of education, and of culture of which we have been deprived, is fraught with some intellectual benefit to the offspring; and on the further ground that the unnatural fathers were, in some cases, moved to give to these children of illegitimate birth educational advantages superior to those within the reach of the unmixed black. Would this justify the assumption that the whites are naturally superior and will always maintain supremacy? By no means. A mere statement of superiority amounts to nothing. It must be proven. The Afro-American is doing his part in schools and colleges, in business and in professional life to confound the advocates of white superiority. Clement Morgans[18] will multiply as the years go by. Let the good work progress. Time will solve the problem; and it is my prediction that despite race prejudice, despite injustice, despite oppression, despite cavillings over race supremacy, the solving will result in the peopling of America with "the man of the new race," the "Minden Armais" of Dr. Jamieson.[19]

17. For information on Kelly Miller Sr., see note 5 in J. J. Turpin, "Wendell Phillips' Memorial Exercises at Howard University," in this volume, p. 121.

18. Clement Garnett Morgan (1859–1929) was born to slave parents in Stafford County, Virginia, and received a law degree from Harvard University in 1893. A Republican, he extended his political influence to close a segregated school in Sheffield, Massachusetts. He was founding member of the Niagara Movement and of the National Association for the Advancement of Colored People (Hayden, "Morgan, Clement G[arrett]," 452).

19. *Minden Armais: The Man of the New Race: A Memoir* (1890) relates the story of a black French abolitionist who traveled to pre–Civil War America with hopes of seeking a better life for himself. Once in America, he was ostracized as a black in every facet of American life. He questioned the right of the white race to subordinate blacks. His strength came from knowing that blacks had a higher mission—to "await the master's coming which shall give them freedom—which shall give them, also, power." Minden Armais represents the man of the new race, one neither fugitive nor slave (Jamieson, *Minden Armais*, 15). "Dr. Jamieson" is a pseudonym for Charles S. Keyser.

PART VIII

WOMEN'S CLUB WORK

Impressions of a Southern Federation

JOSEPHINE T. WASHINGTON

Mobile, city of the sea, true to her name—Mobile—changing, responsive,[1] susceptible, like the waters of her shimmering gulf; tender, dreamy, beautiful, and smiling, she lies under semi-tropic skies.

About her numerous old-fashioned mansions and the rarer structures of modern type, alike, the magnolias bloom in royal splendor and rose-vines grow in rivalry of Jack's renowned bean-stalk. Shaded by giant trees and cooled by falling waters, Bienville Square, in the heart of the town, offers the tired wayfarer ease.

But even in this inviting spot the petty prejudices of our little life obtrude. Yonder swings are not for the dusky children of the sun. Some heart moved to sympathy with childhood's joy, when that childhood is Anglo-Saxon of race, made possible this pleasant pastime. Dark-hued little men and maids look on longingly, but dare not touch the sacred structure. Even in the lovely city of the dead something of the baneful influence follows. Will this ever-present discrimination have effect "when the general roll is called" and we all, according to promise, are "there?"

Down the silvery shell-road we wind our way to the coast, passing what was fairy Frascati,[2] but which, in keeping with the utilitarian spirit of the times, is no longer a park but a railroad yard. Mont Rose, Point Clear, Daphne, Howards, Battle's Wharf, these and other moss-hanging points beck on [sic] to us across the bay.

In the opposite direction is Spring Hill with its long row of beautiful rural residences, among them that of Augusta Evans of St. Elmo fame.[3] Here, too, we

* "Impressions of a Southern Federation," *Colored American Magazine* 7, no. 11 (November 1904): 676–80.

1. The original reads "reponsive."

2. Frascati Park was located on the western side of Mobile Bay. Martin Horst (1830–1878) purchased and developed the land, which became a major postbellum entertainment spot for whites ("Centennial Celebration in Mobile," 1).

3. Augusta Jane Evans (1835–1909), southern Confederate author of nine novels, the third and most popular of which is *St. Elmo* (1866).

find the Colored Orphan's and Old Folk's Home,[4] a commodious structure with spacious and well-kept grounds.

The people who planned and bought this Home for "sweet charity's sake" knew, too, how to provide handsome houses of worship and pretty homes of their own. It is not surprising that a pastor who raised, during a stay of several years, an average of eighteen dollars per day, left behind him a church furnished with stained glass windows and pipe organ, and equal to any in the city in beauty and in convenience.

Business houses there are, owned and controlled by men of color—grocery stores, drug stores, livery stables, undertaking establishments, insurance companies, lawyers' and doctors' offices, etc. etc.

Three public schools, with as many colored principals and an able corps of assistants, together with the Emerson Institute,[5] a Congregational school, and one or two exceptionally good private schools, engage in the pleasant task of teaching the young idea to shoot.

Yet, attractive as we find Mobile, (barring the exhibitions of race prejudice, which the denizens of the Sunny South find everywhere), the place was for the nonce eclipsed in interest by the occasion which brought us thither. This was the Sixth Annual Meeting of the State Federation of Colored Women's Clubs.

To the too-familiar individual with whom all days are either working days on which he adds to his hoarded pile or holidays for spending prodigally in personal gratification, it would have seemed an odd way to pass the "glorious Fourth." The quiet and self-contained company of women that streamed into the city's station was most unlike the usual pleasure-seekers of the season. Twenty clubs responded to the call, and thirty-five representatives of women's organizations came from all sections of the state to this Southern port selected as the place of meeting.

A wholesome-looking set of women they were: sensible, earnest, quiet, cheerful, dignified and courteous. It is true they did not always assemble on time and they failed, in large measure, to adhere to the order of the printed program, but they evidently, came together with a fixed purpose, and when they swerved[6] from

---

4. Mobile Colored Old Folks and Orphans Home was founded in 1904. Located near Springhill Avenue and Mobile Street, it was the only home for the colored aged and orphans in Mobile, Alabama, at the time. It had one employee and a property value of eleven thousand dollars (Owen, *Alabama Official and Statistical Register 1915,* 268; Harris, *Benevolent Institutions,* 174; Polk, *Polk's Medical Register and Directory of the United States and Canada,* 206).

5. The American Missionary Association (AMA) founded Emerson Institute (1865–1927). In 1875, Emerson became Alabama's first African American college (Bailey, *They, Too, Call Alabama Home,* 6).

6. The original reads "sewerved."

a prearranged course it was plain that they thought by so doing the paramount object would be the better promoted. They even took off their hats in the meeting, and when they put them on no one was heard to ask, "Is my hat on straight?" What stronger proof could there be of feminine absorption and self-abnegation?

They dressed simply, many tastefully and prettily, in womanly style, without any straining after mannish effects. The one woman in the audience who, with short-cut hair, plain straw sailor, and masculine looking collar, tie, shirt-front and jacket, might when sitting in the pen have been mistaken for a man, was not a delegate or even a club woman.

Now and then under the tension of excited discussion, there was a little manifestation of hurt feeling and a few quick retorts, but there was no bolting of the convention. Nobody declared, "I won't play because you did so and so that I did not like."

It was a truly representative crowd of women—teachers, wives and daughters of ministers, the mothers of households, one active, white-haired delegate proudly declaring herself the mother of six sons, all grown to vigorous and useful manhood.

Types of the "new woman"[7]—these might be called club women—delegates to a state organization, undertaking the business of establishing a great humanitarian institution, yet, hopeful and reassuring sign, the text of their talk was "home." The mission of motherhood, how to improve the social life, how to help our boys and girls, problems of Negro womanhood, the future Negro woman, character, a single standard of morality, how to help the fallen, mother's meetings, were some of the topics discussed.

"I don't know much, but I do what I know," was the pathetic utterance of one Black Belt delegate. If only all of us would "do what we know!"

Upon the promised land of a realized hope their gaze was fixed. To all else their eyes were closed. Courteously they listened to admonitions from a few cool and cautious ones as to the magnitude and gravity of the task, they were warned to "take care" in deciding to shoulder so great a responsibility. And when it was over, they broke the silence with the old enthusiasm and the persistent cry, "This one thing we do."

Back they came to all three sessions of the two days, braving the heat of a midsummer sun, except the provident half dozen or more who brought their lunch and ate it in the cool recesses of the big church.

---

7. "New woman" was an appellation used in the late nineteenth and early twentieth centuries to designate upward striving among predominantly educated, middle-class Negro women to counter preconceived racist images of black women as licentious, ignorant, and loathsome. Working with churches and club groups, these women emphasized racial uplift through character building, stabilizing the family, and achieving self-sufficiency (Gates, "The Trope of a New Negro," 129–55).

The derelict few who went for drives or graced some social function while the meetings were in progress, were not only soundly scored by the faithful majority but had their remissness nipped in the bud by the passage of a resolution providing that in future delegates so absenting themselves should be reported to their respective clubs.

Most of the women showed a fine spirit of self-denial, staying over an extra day when it was found that the time allotted to the work of the convention was too short, and bravely spending all of that day in session without so much as going out to get a drink of water. Only one woman is on record as pleading with an earnest advocate of an unpopular measure, "O, do stop talking and let it go anyway.[8] I am so tired. Let's get through and go home." Others were willing to stay not only all day but all night if necessary, in order to have such measure adopted as they thought for the best interest of the movement.

The reports showed a club constituency hardly less earnest than these representatives; else, how would such work have been accomplished? "Service" was the watch-word, "forward" the cry. If self-culture was a prominent feature in some of the organizations, it was self-culture associated with benevolent action, self-culture not alone for the sake of the individual, but also for the sake of the many. If some of the clubs had social evenings or served refreshments at the close of a strenuous session, such diversions were never confounded with the purpose of the body, the thing for which it stood, the reason for its being, and money raised for charity was not touched for such uses. Garments were made for the poor, other articles begged from overstocked wardrobes and bestowed where needed, food and fuel and medicine furnished the sick, tuition paid in private institutions for children crowded[9] out of the public schools. A room had been furnished in the charity ward of a hospital. One club had secured a gift of land and a cottage and was working to establish a hospital. One had bought land and had as its object the building of a High School in a town where no such provision was made for colored youth. One is furnishing the rooms of a local Young Men's Christian Association. Where fire or flood caused loss of life and property these clubs respond to appeal for aid.

Nor do they make the giving of alms the limit of their service. They seek to elevate the tone of life in their communities; they stand for "purity, for progress, for philanthropy, for peace."

Mothers' meetings are held in which topics relating to the care of the home and children are informally discussed, popular lectures are provided, schools are visited, and a helpful interest shown in educational matters.

One club celebrates yearly the birthday of Douglass,[10] and otherwise fosters race pride by giving an annual prize for the best essay on a race subject.

8. The original reads "any way."
9. The original reads "crowed."
10. Reference to Frederick Douglass.

And so the reports go on, telling the tale of varied activity, all helpful and inspiring, but all subordinate to the larger object for which the clubs unite in the State Federation.

And what is this aim, this united undertaking? A great aim, a stupendous undertaking it is; yet not too great for courageous hearts and untiring hands—the establishment of a reformatory for wayward boys.

More than five years ago, in the city of Montgomery, a little group of earnest women, moved with compassion for youthful lawbreakers of the race, arrested for minor offenses, convicted and sentenced to penitentiary and to mines, there to consort with hardened criminals, consecrated themselves to the task of awakening the public conscience and arousing interest looking to the establishment of a reformatory.

A club was formed for this purpose, but the magnitude of the work caused its promoters, upon the organization of the State Federation, to bring the work before that body as a fitting object for the united efforts of the women of the state. Three years ago the state organization adopted this work. The clubs were few and young, and weak; laboring, too, under the obligation of local charities already undertaken. Progress was slow, contributions coming in uncertainly and irregularly, many clubs being too poor to do more than send their delegates to the meetings with the requisite ten cents per capita.

Refusing to abandon hope, the purpose was held to tenaciously. Last year the clubs were asked to try to bring fifty dollars each. Several responded this year at the meeting in Mobile, the Mobile Century Club leading the van with seventy-five[11] dollars.

Banded together by this common purpose, a degree of unanimity prevails well nigh incomprehensible to the average attendant on men's conventions. Differing in tastes, pursuits, attainment, and station, a common hope levels all distinctions.

Not varying greatly from similar gatherings among their sisters in other sections is this assemblage of Afro-American women of the South. Perhaps the most marked feature is the gravity of their mien, their seriousness of aspect.

That was the comment, perhaps the criticism, on the educated Afro-American woman of the South by a distinguished Northern woman of the race: "Your women are so solemn." The fault is not in ourselves, but in our stars—that we are weighted with care.

There is a blur on the sunshine of the fair South, there is a jar in the tones of her tender lute; the atmosphere is surcharged with elements that threaten. The sensitive soul of the discerning black woman thrills to the situation, and merriment dies out of her heart.

11. The original reads "seyenty-five."

Child Saving in Alabama

JOSEPHINE TURPIN WASHINGTON

A recent issue of a well-known race weekly sounded a "warning to club women" based on the prognostication of one Dr. Thomas Hunt Stucky[1] of Louisville, Kentucky. The learned doctor is quoted as saying, "The manner of life of the ordinary club woman of today is helping to ruin her digestion."

The editorial comment expresses the opinion that "the ordinary card games played in the average club or social function are a drain on the nervous vitality of women."

Afro-American club women may well stand aghast at this statement. The ordinary club woman devoting herself to cards. The extraordinary one, forsooth, if any at all. Such may be the clubs of the idle rich, of the self-indulgent votaries of fashion; and doubtless there are, in some of the large cities, Afro-American women who ape the follies of this class, but the average club woman, certainly the club woman of this section, is a creature of another type. The colored woman's club is an eleemosynary organization. There may be a social feature and some attention may be given to self-culture, but these are secondary aims. The main purposes are to relieve suffering, to reclaim the erring, and to advance the cause of education.

Down here in Alabama many forms of altruistic work are carried on, with varying degrees of success. Here and there may be found an organization that adopts some special work, entailing much labor and expense, yet maintains it with unflagging zeal and devotion. Such a club is the Sojourner Truth Club[2] of this city, that maintains a free reading room which it established four years ago. Our City Federation supports an infirmary for the aged and invalid. These and kindred facts indicate the spirit of service characteristic of Afro-American clubs.

---

* "Child Saving in Alabama," *Colored American Magazine* 14, no. 1 (January 1908): 48–51.

1. Dr. Thomas Hunt Stucky (1859–1917), a Louisville, Kentucky, surgeon and advocate for women's health.

2. The Sojourner Truth Club is named after Sojourner Truth (1799–1883), black anti-slavery lecturer and women's rights activist. The club was devoted to the intellectual and educational uplift of black women.

It may be interesting to your readers, however, to learn something of a work which has been undertaken by the Alabama State Federation of Colored Women's Clubs. This is a reform school for wayward boys. This movement originated ten years ago with a little band of women under the gentle leadership of Miss Anna Duncan,[3] until her death a teacher in the Montgomery public schools. Meetings were held from house to house and plans discussed for saving the youth. The hearts of these mothers and daughters ached over the boys of tender age who, convicted of petty misdemeanors, were sent to penitentiaries and mines, to be herded with hardened and contaminating criminals.

As club life grew and strengthened in Alabama, and a State Federation was formed, the movers of the reformatory idea, recognizing the magnitude of their undertaking, urged its adoption by the state organization. Then followed years of planning, of educating public sentiment, and of more or less strenuous efforts to raise money and to realize the hope of a Reform School. At one time a gift of land was accepted, but the land was found to be encumbered and a legal deed could not be secured. This was a severe blow to this band of struggling women who had thought themselves so near the goal. Nothing daunted, however, they bravely faced the situation and started anew to raise funds for the purchase of land and the erection and equipment of a building. The clubs were asked to send fifty dollars each to the next annual convention. A few complied with this request; many did not succeed in raising the amount, and a few others volunteered the information that they had the money ready to hand in after something definite was done. In time this last class was convinced that it was their duty to turn over funds held for this purpose and so aid in making it possible to "do something"; more money was accumulated; and, at a memorable meeting held in Birmingham eighteen months ago, it was decided to buy twenty acres of land twelve miles from Montgomery. This location is not only central, but, being easily accessible to the capital, it was hoped that legislators might be induced to visit the institution and so be led to favor a State appropriation for its maintenance.

At the Selma meeting, a year later, a superintendent was employed. Already the executive board had appointed a building committee, and the work of building had begun. At this gathering, which was more than usually well attended, the greatest enthusiasm and unanimity of purpose prevailed. Most of the clubs had met all the requirements of the State organization. Some had done more than was asked of them. The Gulf City Woman's Club brought in $100. Ministers and other leading men in attendance on the meeting expressed gratification at the progress the cause was making, and promised hearty co-operation.

3. Anna Duncan served as the first president of Alabama's State Federation of Colored Women's Clubs from 1899–1901 (Wesley, *The History of the National Association*, 262, 280).

On August 18, the reformatory was opened. The cottage was still unfinished and the most scanty furnishings were on hand. Judge Feagin,[4] of Birmingham, who has shown a marked interest in the salvation of the Negro boy, had written urgently, asking that a number of boys brought before his court be accepted as inmates of the school. If not taken promptly, they would have to be sent to the penitentiary.

So the superintendent was authorized to go for them, and he brought them home to Mt. Meigs. Home![5]—poor little outcasts, chained, rebellious, terror-stricken, the word had no meaning nor charm for them. No one would have dreamed then of the change which a few months of kind and humane treatment would make in their appearance, as well as in their demeanor.

The home or school, to which these boys were taken and in which twenty boys now live with Superintendent Tyrrel, is a five-room cottage, painted white, with green blinds set in a clearing and surrounded by a thick grove which, when I saw it on Thanksgiving Day was ablaze with glory, of autumn tints. Like most Southern cottages, it has a hall running through the house. The back part of this hall is separated from the front part by a screened door, and is used as a dining-room and a sitting-room. There are front and back galleries, the back gallery being latticed and having a door that is furnished with lock and key. Here the boys may sit or play on warm evenings. The rooms are not yet fully furnished, but the boys have pretty white iron bedsteads and are supplied with clean and comfortable, though coarse, bedding. Superintendent Tyrrell kindly furnished his own room.

The superintendent is a man who has had unusual advantages of education and travel, yet he is eminently practical and makes no odds of doing and teaching the most common kinds of labor. He has had experience in this sort of work, having been connected with a reform institution in Virginia before coming to this State. His remarkable success in dealing with boys was strikingly demonstrated during the few months he filled a temporary vacancy in the Mt. Meigs' Village School, a Hampton offshoot in this vicinity.

The boys in the reformatory were committed by Alabama courts, most of them from the court presided over by Judge Feagan, who has been mentioned already. At its last sitting the Alabama Legislature repealed the Juvenile Court Law, on the grounds that the ends of justice were defeated by the prevalence of lying in connection with the age of the youthful law-breaker. At the discretion of the court, however, boys may be sent to a reform school, if there is such a place to receive them. At East Lake, near Birmingham, there is a commodious and well-

4. The original incorrectly reads "Feagan." Noah B. Feagin (1843–1920) served as judge on the Jefferson County Inferior Criminal Court in Birmingham, Alabama (Owen, *Alabama Official and Statistical Register 1915*, 565–66).

5. Mt. Meigs Home, also known as Mt. Meigs Village School (1890s–1919), was started by concerned mothers and by an understanding criminal court judge.

appointed reform school for white boys. At the last meeting of the Legislature $50,000 was appropriated to this institution. No provision is made for colored boys. Leading white men, members of the last legislature, when approached on this subject by representatives from the State Federation, told the women that there was too much legislation at this session to give the matter attention, but that they would certainly give it support at the next session—four years hence.

In the meantime the cottage is filled to its utmost capacity, these children to remain there until reformed, or until grown; then passing into homes or into the great world of employment, they will make way for other unfortunate waifs. Oh, happy fate for these ill-starved little ones! Saved from the slavery of an iniquitous prison system, they are busy, happy, loving and being loved; with God's blue sky above their heads, the fields and woods about them, and the glad voices of nature in their ears. There are so many things they have to be taught—to be clean, decent, self-respecting, regardful of the rights of others, diligent in study, faithful in the performance of tasks; even some things that most of us seem to breathe in, not knowing when or how we learn them.

"Do you know anything about God, son?" a little fellow was asked.

"Yas, Marse; he is a big white man who lives up North and sot the nigger free!"

It is pleasant to be able to record that these children already show signs of improvement. There are but few attempts to run away. They respond readily to kindness and are quick to take on the ways of civilized life. Some of them may be trusted, even, to do errands at the village store, "a good piece" away from the school, to use the country vernacular. The superintendent's methods of management place[6] responsibility upon a boy as soon as there are encouraging signs, and the more trustworthy boys help in the care and training of the others. They like to have visitors and enjoy the talks and songs that sometimes mark the occasion. They know some jubilee songs and sing them with great gusto, led by one of their number, who seems to have the spirit of leadership as well as of music. When an attempt was made by a recent visitor to teach them the "Glory Song," they showed the usual race readiness in "catching on" to new tunes.

The need of such an institution is generally conceded, and this effort on the part of the womanhood of the state meets with approval from all classes. The Journal, the leading evening daily of Montgomery, in a recent issue quoted lengthily from an interview with the superintendent and said, "The institution is doing a noble work," The school has won the good opinion of the citizens of Mt. Meigs, although at first there were protests against its being located there. In four years the Legislature reassembles. Then we trust that an appropriation will be made, so that the work may be enlarged and placed on a stable foundation. In the meantime our women, supported by loyal husbands and fathers and brothers, must carry this load.

6. The original reads "places."

Four Years' Growth

JOSEPHINE T. WASHINGTON

Chairman Executive Board

To those acquainted with the inception of the reformatory idea among our women in Alabama and who have watched its growth from year to year, it is particularly interesting at this time to take a retrospect of the movement.

The cause received a fresh impetus in the Mobile meeting of 1904. Probably this was due, in large measure, to the fact that in this meeting decisive steps were taken towards the establishment of the long-talked of Reformatory. The four or five years antedating this period had been given to creating sentiment in favor of the undertaking and raising funds in order to make a beginning. Necessary foundation work, to be sure, but not likely to arouse the enthusiasm won by a practical application of theories. In the Mobile meeting, it was voted to begin the operation of a reformatory on the tract of land near Tuscaloosa, previously offered for this purpose by Mr. Samuel Dailey, a colored farmer of that locality.

Four Clubs met the appeal made the year before that a donation of fifty dollars be made towards the erection of a building. These Clubs were the Sojourner Truth Club, Montgomery; the Married Ladies Social, Selma; the Sojourner Truth Club, Birmingham; and the 20th Century Club, Mobile, the last-named giving twenty-five dollars beyond the sum asked. Several other Clubs made the fifty-dollar donation later.

The following officers were elected: Mrs. A. P. Kingston, President; Miss Cornelia Bowen, first Vice-President; Mrs. L. B. Bailey, Second Vice-President; Mrs. R. S. Caldwell, Recording Secretary; Mrs. F. E. Morin, Corresponding Secretary; Mrs. L. B. Dungee, State Organizer; Mrs. Lena Hadnott, Treasurer, and Mrs. J. T. Washington, Chairman Executive Board.

These officers accepted their positions with the understanding that the work of rescuing our boys from the criminal courts would begin at once under the auspices of the Federation.

Untoward developments, however, prevented the carrying out of this purpose. At the Greenville meeting the following year the Executive Board reported that at a called meeting held, Dec. 28th, in Montgomery, steps had been taken

---

* "Four Years' Growth," *Colored Alabamian* 2, no. 21 (25 July 1908): 2–3.

to have the title to the Dailey property examined, and that as a result of said investigation it had been ascertained that the land donated the Federation by Mr. Dailey was encumbered. The Federation being without land, a committee was recommended to advertise that a location for the Reformatory was being sought and that offers were invited from any community desiring the Reformatory.

This meeting was presided over by the Vice-President, Miss Cornelia Bowen, who managed the business with skill and showed such marked ability as a leader that all eyes turned to her as the natural successor to the president, Mrs. Kingston, who was incapacitated by illness. A telegram of sympathy was sent the president and words of greeting were received from her.

Trustees were elected as follows, for six years: Miss Cornelia Bowen, Mesdames J. T. Washington, E. J. Penny; four years, Mrs. R. T. Pollard; two years, Mrs. R. S. Caldwell. Miss Bowen was elected chairman of the Trustee Board.

It was decided by motion that the monies of the Federation be deposited in the Penny Savings Bank of Birmingham.[1]

In this meeting, as in others, the trend of the subjects discussed was the saving of childhood, the sanctity of the home, and the elevation of race standards.

Among the excellent thoughts presented in a paper on "Home Training for Girls," by Mrs. L. R. Burwell,[2] were these: "A well-trained girl is the result of a well-trained home. If the home training is not what it should be, the school room can do but little. The gentle graces of the mother live in her daughter long after her head lies pillowed in the dust."

Mrs. R. B. Hudson, in a helpful paper on "Housekeeping and Home-making" said: "Mothers of today make a great mistake in doing all the work and allowing the girls to go free. At the end of school-days girls should be made to feel that they should begin a new school study. Incompetency in housekeeping is the cause of failure in many young housewives."

Mrs. S. H. Wright sounded a note of warning, as well as a call to service, when she said: "While the work needs woman, let her guard against the neglected home."

Miss S. C. V. Foster read the report of the President as delegate to the National Association of Colored Women's Clubs, which met in St. Louis in 1904. This newly installed president, Miss Bowen, was elected to represent the Alabama State Federation at the next meeting of the National, to be held in Detroit, in 1906.

1. Reverend William Reuben Pettiford founded the Penny Savings Bank of Birmingham (1890–1915). It was the first bank that blacks owned and operated in Alabama ("Penny Savings Bank of Alabama," *The Encyclopedia of Alabama*, 2012).

2. Luvenia R. Burwell served as president of National Association of Colored Women's Clubs from 1918 to 1919 (Wesley, *The History of the National Association of Colored Women's Clubs*, 262).

The next State meeting was held in Birmingham and was largely attended. Much interest was manifested on the part of citizens, leading ministers and other prominent citizens expressed approval of the women's plans and promised support. The Federation had the privilege of being addressed by Mrs. R. D. Johnston, president and founder of the Reformatory for white boys. Mrs. Johnston expressed her pleasure at the ability, displayed by the members of the Federation in the proceedings which she had witnessed and gave very valuable information relative to the establishment of the institution planned. Judge Feagan, of the Jefferson County criminal court, pledged his support in the effort to save youthful Negro[3] law-breakers from the penitentiary.

In this convention Miss M. A. Jenkins, of Montgomery, was made corresponding secretary and brought to the work the zeal, originality, and devotion to duty for which this young woman is known.

The Federation accepted the recommendation of the board that twenty acres of land, located at Mt. Meigs and offered at twenty-five dollars an acre, be purchased as a site for the Reformatory, the understanding being that more ground could be purchased when desired.

The Birmingham meeting closed with a balance in the treasury of $686.89.

The next year's meeting in Selma was attended by fifty-five delegates, representing forty-eight clubs, and approximately eight hundred club women,— showing a decided gain during the year.

The corresponding secretary who, on March 1, 1907, had been given credentials as financial agent, made an excellent report, showing more than three hundred dollars raised since her appointment, much of this amount was raised through mass meetings in Montgomery, Birmingham, Talladega, and other places, in which the Secretary was ably assisted by the President and the Vice-President-at-large, Mrs. Booker T. Washington and others.

We quote the following from the report of the Committee on Resolutions, showing how near to the hearts of these club-women lay the interest of the child: "Be it resolved, That we pledge ourselves anew to the work of child saving, realizing that in our young lies the hope of the race, and that when we save the boy or girl of today, we save the man or the woman of tomorrow.["]

A donation of ten dollars from the girls of the Clioian Society of the State Normal School, located in Montgomery, was noted with special pleasure as the beginning of a movement to arouse among the young people an interest in the Reformatory. Another special donation was five dollars from the Tuskegee Alumni Association of Montgomery.

Among the resolutions was the following reference to one universally loved and now absent in the Spirit World: "Resolved, That as we rejoice over these energetic workers, like busy harvesters amid the golden grain, our tender rever-

3. The original reads "negro."

ent thought goes out to those who have laid aside the finished sheaf, numbered among whom is Miss S. C. V. Foster, whose gentle, gracious spirit will be ever an inspiration, though her bodily presence is with us no more."

The Selma session was, from all standpoints, one of the best in the history of the Federation and a fitting forerunner to the splendid convention just closed in Montgomery. Between these two gatherings, however, was a long and eventful year, a year which meant not only strenuous efforts on the part of the Clubs but much anxious thought for those in positions of responsibility.

According to contract with Mr. Jas. Puckett, of Mt. Meigs, a cottage of five rooms was erected at a cost of $1,178. Owing to an urgent call from Judge Feagan, the Reformatory was opened August 18th, prior to the completion of the building. Special acknowledgment is due the people at Mt. Meigs for kindnesses begun in those early days and continued to the present time. Many a good wife in the Mt. Meigs community has helped in some way to "mother" the little stray waifs cast upon our shores, and many a kind-hearted farmer has hailed the Reformatory wagon and added to its load a part of the produce from his own garden. Donations of quilts, spreads, sheets, pillow cases, towels and other household necessities came in from Clubs and friendly individuals. Other furnishings were bought as speedily as means permitted; and gradually the little white cottage, glistening in the sunshine, took on somewhat of the appearance and the atmosphere of a home.

When the Board met in December, 1907, the institution was put upon a more business-like basis by the appointment of a committee of management, whose duties, as outlined by the Executive Board, comprise a general supervision of the affairs of the Home, purchasing supplies, including the making of bills in the name of the State Federation, and the answering of emergency calls for boys. This committee consists of Miss Bowen, President; Miss M. A. Jenkins, Corresponding Secretary; Mrs. S. H. Wright, member of Board of Montgomery county; Mrs. J. T. Washington, Chairman Executive Board; with Mrs. L. B. Dungee as Chairman. The Board considered itself fortunate in securing the services in this capacity of Mrs. Dungee, who to an attractive personality which wins friends for the work adds a fine enthusiasm and untiring industry in the cause she has espoused.

But troublous times were ahead of the committee. Not one of the number will ever forget the long, drawn-out meetings and the care-freighted consultations of those days. The committee was fortunate in having in one of its meetings of most serious importance the presence and advice of Mrs. Booker T. Washington, who, as Vice-President-at-large, came from Tuskegee to help at a time when help was most needed.

At a call meeting of the executive board, held March 14, the resignation of Superintendent Tyrrell was accepted. Mr. Wm. D. Hargwood, a graduate of

Hampton [and] a former employee of the Calhoun School, was elected to the position made vacant.

Mr. Hargwood had before him a particularly difficult task, entering, as he did, upon the management of more than a score of wayward boys, all of whom regarded him with feelings of distrust. At the solicitation of the chairman, a generous spirited young friend went out from his Montgomery home to give a week's help to the new Superintendent. The temporary services of Miss Anna Davis, of Tuskegee, were secured as Matron. Living though she does in a neighbor's home and coming out daily to help as she can, her influence over the boys has been noticeably refining.

The Committee of Management reports a satisfactory condition of affairs in the Home and considerable reduction of expenses.

The boys have nearly paid for a cow, out of their earnings. They have also bought a pig, purchased shoes for themselves, and raised a large percent of the vegetables used. This relief has left the Committee freer to cope with the debts made by the former superintendent.

The committee feels grateful to the Anna M. Duncan Club and the Sojourner Truth Club of Montgomery for loans made at this embarrassing juncture. Creditors, in general, agreed to wait for a full settlement till after the July meeting of the Federation; and Mr. Tulane, Montgomery's leading Colored grocer, went on supplying goods at the order of the committee, with the most undisturbed certainty.

The Montgomery session of the Federation, just closed, brought in collections amounting to $1,078.92. All debts have been paid and we have a few hundred dollars in the treasury. The people have responded with open hearts and hands to the call for help. Had it been otherwise, our clubs could never have made the splendid reports that they did make. The Anna M. Duncan Club reported $222.25; the 20th Century Club of Mobile $185.00. Other organizations have given out of generous hearts all that their opportunities permitted. Individual friends have lightened the load for the committee by helpful service of various kinds, through all the months since this work began. Mr. P. W. Ross interested others to unite with him in giving a mule—a most valuable addition to our farm possessions. Prof. Wm. Pickens[4] has turned hearts to this call by his eloquent appeals. The writer remembers one especially touching and convincing at the State Teacher's meeting in Tuscaloosa. President Pollard, of Selma University, and Hon. C. F. Johnson of insurance fame left their business interest and came to Montgomery to spend a long afternoon in a Board meeting, in conference with our women from various parts of the state. These members

4. William Pickens (1881–1954), South Carolina native, founding member and field secretary of the NAACP. In 1942, the House Un-American Activities Committee cited him as subversive (Cobb, "Pickens, William," 338–40).

of the Advisory Board and other leading men of both races, who compose this body, stand ready to help.

Let every individual who reads this record resolve to do the same.

We need more room at the Reformatory; more room for the children already there; and room for those who ought to come.

When the Legislature meets, we hope for State aid. Now we are wholly dependent[5] upon our own efforts. What will you give of money, of materials, of labor, of influence?

---

5. The original reads "dependnt."

12th Annual Meeting of the State Federation of Colored Women's Clubs

JOSEPHINE T. WASHINGTON

The State Federation of Colored Women's Clubs held its twelfth annual session at Auburn and at Opelika July 3, 4, 5, and 6.

The Federation opened with a mass meeting in Auburn which was attended by a goodly number of delegates and citizens, despite wet weather and muddy streets. The church was beautifully decorated with flowers and potted plants, and these breathed their welcome and emphasized the cordial greeting extended by speakers appointed to represent the churches, the clubs, and the citizens.

The main feature of this meeting was a symposium on "Our Work," discussed under the heads: "Its Aims," "Its Workers," "Its Accomplishments" and "Its Needs" by Mrs. M. Jenkins-Lewis, of Montgomery, Miss Georgia Washington, of St. Meigs, Mrs. Beatrice Campbell, of Montgomery and Prof. Silsby[1] of Talladega College. In presenting the needs of the work, Prof. Silsby dwelt less on the need of more money, more land, more buildings, and more and better furnishings than on the need of the constant cultivation of a prayerful, earnest and consecrated spirit on the part of the workers.

The meetings held in Opelika began on Monday morning with an early session of the executive board. They closed on Wednesday with the last session of the board, adjourning in time to permit the delegates to leave on afternoon trains for home.

The delegates showed the deepest interest in their work. Coming to the meetings in rain as well as in sunshine, and remaining in session practically all day with but a brief intermission for dinner. With commendable zeal and a large measure of wisdom, they discussed questions relating to their work, heard reports and outlined plans for future action.

The evening sessions were given over to listening to addresses, prominent

---

* "12th Annual Meeting of the State Federation of Women's Clubs," *Colored Alabamian* 4, no. 20 (9 July 1910): 1.

1. Edwin Chalmers Silsby (1851–1922), born in Siam. He served as secretary-treasurer of Talladega College (1886–1907), and then as dean, register and professor (1907–13) ("To Edwin Chalmers Silsby," 69).

among which was that delivered by Prof. William Pickens on Tuesday night. An interesting feature of the last day's meeting was a talk by Mrs. Booker T. Washington,[2] who spoke eloquently on the duty of the state organization to the national body, represented by the national association of Colored Women's Clubs.

Prof. Silsby of Talladega College and Major Ramsey[3] of Tuskegee, were present in the business sessions and with Prof. Pickens and Rev. C. J. Davis, of Mt. Meigs, all members of the Advisory Board rendered valuable series.

The reports from clubs showed an interesting variety of philanthropic effort. Care is given to the sick and needy, children are kept in school, pure literature is circulated, prisons are visited, juvenile criminals rescued, and helping hands held out in all directions. Some attention is also given to self-culture, many of the clubs reporting literary exercises as a regular feature of their meetings.

A message from the Department of Literature of the National Association, which is presided over by an Alabama woman, was among the leaflets given out to the delegates.

The keynote of the Federation, however and the center of interest for every worker, was the Reformatory. The cash contributions for this cause amounted to one thousand one hundred and two dollars and thirty-four cents. This means the amount raised in this Auburn-Opelika meeting, and does not include either donations made during the year by clubs, individuals, or the payment of the salary of one teacher by the Jeanes Fund, a gift secured through the influence of our active Vice-President at large, Mrs. Booker T. Washington.

The banner was awarded to the Tuskegee Woman's Club, which brought in the largest amount, two hundred and fifty dollars. The Mobile club came next, the Twentieth Century League giving one hundred and seventy-five dollars. The Anna M. Duncan Club[4] of Montgomery came close behind the Mobile club, both of these clubs making a remarkably good showing when it is remembered that the president of each has suffered from extended illness, covering many months of the past year. Large donations came from individual clubs in Selma, Birmingham and other places, and while the Federation was thankful for the splendid strength and generosity of these favored organizations, the smaller gifts made with the full heart and in the Christ spirit were as gratefully received.

2. Mrs. Margaret Murray Washington (1865–1925), third wife of Booker T. Washington, served as president of the National Association of Colored Women (1912–16) and president of the Alabama Association of Women's Clubs (1919–25) (Rief, "Washington, Margaret Murray," 327).

3. Julius B. Ramsey was commandant and strict disciplinarian at Tuskegee in 1915 (Harlan and Smock, eds., *The Booker T. Washington Papers*, 3:350).

4. Anna Duncan Club was established as a memorial to Anna Duncan, first president of the Alabama Association of Colored Women's Clubs (Wesley, *The History of the National Association of Colored Women's Clubs*, 262).

A very interesting report was made by the chairman of the committee of management Mrs. L. B. Dungee.[5] This report showed that there are thirty-one boys in the Reformatory at this time, and that during the past year the boys have earned one hundred and seventy-eight dollars toward their own support.

Steps were taken looking to the circulating of a petition setting forth the claims of this work and asking for endorsement from influential white citizens in our effort to secure an appropriation from the legislature.

A touching little incident was the recital of the story of the "Baby Fund," by the corresponding secretary, Mrs. M. Jenkins-Lewis, who investing in various ways the handful of pennies given by a mother from the bank of her dead child, has in the past two years raised fifty dollars.

The Federation song, "Mother Alabama," written by a member of the Federation,[6] and formally adopted as the rallying song of the club women of Alabama, was sung for the first time in this meeting.

The president's annual address was an inspiring call to undertake great things, and aroused great enthusiasm.

With but few exceptions the old officers were reelected. One important change was the securing of Miss. Sarah Hunt of Tuskegee, as state organizer. Miss Hunt has already begun to plan her work, and gives promise of being a most capable officer. It is hoped that interested persons in communities having no clubs or needing to be aroused to renewed club activity, will write to Miss Hunt and make arrangements for a visit from her.

Resolutions expressing gratitude for the work the women have been enabled to accomplish and calling upon friends everywhere for even greater loyalty in the year before us, were read at the closing session. Thanks were also expressed for the kindly treatment given the visitors in the towns of Auburn and of Opelika.

The place of meeting is to be announced later.

So closed the twelfth year of the federated movement among the colored club women of Alabama, and the third year of the maintenance of the reformatory for our wayward boys in this State.

May the movement spread and the work progress until all over the land our people are united in the effort to save the youth and redeem the race from the reign of ignorance and of crime.

---

5. Lillian Brewster Dungee (1868–1939) was the first black to be appointed to the court of Domestic Relations in Montgomery, Alabama (ibid., 282).

6. Josephine Turpin Washington wrote the lyrics to "Mother Alabama," the song for the Alabama State Federation of Colored Women's Clubs (see appendix A).

A Card—To the Women's Clubs of Alabama

JOS. T. WASHINGTON

Chrmn. Ex. Bd. State Fed.

Beginning with Saturday, August 31, *The Colored Alabamian* will contain a State Federation Department. This new feature is the outcome of action taken at the last session of the Executive Board of the State Federation of Women's Clubs, held in Opelika, July 3–6. In this meeting, a committee consisting of Mesdames L. B. Dungee and M. Jenkins-Lewis, was appointed to confer with Rev. R. C. Judkins,[1] relative to securing space in his paper. The result of the interview is that Rev. Judkins gives a column a month to the Federation.

The Federation Department will be conducted by Mrs. Josephine T. Washington, chairman of the Executive Board, and will be devoted to the interests of the clubs composing the Federation, especially to the Federation's chief object, the maintenance of the Reformatory for Negro Youth. Mrs. Washington will be assisted by Miss Etta B. Smyly, of Montgomery. Clubs are invited to contribute news items, through their duly elected reporters, or through any other member in good and regular standing. Liberty must be allowed the editor, however to abridge or to modify in any other way, articles too lengthy, or for any other reason deemed unsuitable. Information of what is going on in the clubs is greatly desired, however, and will be gratefully received and used as far as practical.

The club women of Alabama are greatly indebted to Rev. Judkins for the generosity which prompted him to refuse to make any charge for the use of a monthly column in his paper, more than ever we should rally to The Colored Alabamian. Send in your subscription to the paper, and notes of your club work to the editor of the Federation Department. The fourth column of the front page will be ours the last Saturday of every month. Help to make the Department interesting and pay for the paper in which it appears.

Yours for "Lifting as we climb."

* "A Card—To the Women's Clubs of Alabama," *Colored Alabamian* 4, no. 23 (30 July 1910): 1.

1. Reverend Robert Chapman Judkins (1868–1919) pastored Dexter Avenue Baptist Church in Montgomery, Alabama, and founded and published a weekly newspaper, the *Colored Alabamian,* in his home (Robertson, *Fighting the Good Fight,* chap. 2).

APPENDICES

APPENDIX A

Alabama Federation of Colored Women's Clubs Association Song: "Mother Alabama"

JOSEPHINE T. WASHINGTON

Sung to the tune of "Onward Christian Soldiers"

Mother Alabama	Mother Alabama
Saving Wayward Ones—	Great in thought and deed
May thine arms grow stronger	As we hear the summons
With successive suns	So thy daughters heed
Christ, whose love for children	One in faith and purpose
Drew them to His Knee	Firmly now we stand;
Loves them still and saves them	Joined to save the children
Through His keeping thee.	Pledging heart and hand.

CHORUS
Mother Alabama
Saving wayward ones—
May thine arms grow stronger
With successive suns.

---

* Qtd. in Charles Harris Wesley, *The History of the National Association of Colored Women's Clubs* (Washington, D.C.: National Association of Colored Women's Clubs, 1984).

APPENDIX B

Cedar Hill Saved

JOSEPHINE T. WASHINGTON

Dedicated to the National Association of Colored Women's Clubs

Above Potomac's rhythmic flow
    To Cedar Hill I go;
Its charm o'er sense and spirit steals,
And as of yore appeals
In cadence sweet and low.

Once lived the hero of his race,
Within this sacred place;
        The magic of his presence still
        The old home seems to fill,
And mem'ry paints his face.

Far famed the spot where Douglass dwelt,
Here pilgrims oft have knelt
        In homage to his noble fame,
        With blessings on his name,
And gratitude heart-felt.

And now before a double shrine,
In praises we combine
        With Douglass, great and wise and good,
        Devoted womanhood—
'Round both our garlands twine.

* "Cedar Hill Saved," *Crisis* 17, no. 4 (February 1919): 179.

In union strong throughout the land,
A consecrated band,
    A service measureless they wrought
    When Cedar Hill they bought
And saved from alien hand.

Fear not, faint not, O sable race!
The truth naught can efface
    Is writ on ev'ry passing breeze;
    With women such as these
Our fight is won a-pace.

APPENDIX C

Out Doors in Summer

"JOYCE"

The world is always in its prime. It is always beautiful, glowing, soul inspiring; as our poet Longfellow happily expressed it—"With what a glory comes and goes the year!"[1]

Each season possesses its own delights and the share of discomforts it must necessarily bring, to give a touch of reality to the fact that we live on a planet where "life is but an empty dream."[2] Well might one be tempted to exclaim with the boy in the story with a moral: "I wish it were always"—whatever it is! "Whatever it is, is right."[3]

Surely whatever *God* ordains is right. No other climate or season would prove us advantageous and agreeable as that which is so much complained of as "too hot," "too cold," "too wet," "too dry."

The "heated term" has now arrived when devotees of Fashion must needs betake themselves to the springs, the mountains, or the seaside, where society leaders, as mute advertisers of the pecuniary prosperity of their masculine relations, flash their diamonds at midnight ball and sweep their silken trains through carpeted halls. All who fain would follow in the wake of these belles do not spend the "season" in a like manner. Ah! Reader, are you not acquainted with the novel method adopted by modern, necessity-made economists? Darken the front parlors and chambers, by tightly closed doors and hermetically-sealed shutters; close the piano; hush the sound of merriment; lounge around in slippers, easy wrappers and favorite curl-papers, and order the polite waiting-maid to announce to the former visitor that "madam is out of town."

Do you really want to spend your summer vacation where you can rest and enjoy yourself, where you can for a time be as free and indolent, and happy as a

---

* "Out Doors in Summer," *People's Advocate* (Washington, D.C.), 21 August 1880, 1.

1. Longfellow, "Autumn," 1:13, stanza 1. Longfellow's line reads, "[With] what a glory comes and [goes] the year!"

2. Longfellow, "A Psalm of Life," 1:6, stanza 1.

3. Pope, "Essay on Man, Epistle 1," 53. Pope's line reads, "Whatever is, is right."

non-society man may wish to be? Then shun these popular resorts, whose inmates one could easily believe exist on a lavish allowance or undiluted oxygen; and seek some sequestered nook and rural scenes. Here, free from the "duties we owe to our fellow beings"[4]—of the club and parlor, we wander at will through fields of ripening grain, receiving a lesson from the honest toil and simple content of the farmer and his workmen; down lanes where gleams of sunny rays lead to unknown brightness; into deep, cool woods with their wealth of spreading foliage.

The caroling of birds in neighboring groves is a *reveille* that might arrest the listlessness of a bead counting devotee, and inspire him with a gush of real feeling, a strain breathing praise to the Giver of all good. Shut in the shade from homes and houses, fields and fallows beyond, we seem drawn forth by a protecting Hand for communion with nature in one of her brightest moods. The sun shines through on patches of fresh, damp moss, like gleams of gold on an emerald sea; and, glancing aside, its brightness makes rainbows on tiny drops of dew on tender blades of grass. Its light reveals dainty coverlets of spider's web, spread on glossy, green leaves, clinging caressingly as though both to cease to beautify that which is so charmingly fairylike without them.

Through these vast repositories of plants and flowers, botanists love to wander where green things innumerable grow, and great banks of violets rear their modest bloom in hues of Sun and sky. Wordsworth mentions;

> "A violet, by a mossy stone
> Half hidden from the eye,
> Fair as a star when only one
> Is shining in the sky."[5]

Daisies with pure white petals encircling a heart of gold, throng one's pathway and cause the feet to turn instinctively aside, dreading to crush the little life from so beauteous a ting. Ivy blossoms, with a pink like the faint flush of a morning sky, draw the eyes to their height; honeysuckles scent the air with delicious fragrance; and, towering above all these, are the mighty forest trees, among which ranks conspicuously[6] the oak, that "monarch of the wood"—so strong, so mighty, so high, like noble men among the nations. Here one great oak, on the side of a ravine, breasts the storms with half of its roots bare and brown, and exposed on the rocky steep, but, on the other side, the vital portion dives deep down into the earth and draws forth the sustenance needed, like dutiful children recompensing the neglect of their wayward brothers. The trunk of another, rugged and worn and dead, serves as a hive for busy bees that

4. Hoyt, "The Prayer-Meeting Service," 447.
5. Wordsworth, "She Dwelt among the Untrodden Ways," 1:250, stanza 2.
6. The original reads "conspicously."

"gather honey all the day from every opening flower."[7] Insects of woody habitation, intent on duties of the day, dart by with noisy buzz. Butterflies lazily flash their wings of brilliant colors; and, after draughts of dew-distilled nectar from fragrant flowers, the throats[8] of warbling songsters seem in sweetest tune. It is a pretty fancy of an American poetess that butterflies are disembodied spirits of early springtime flowers.

Crashing the music, making twigs under foot, as we approached the brook we startle the timid squirrel that had dropped[9] its pretty head to drink. And, with a slight shade of disappointment, we watch it scamper away into the thickest coverts. What melody lives in the rippling waters! What beauty in the scene of white stones underlying and with what never ceasing admiration we note the silver gleaming fish dart in the current.

> "And I have a notion
> All beautiful motion
> Itself a sweet melody makes."[10]

After a walk amid such surroundings, the city boarder might return to his rural residence, and devour his morning repast of snowy rolls and golden butter and delicious milk with a hearty appreciation of the culinary skill and a self-satisfied assurance of the wisdom of his morning occupation.

> "Nature never did betray
> The heart that loved her. 'Tis her privilege
> Through all the years of all this our life, to lead
> From joy to joy! for she can so inform
>   That is within us, so impress
> With quietness[11] and beauty and so feed
> With lofty thoughts, that neither evil tongues,
> Rash judgements, nor the sneer of selfish men,
> Nor greetings where no kindness is, nor all
> The dreary intercourse of daily life
> Shall e'er prevail against us, to disturb
> Our cheerful faith that all which we behold
>   Is full of blessings.[12]

7. Watts, "Song XX: Against Idleness and Mischief," stanza 1, lines 3–4, p. 65. Watts's line reads, "[And] gather honey all the day / From every opening flower!"

8. The original reads "the the throats."

9. The original reads "drooped."

10. Tennyson, "The Beautiful Snow," 202.

11. The original reads "quiless."

12. Wordsworth, "Lines, Composed a Few Miles above Tintern Abbey," 2:164.

The Origin and Progress
of the English Language

JOSEPHINE J. TURPIN

All the languages of Europe were originally one. This they evince by similarity of structure and the common possession of certain fundamental principles. We have reason to believe that ages ago, in the prehistoric period, these now widely varying tongues were identically the same, and that the peoples now using them once dwelt together in pastoral tents, a simple, harmonious state. The earliest name by which this primitive European speech is known is Aryan or Indo-European, a name indicative of the region whence it sprung. Branching off, various tribes left their native home and settled throughout Europe. Where they went and where they settled and grew, so likewise did the language; and in consequence of the changes brought about by different surroundings, different modes of living, different kinds of influence, there arose different dialects of the language, in which the changes became so great, as years went by, as to form practically new languages.

Of this species is the English language. Though now spoken in every part of the world, its history is confined to Great Britain. We hear first of this island from Julius Caesar,[1] who made an invasion into it fifty-five years before Christ. The inhabitants were a wild and barbarous people called Celts. Their language was, however, not the English, but simply one of the ingredients—and, withal, one of secondary importance—which went to make up this great speech. The English is a composite tongue. It is formed by the blending of many tongues. Its history may be said properly to begin with the date of the entrance into Britain of the Germanic hordes. These tribes, designated by the common term Anglo Saxon, conquered and subdued the half-Romanized Britons, introducing their customs and giving prevalence to their own language. This tongue, which now became the ruling one of the island, was akin to modern Dutch. Undergoing little alteration, save the accession of a small number of Celtic words chiefly the names of rivers and towns, it held, for nearly six centuries, undisputed sway in Britain.

---

* "The Origin and Progress of the English Language," *A.M.E. Church Review* 1, no. 1 (January 1884): 280–84.

1. Julius Caesar (100?–44 BC), Roman general and dictator.

But there came a change, and this began with the Battle of Hastings, Oct. 14, 1066. As the Anglo-Saxons had conquered the Celts, so in turn were they themselves conquered by the Normans. Linguistic supremacy is a natural attendant of political ascendancy. French became the language spoken at court, the language taught in the schools and used in all judicial proceedings. The common people clung to their native vernacular with the greatest tenacity. It was their speech; they knew no other, they wanted no other. Their allegiance saved it from absorption and preserved it from decay. The hostility between the dominant Norman and the fettered Briton was an effectual barrier to a commingling of tongues. We have here the strange spectacle of two languages, spoken in the same state and under the same government, each adhered to by its own particular class of followers, each remaining separate and distinct from the other, with no apparent probability of a union.

In the thirteenth century the Normans in England suffered a defeat whereby they lost all their French possessions. Excluded from France, the Norman felt himself no longer a foreigner in possession of English soil, but a citizen and a countryman. The recognition of a common interest bred sympathy and friendliness. A tendency towards an assimilation of languages manifested itself. This was further accelerated by the fact that the French spoken in England had, from various causes, become so corrupt and so unlike French as spoken in France, that it had grown to be an object of ridicule. Besides it was exceedingly awkward for the Norman lord to maintain those necessary relations and carry on that needed intercourse with the Saxon dependents without an acquaintance with the only tongue they understood. Then began that blending of languages which resulted in the gradual adoption, by all classes, of what afterwards came to be known as the English language.

The Anglo-Saxon of this period differed materially from that used before the Norman conquest. Anglo-Saxon was an inflected language. Like the Latin and the Greek it showed the relations of its words by a correspondence of form; it was in this unlike its English offspring, which by arrangement, auxiliaries, and particles, does the work of inflections. These inflections had not, however, remained undisturbed through all these years of French dominancy. There is a tendency in language to rid itself of inflections; and Anglo-Saxon had, in great measure, yielded to this tendency. Excluded from literature, it had no standard by which to regulate itself; confined to the common and ignorant classes, it had suffered all those mutilations, which are the results of the expediencies to which men resort for the saving of time and breath. The hitherto hostile languages began rapidly to coalesce. The groundwork was still Anglo-Saxon, it was the grammatical foundation upon which the new speech was built. The changes were mainly in the loss of flexible endings, a variation in pronunciation and spelling, and the introduction of many new words, principally French derivatives. Latin had, since the advent of the Christian missionaries in the sixth century, been the dialect of the church and of moral and religious instruction. Many Latinisms of this character were transferred into the new language.

There were, too, in common use a small number of Latin terms, which found their way into the speech in consequence of the Roman invasion and conquest. A greater profusion of French derivatives was accepted, and the new language gained much by incorporating into itself so much of the delicacy and refinement native to the Romance tongues. Law gave into the language many French terms; for until the middle of this century, all pleas made in court had been required to be in the speech of the Normans. Commerce led to the adoption of others, and still others were received through the sciences, for medicine, physics, geography, alchemy, astrology, all became known to the Saxons through French channels. Among the many changes of this period was the abandonment of grammatical gender, and the substitution of one corresponding to the natural distinction of sex.

The "Vision of Piers the Plowman"[2] was the first composition in which the English spirit and genius are distinctly perceptible. Three dialects of the language arose in the different localities; but that designated the midland dialect became, because of its adoption by Chaucer,[3] the speech of the English people. Chaucer was great benefactor of the language. His works gave to it a definite form and permanence, which it had not before possessed, and did much in the way of polishing, refining and spiritualizing expression.

The chief feature of Anglo-Saxon poetry was alliteration. The influence of Chaucer's example contributed largely to the important place rhythm and rhyme occupy in poetic composition. Wycliffe[4] did inestimable service in the establishment of a religious dialect, which with but slight changes has remained the same. The art of printing introduced into England in the latter part of the fifteenth century, stereotyped the language and rendered easier the universal adoption of a uniform standard of speech.

The War of the Roses brought immediate confusion into the language, but its final effects were beneficial. So also was it with the Reformation.

New ideas were forming in men's minds, new thoughts were struggling for utterance, new circumstances were developing; the natural consequence was that the language was enriched by many terms, embodying new and important significance.

The Elizabethan period, extending from 1580 to 1625, is pronounced by many the greatest in the history of the English language. It was a period of transition, a period of new ideas and new discoveries. In thirty years the language was almost

2. Protagonist in the alliterative poem, "The Vision of William Concerning Piers Plowman," attributed to William Langland.

3. Geoffrey Chaucer (1340–1400), English author of *The Canterbury Tales.*

4. John Wycliffe (1330–1380), authored the first complete English translation of the Bible from the Vulgate.

altogether refashioned and reorganized. Elizabeth[5] herself a scholar and a patron of learning, hers was pre-eminently an age of literature. Roger Ascham[6] was one of the founders of a cultivated English prose style; and Tyndale,[7] by his version of the Scriptures, did important linguistic service. This was the era in which appeared Sydney[8] of pure and simple style, Spencer[9] of fairy strains, Shakespeare[10] of immoral fame, Hooker,[11] Bacon[12] and Ben Johnson.[13]

It was, though, a period of marked irregularity in the formation of words and their combination into sentences. Men thought much of what they were to say, little of the manner of saying it. A critical age was later to rectify this.

The restoration of Charles II[14] to the throne caused the language to suffer under a pernicious influence. The evil doings countenanced by Charles and his followers, the low state of morals at court, caused many words suggestive of profane and vulgar meanings, to find their way into the vocabulary. In spite of the denigrating tendency of the times, Milton[15] sung his lofty verse and Bunyan[16] wrote in pure, sweet prose.

The critical age developed Pope,[17] Dryden,[18] Addison,[19] Bolingbroke,[20] Dr. Samuel Johnson.[21] A chaste and polished style was the desideratum, and the language lost the irregularities of Elizabeth's time. The age following this was characterized by a union of the genius and spirit of the creative era and the graces of the critical; the products of which union were Cowper,[22] Keats,[23] Shelley,[24] Byron,[25]

5. Queen Elizabeth (1533–1603), queen of England from 1558 to 1603.

6. Roger Ascham (1515–1568), tutor of Queen Elizabeth I.

7. William Tyndale (1494–1536), translator of the Bible.

8. Sir Philip Sidney (1554–1586), English poet and essayist.

9. Edmund Spenser (1552–1599), English poet and author of *The Faerie Queene.*

10. William Shakespeare (1564–1616), English poet and playwright.

11. Richard Hooker (1554–1600), English writer.

12. Francis Bacon (1561–1626), English essayist.

13. Ben Jonson (1572–1637), English playwright.

14. Charles II (1630–1685), king of England, Scotland, and Ireland (1660–85).

15. John Milton (1608–1674), English poet and author of *Paradise Lost.*

16. John Bunyan (1628–1688), English author of *Pilgrim's Progress.*

17. Alexander Pope (1688–1744), English poet.

18. John Dryden (1631–1700), poet laureate of England (1670–88).

19. Joseph Addison (1672–1719), English essayist and poet.

20. 1st Viscount Bolingbroke (1678–1751), English political writer.

21. Samuel Johnson (1709–1784), English critic and writer.

22. William Cowper (1731–1800), English poet.

23. John Keats (1795–1821), English Romantic poet.

24. Percy Bysshe Shelley (1792–1822), English Romantic poet.

25. George Gordon Byron (1788–1824), English poet.

Scott,[26] Moore,[27] Coleridge,[28] Campbell,[29] Wordsworth.[30] This period marks the ascendency of prose, to which species of literature De Quincy[31] and Macaulay[32] devoted their genius.

It is in the nature of language to undergo changes. No language spoken by a people, will remain stationary; it will grow as they grow, progress as they progress. The English language has undergone no material change since its style was determined by the later poets and great prose writers; its structure is fixed, its principles defined; but as thought progresses, discoveries are made, inventions are brought forward, modifications are necessarily made. Language is but the vehicle by which thought is conveyed, and new thoughts demand adequate expression.

English is surpassed by no tongue in the combination of those qualities which render a language an effective transmitter[33] of ideas. It possesses a vocabulary of 104,000 words, exclusive of provincial terms and local usages. It has a large number of synonyms, by means of which fine shades of thought may be expressed and accurate discrimination made. It has a dialect for common objects and feelings, composed mainly of Anglo-Saxon words; an ecclesiastic, drawn largely from the Latin; and scientific nomenclature, made up almost entirely of words of Greek origin. Each class of ideas may be give appropriate expression. The structure of sentences and the style may be varied by the use of Anglo-Saxon or Latin words. Deficiencies may be supplied by drawing from obsolete words, from classical sources, and from other living tongues.

No language is so widely spoken as is the English. What it will ultimately accomplish we cannot know. It will be neither stronger nor weaker than the men who use it. Language is but a sign, a symbol, a token, a representative of something which lies back of it. Representatives lose force when that represented has no existence. Upon the future of the English-speaking people, depends what the English language will be.

Howard University, Washington, D.C.

26. Sir Walter Scott (1771–1832), Scottish poet and novelist.

27. Thomas Moore (1779–1852), Irish poet.

28. Samuel Taylor Coleridge (1772–1834), English poet and critic.

29. Thomas Campbell (1777–1844), Scottish poet.

30. William Wordsworth (1770–1850), poet laureate of England (1843–50).

31. Thomas De Quincey (1785–1859), English essayist.

32. Thomas Babington Macaulay (1800–1859), English essayist and historian.

33. The original reads "transmuter."

What of the Children?

JOSEPHINE T. WASHINGTON

Victor Hugo called the nineteenth century "woman's century." The beginning of
the twentieth century, however, sees the fuller triumph of her cause.

Without doubt, the events of the Great War accelerated the movement in
behalf of equal rights. The nation needed its women in unusual ways. Loyally
they responded; they came; they *were seen;* they conquered. Their ability to fill
the positions men had filled was clearly demonstrated. A new status was won; a
new self-confidence grew in feminine consciousness.

From every walk in life came the army of women who had left their homes
to meet the crisis. Women whom no lesser motive would have taken from the
affairs of their own household; women whose financial circumstances were such
as to offer no temptation to go out to earn money; other women too, who had
felt the pinch of poverty, yet had never thought they had either strength or
skill for outside employment—all arranged matters at home as best they could,
found courage for unwonted tasks, and answered their country's call.

The question which these and other women are now facing is of a different
sort. What is to be their future relation to the world of work? Are they to find
their places in the home, or outside as well? For never can women escape altogether the claims of the home. The cord which binds them to the age-old institution may stretch, but it will not break. And herein lie some of the dangers of
the new order.

It is not the exactions of newly acquired citizenship which raises the question
of woman's relation to world affairs. The strictures of opponents to woman's
suffrage notwithstanding the obligations of citizenship require but a modicum
of time and energy. Reading and discussion in the family circle will keep any
woman at least fairly well posted on the issues of the day. And, to repeat a trite
illustration, a visit to the polls is as easily made as a visit to the store or the
home of a neighbor. When it comes to the question of positions which demand
too much of the housewife's time, it must be remembered that neither government nor corporation forces anybody to take office. It is accepted at one's own
option.

But public posts are not the only openings for women. They are finding their

* "What of the Children?" *A.M.E. Church Review* 39, no. 1 (July 1922): 8–10.

way into industry, business, and professions as never before. In many instances, successful men are pleased to see the clever woman filling a position commonly counted beyond her powers. Many welcome a woman's viewpoint where a few years ago, they would not have expected her to have an opinion.

As a writer in the *Atlantic Monthly* expresses it "To the woman of courage, capacity and training the world seems already a very open field. The pioneering has been done; the paths are broken in all directions, and a vast deal of work and money is going into the improvement of the roads." Woman is to "have a fair chance; a full, even share of all the education, all the power, all the good employments, and all the money that is in process of distribution." In the attainment of these rights Mr. George places "a good deal of reliance on the ennobling of the nature of the male," a process which, he says, is steadily going on. He thinks, too, that this new movement "should go no faster than women can be trained to meet the new expectations which are geared to it."

To quote further the same article "More education for girls, new employments, more pay, more independence, more freedom of action, half of what there is generally—seem to be prosperously on their way with the applause of the nations. Surely nobody can doubt that the present woman movement will go along as far as present conditions of human life can stand and will produce considerable changes."

Clearly, womanhood is coming into its own. But while the distance traveled may well evoke a thrill of pleasurable pride, it must be recognized that growing out of these new conditions are new dangers. Certainly such recognition does not imply regret for the old order of things. There can be no desire to have women retreat into the background from which they have emerged. That the new path may mean progress, however, it must be pursued with sanity and a thoughtful consideration of values. Walking with sure tread, women must not permit the breezes of a new-found freedom to sweep them off their feet.

Financial continuations do not always explain the unwillingness of women to relinquish positions held while the men were at war. Contributory causes were the lure of independence, the charm of varied experience, the gratification of using their talents with recognized success, the conviction that they were doing *something really worthwhile*.[1]

Aye, there's the rub—the belief that outside of the home is the work "worthwhile." Let women enter the world of competition if they must; even if they will. Let them do a necessary piece of work which appeals to them; let them give expression to every gift with which they have been endowed; let them, if need be, augment the family income by their daily earnings, but never let them choose the work of the world as *more worthwhile* than the duties of the home.

There is much in twentieth century living conditions to afford comparative

1. The original reads "worth while."

leisure to the childless married woman. The press-a-button and put-a-nickel[2]-in-the-slot existence we moderns lead is quite unlike the spinning and weaving days of our forebears. The present age is characterized by a wealth of labor-saving devices. Electricity will launder the clothes, sweep the floor, cook the meals, wash the dishes and perform, as by magic countless tasks—which in earlier ages the hands unaided wrought. Unfortunately, too, apartment homes are on the increase. There is less room space to be taken care of; no yards to be kept neat and attractive.

Small wonder that with so much time and so many calls for money, with the modern craze for possession and the enticements of city pleasures, the wife wishes to find employment outside of the home. The husband strained almost to the breaking point in efforts to meet the clamorous demands of a money-mad family, accepts the relief, albeit reluctantly. In other cases, the money pressure lacking, he may be unwilling to appear obstinate or "non-progressive"—hence, like Barcus, "is willing."[3]

Is there danger that the allurements of money-getting and money-spending may foster the desire to keep that childless home? The Roman Catholic Church teaches that married people who for purely selfish reasons refuse the burden of children are not truly religious. Is the church wrong?

Where already there are children, the condition is still more critical. If the mother is compelled to leave home to work because of a husband invalid, or out of a job, or that she may eke out his starvation salary, the necessity, regrettable as it is, must be met as best it may.

But where there is no urgent reason why the mother should be a wage earner, she should pause long before turning her face away from her own fireside. Neither kindergarten nor hired care-taker, nor boarding-school too early entered, can take the mother's place. Better less of material wealth and more of riches in the lives of the boys and girls. Better forego the elegancies of dress, entertaining, furnishing a parlor, or any number of the hundred and one things we vain mortals like, but can get along very well without.

If the aim is civic betterment, that is not to be attained at the expense of childhood. Can there be any sort of world progress unless the children have the growth, physical and moral, as well as mental, which will fit them to take their places in the ever-passing procession? What can the mother give society which will compensate for failure in this direction? G. Stanley Hall says that our highest duty is to pass on, to those who come after us the torch of life burning more brightly than when we received it.[4]

2. The original reads "nickle."

3. Reference is to Barkis, a character willing to marry, in Charles Dickens's *David Copperfield*.

4. Fisher, *Self-Reliance*, 236.

"But the mother's nature craves expression, a field for activity. Is she not human being as well as parent? In return, we ask, what greater scope can she find for the exercise of all her faculties, than the training and companionship of her children? There is a task which calls for all of knowledge, taste, tact, skill, patience, love, wisdom, that any human being can possess.

As for the ultimate satisfaction, as Dorothy Canfield Fisher says in "Self-Reliance:" They are an unusually fortunate and gifted pair of parents, who can find in life anything at all comparable to the job of bringing up their children, for interest, for unexpectedness, for sanity and laughter and health and pure joy." But such acquaintance with the higher values can come only from experience.

After all, it is not so much a condition as an attitude about which we need to be concerned. If we place the child where he belongs in our hearts and lives, the rest will follow. The woman who reverences the young life, who recognizes child-rearing as the greatest opportunity for service, who looks upon a mother as one, like Mary, blessed among women, will not abandon her divinely-appointed mission. She will realize that no vocation or career can equal it in importance. Nothing will be permitted to take precedence of her primal duty. Her relation to the world's work, to civic claims, to society, to the church will be adjusted to meet the requirements of her duty to the child. Putting this high mission first, whatever else she can do by way of self-cultivation, self-expression, or community helpfulness, with or without financial considerations, let her do—and none should say her nay. Impressed with the lofty character of her calling and the bigness of her job in being the right sort of mother, she will guard carefully her powers, lest she undertake too much of what is non-essential.

Should circumstances force upon her the cruel necessity of going out to earn bread for her children, God help her (the nation should!)

Someday the universality of mothers' pension laws will do away with tis unnatural condition—but that, as Kipling says, is "another story."

Of Mr. Turpin and Dr. Crump: Two Southern Gentlemen of Quality

Autobiographical Notes

JOSEPHINE TURPIN WASHINGTON

The following manuscript was supplied to [Goochland County Historical Society] by Augustus Turpin Granger.[1] The author was the granddaughter of Edwin Turpin and made these notes about her family at the age of eighty on March 19 and 20 of 1941.—Editor

At the request of my grandson Joe, I am jotting down at random a few items about my family as I recall or heard them.

I was born in Goochland County, Virginia July 31, 1861. My father was Augustus Adolphus Turpin and my mother, Louise Victoria Crump Turpin. My mother was only seventeen when she married, and my father about twenty-nine. My child-bride mother went at once to Turpin's home in Goochland County.

Probably, my mother married so early because the home was broken up by the death of her mother and the marriage of her older sister, Mary Jane Crump, to a Mr. Hickman, a prosperous barber from St. Louis, Missouri. When my sisters and I were small, we always spoke of "Aunt Mary Jane" with awe and admiration, and later, with a little amusement, for she showed plainly in her face and bearing her high estimate of herself. This was fostered, no doubt, by the fact that after the demise of her mother, she was, in a way, the head of the family, taking with her to St. Louis the younger children for whom she and her husband became responsible. Personally, I did not know my mother's father, Dr. Abner Crump. I was acquainted with but a few facts concerning my grandpar-

---

* "Of Mr. Turpin and Dr. Crump: Two Southern Gentlemen of Quality," *Goochland County Historical Society Magazine* 25 (1993): 29–33.

1. Augustus Turpin Granger (1892–1942), nephew of Washington and son of her sister Sarah Jane Turpin Granger, who married William Randolph Granger (see the Turpin family tree outlined in Rollins, *All Is Never Said,* n.p.).

ents. My grandfathers were both white. I do not even know if my grandmothers were owned by them or whether they were free women kept by Dr. Crump, my mother's father, and Mr. Turpin my father's father.[2] It is more likely the former supposition was true. As was common among Southern gentlemen "of quality," Dr. Crump had this colored family and, in another county, a white family. He spent a considerable time with the colored "wife" and was fond and proud of their children, of whom my mother was one of the younger.

These colored children with the white father were told very little concerning their ancestry. It seems strange to me that we did not ask. We merely heard what was told us and were not particularly curious. There was a reticence, no doubt due to the fact that the relationship between the parents was not legal. Colored people were beginning to get very conscious of such relationships. I've heard my mother, however, refer more than once to the fact that we had "good blood."

As to my lack of knowledge of the family relationships of those days, I can truthfully (and ignorantly) say that I do not even now—and I am nearly 80—know whether my grandmothers were slaves or free women in those days when they bore their children to Dr. Crump and Mr. Turpin.

My father's father [Mr. Turpin] had no other wife than my grandmother[3] who lived in an attractive two story frame house a few yards from the big brick house where my grandfather Turpin lived. I did not know my grandmother Turpin, but I knew well the sons and daughters, several of them living at the old home or visiting there often during the period of my childhood.

There were but two of them aunts, Aunt Jane [Elizabeth Jane Turpin] and Aunt Kate [Martha Catherine Turpin]. Aunt Jane made an unhappy marriage to a Mr. Green whom I never saw. I recall her as a sad-faced buxom woman, deeply devoted to her only child, Laura. My grandfather's other daughter, Aunt Kate, was a small, gentle, self-effacing woman. She married a Mr. Moseley,[4] a

2. Washington's paternal grandfather was Edwin Durock Turpin (1783–1868), a white Englishman, who settled in Goochland and owned as many as fifty slaves. His father, also Washington's great-grandfather, was first cousin to Thomas Jefferson, third president of the United States (Rollins, *All Is Never Said,* 20).

3. Washington's grandmother's name is listed only as 'Mary" in the Turpin family tree (Rollins, *All Is Never Said,* n.p.).

4. William P. Moseley (1819–1890), a literate ex-slave and Virginia native. He was one of twenty-four African American delegates elected to serve on Virginia's Constitutional Convention (1867–68) and one of fourteen senators nominated to serve in the state senate (1869–91), where he represented Goochland. He had an unsuccessful run for Congress in 1880. He acquired the five-hundred-acre farm at Elk Hill, near Pemberton, in Goochland, the homestead bequeathed to the colored children of Edwin Durock Turpin, father of Martha Katherine Turpin, Moseley's wife ("A Visit to Goochland," *Virginia Star,* 11 May 1878, 8; the typescript of this essay is found in Edwin Durock Turpin's folder at Goochland County Historical Society).

heavy-set, brown-skinned man who, in time, became a member of the legislature of Virginia. The Moseley family then spent most of their time in Richmond, the capital city.

The Moseleys had a large family; there were three girls, Mary, Ellie, and Mat-
tie, and boys: Willie the oldest, I remember especially well because shortly after
he moved with the family to Richmond, he had an eye put out by a snowball
thrown by a playmate; Junius I recall plainly as he was about my age, and we
played together in our country home—chopping down branches and building
a "house" in the woods, and stealing coals from the cabin fire of old "Uncle
Robin" while he was taking his daily nap. We had been forbidden to handle fire,
for fear we would set ourselves on fire or do some other damage.

Ellie is another of the Moseley children that I distinctly recall. She was
younger than I and the special chum of my sister Mary Lou. The characteristic
that particularly caused me to remember Ellie was that all through life she was
given to boasting that her father had been a member of the state legislature.

The union of my grandfather Turpin and his wife in all but name produced
seven fine boys: Robert, William, Thomas, Augustus, Henry, Junius and Durock
[sic]. Mr. Turpin was not only fond of them, but he was proud of them. Of my
father, Augustus, he once said of the boy as he rode past his window, "What a
fine boy he is!"

My mother was seventeen when she married. She probably would not have
married so young had it not been that her mother died and the family was broken (as I have already mentioned). Of this marriage there were ten children:
Josephine Jewett (myself), Mary Louisa, Augusta, Sarah Jane, Brittania, Robert
Lincoln, Constance, Laura, Estelle (Essie we called her) and Edwin Abner, the
youngest who lived with me after the death of our mother as he was only nine
years old.

At that time, we were living at Tuskegee Institute, Alabama where my husband,
Dr. Samuel Somerville Hawkins Washington,[5] was resident physician. When we
went there, our daughter Jewett Elizabeth was little more than five years old.
The famed Dr. Booker T. Washington, founder of Tuskegee, was living and, as
throughout his life-time, was the Principal of the institution. My husband was
glad of the opportunity to serve there, for it meant a certain kind of interesting

5. Dr. Samuel Somerville Hawkins Washington (1858–1913), a native of Nevis in British West Indies. He moved with his family to Philadelphia, Pennsylvania, in 1874. He
attended Howard University's Preparatory School and Collegiate Division (1877–82) and
Medical School (1883–86). After working in the War Department in Washington, D.C.,
he married Josephine Turpin, and they moved to Alabama. He became a licensed physician in the state and worked as a resident physician at Tuskegee Institute (1895–99),
and then entered private practice in Montgomery (Lamb, *Howard University Medical
Department*, 226–27).

opportunity to get acquainted with Negro youth in America. (He was a West Indian who came to this country when he was a youth of sixteen). Still, he did not feel it would be to his advantage as a physician to remain in practice as a resident physician in a school. So, after a few years at Tuskegee, he resigned and went to Montgomery, Alabama. There, I resumed my career as a teacher.

When the young man who later became my husband met me, I was a student in college at Howard University in Washington, D.C. After graduation, I taught there. But that was not my first entrance into the teaching field.

We married in 1888. (I remember how beautiful the figures—three eights— looked to me on the announcement cards.) A short time after, my sister Mary Lou married. Her husband was William Randolph Granger, also a physician. Brittie married a Mr. Poindexter, a farmer in Louisa County, Virginia, a man several years older than herself. Sarah, Connie, and Laura died young, unmarried. They had all graduated from the State Normal School and been teaching for a few years. They were all victims of tuberculosis. Connie was the first to contract the disease and to succumb to it. In those days, little was known as to the contagious nature of consumption, as it was generally termed, and less, if possible, as to its cure. A neglected cold or some other cause weakened the young person, and he or she fell a prey to the dread malady. The result was that all the members of a family, especially its youth, fell under the doom. Essie (Estelle) did not go in this way, but she had pneumonia after a few days illness.

We all grieved much at the death of Essie. She was a lovely, laughing child, the youngest, and, as I recall, the favorite in the family. But, it always seemed to the older ones that whoever was the youngest was the favorite, particularly of our father. Our father never got over his fondness for life in the country. He was a carpenter and one unusually skilled in his trade. It was not possible to get regular work in Goochland, our grandfather's home, our home. Often, my father went to Richmond to find work. This being the case so frequently, our parents finally decided it was better to go to Richmond to live.

I don't know that we were any better off financially after we moved to "the big city," but at least we were all together. My grandfather Turpin had died (our grandmother on our father's side had died long before our mother and father were married), the numerous uncles (my father's brothers) had grown up and gone to the city to work, or they had accepted their father's offer to send them North to school. Mr. Moseley, my Aunt Kate's husband, had already moved his wife and numerous progeny to Richmond.

It seems to me that about this time I was nine or ten years old. Our first place of residence in Richmond was in a small, white painted, one and a half story cottage on a hill near the cemetery. There was no paved street anywhere near. I remember how cautiously I got around the corner where the earth had been worn away by successive rains and erosions, or else went down a steep declivity, across a narrow ravine, up a high hill and then went fearfully along a wide space to reach my school, located in the upper story of the orphan asylum of the neighborhood. Of course, the school being a colored school, the asylum was colored also. In those early days, I think all of the teachers in the colored school were white teachers from the North. Of this, however, I am not quite sure. We studied in a stoop shouldered fashion, seated two to a desk, one large room accommodating, or at least containing, all of the girls and boys in the school. Once we had the "young and pretty" teacher to tea at our house. That circumstance is one reason why I think the teacher was from the North.

The next school I remember having attended was the Baker Street School where I feel certain that, in the early days, the teachers were white and of the city. Later, young colored girls, graduates of the State Normal School (Colored) were the teachers. Miss Pattie Payne, an unforgettable maiden lady of many years, was one of my early teachers, I think in the Baker Street School.

****

One is left at this point, wishing that Mrs. Washington had been able to continue her fascinating narrative.—Editor.

Bibliography

Works by Josephine J. Turpin Washington (pseudonym "Joyce")

Joyce. "'Joyce' to 'Quiz.'" *People's Advocate* (Washington, D.C.), 18 June 1881, 2.

———. "Notes to Girls. No. 1." *People's Advocate* (Washington, D.C.), 20 November 1880, 1.

———. "Notes to Girls. No. 2." *People's Advocate* (Washington, D.C.), 27 November 1880, 1.

———. "Notes to Girls. No. 3." *People's Advocate* (Washington, D.C.), 11 December 1880, 1.

———. "Notes to Girls. No. 4." *People's Advocate* (Washington, D.C.), 18 December 1880, 1.

———. "Notes to Girls. No. 5." *People's Advocate* (Washington, D.C.), 25 December 1880, 1.

———. "Notes to Girls. No. 6." *People's Advocate* (Washington, D.C.), 8 January 1881, 1.

———. "On the Street Car." *Virginia Star,* 30 April 1881, 4.

———. "Out Doors in Summer." *People's Advocate* (Washington, D.C.), 21 August 1880, 1.

———. "A Reply to Quiz's Baptismal Queries." *People's Advocate* (Washington, D.C.), 2 July 1881, 2.

———. "Unwise Talkers." *People's Advocate* (Washington, D.C.), 18 June 1881, 2.

Turpin, J. J. "The Benefits of Trouble." *Virginia Star,* 11 November 1882, 1.

———. "The Good Old Times." *People's Advocate* (Washington, D.C.), 8 September 1883, 1 (republished 15 September 1883, 1).

———. "Wendell Phillips' Memorial Exercises at Howard University." *People's Advocate* (Washington, D.C.), 8 March 1884, 2.

Turpin, Josephine. "Teaching as a Profession." *A.M.E. Church Review* 5, no. 2 (October 1888): 103–11.

Turpin, Josephine J. "Anglo-African Magazine." *New York Globe,* 13 October 1883, 1.

———. "Charles Dickens." A.M.E. Church Review 2 (July 1885): 34–40.

———. "Frederick Douglass." *New York Globe,* 24 May 1884, 2.

———. "'A Great Danger': Annie Porter Excoriated." *New York Globe,* 2 February 1884, 1.

———. "Higher Education for Women." *People's Advocate* (Washington, D.C.), 12 April 1884, 1.

———. "Holland's 'Kathrina.'" *People's Advocate* (Washington, D.C.), 30 June 1883, 1.

———. "The Origin and Progress of the English Language." *A.M.E. Church Review* 1, no. 1 (January 1884): 280–84.

———. "Paul's Trade and What Use He Made of It." *Christian Recorder* 22, no. 7 (14 February 1884): 1.

———. "A Plea for the Co-Education of the Sexes." *A.M.E. Church Review* 3, no. 3 (January 1887): 267–71.

———. "The Remedy for War." *A.M.E. Church Review* 4, no. 2 (October 1887): 161–66.

———. "What the Citizen Owes to the Government." *New York Globe,* 9 June 1883, 2.

Washington, J. T. "Lessons from the Life of President Paterson." *Alumni Reporter* (Montgomery, Alabama) 1, no. 7 (February 1909): 1–2.

———. 12th Annual Meeting of the State Federation of Women's Clubs." *Colored Alabamian* 4, no. 20 (9 July 1910): 1.

Washington, Jos. T. "A Card—To the Women's Clubs of Alabama." *Colored Alabamian* 4, no. 23 (30 July 1910): 1.

Washington, Josephine T. "Cedar Hill Saved." *Crisis* 17, no. 4 (February 1919): 179.

———. "Child Saving in Alabama." *Colored American Magazine* 14, no. 1 (January 1908): 48–51

———. "Federation Department." *Colored Alabamian* 6, no. 6 (30 March 1912): 1–2.

———. "Four Years' Growth." *Colored Alabamian* 2, no. 21 (25 July 1908): 2–3.

———. "Impressions of a Southern Federation." *Colored American Magazine* 7, no. 11 (November 1904): 676–80.

———. "Josephine T. Washington Writes of Tuskegee's Commencement Week—A Splendid Occasion." *Freeman*, 15 June 1895, 2.

———. "Lessons from the Life of McKinley." *A.M.E. Church Review* 18, no. 3 (January 1902): 210–15.

———. "Mother Alabama." In *The History of the National Association of Colored Women's Clubs: A Legacy of Service,* edited by Charles Harris Wesley, 283. Washington, D.C.: National Association of Colored Women's Clubs, 1984.

———. "A Mother's New Year Resolutions." *Crisis* 15, no. 3 (January 1918): 124–25.

———. "A Plea for the Moral Aim in Education." *A.M.E. Church Review* 38, no. 2 (October 1921): 67–71.

———. "The Problem of the Fallen." *Colored Alabamian* 14, no. 3 (15 May 1909): 1+.

———. "What of the Children?" *A.M.E. Church Review* 39, no. 1 (1922): 8–10.

Washington, Josephine Turpin. "Anglo Saxon Supremacy." *New York Age,* 23 August 1890, 2–3.

———. "Josephine Turpin Washington Nominates T. Thomas Fortune." *Cleveland Gazette,* 9 November 1889, 1.

———. "Needs of Our Newspapers: Some Reasons for Their Existence." *New York Age,* 19 October 1889, 1.

———. "Of Mr. Turpin and Dr. Crump: Two Southern Gentlemen of Quality." *Goochland County Historical Society Magazine,* 25th anniversary issue, vol. 25 (1993): 29–33.

———. "The Province of Poetry." *A.M.E. Church Review* 6, no. 2 (October 1889): 137–47.

Works Consulted

Adams, F. P. "Grammar Department." *Normal Teacher: A Monthly School* 4, no. 4 (June 1880): 147–48.

"Address of Josephine St. P. Ruffin, President of the Conference." In *A History of the Club Movement among the Colored Women of the United States of America as Containing in the Minutes of the Convention, Held in Boston, July 29, 30, 31, 1895 and of the National Federation of Afro-American Women, Held in Washington D.C., July 20, 21, 22, 1896,* 31–34. National Association of Colored Women's Clubs, 1902.

Aiken, P. F. *Memorials of Robert Burns and of Some of His Contemporaries and Their Descendants.* Sampson Low, Marston, Searle and Rivington, 1876.

Akenside, Mark. *The Pleasures of the Imagination and Other Poems.* R and W. A. Bartow, 1819.

Alexander, Ann Field. *Race Man: The Rise and Fall of the "Fighting Editor" John Mitchell Jr.* Charlottesville: University of Virginia Press, 2002.

"Apology: Introductory." *Anglo-African Magazine* 1, no. 1 (January 1859): 1.

Aristotle. *The Poetics of Aristotle.* Edited by S. H. Butcher. Macmillan, 1902.

Arnold, Matthew. "Heinrich Heine." *Cornhill Magazine* 8, no. 44 (August 1863): 233–49.

Bacon, Francis. "Of the Proficience and Advancement of Learning Divine and Human." In *The Works of Francis Bacon, Baron of Verulam, Viscount St. Alban, and High Chancellor of England,* edited by James Spedding and others, vol. 3. Longman, 1857.

Bailey, Richard. *They, Too, Call Alabama Home: African American Profiles.* Montgomery, Ala.: Pyramid, 1999.

Bauch, William Ralston. *The Complete Compendium of Universal Knowledge Containing All You Want to Know of Language, History, Government, Business, and Social Forms, and a Thousand Other Useful Subjects.* 1895.

"The Beautiful Snow." In *Holmes' Fourth Reader with an Elocutionary Introduction,* edited by George F. Holmes, 201–2. University Publishing, 1870.

Blair, Lewis Harvie. *Encyclopedia Virginia.* Virginia Foundation for the Humanities. https://www.encyclopediavirginia.org/Blair_Lewis_Harvie_1834-1916.

Blanton, Wyndham B. *Medicine in Virginia in the Nineteenth Century.* Richmond, Va.: Garrett and Massie, 1933.

Blume, Kenneth J. "John Mercer Langston." In *Encyclopedia of African American History,* edited by Leslie M. Alexander and Walter C. Rucker, vol. 2. Santa Barbara, Calif.: ABC-CLIO, 2010.

"Books and Reading: Poetry and Poets." *Hours at Home: A Popular Monthly of Instruction and Recreation* 10, no. 6 (April 1870): 498–510.

Bowles, Samuel, and Helen Gintis. *Schooling in Capitalist America: Educational Reform and the Contradictions of Economic Life.* New York: Basic, 1976.

Bragg, George. *History of the Afro-American Group of the Episcopal Church.* Baltimore, Md.: Church Advocate Press, 1922.

Brewster, David. *Memoirs of the Life, Writings, and Discoveries of Sir Isaac Newton.* Vol. 2. T. Constable, 1855.

Brooks, Phillips. "February 12th." In *Daily Thoughts,* 29–30. R. H. Woodward, 1893.

Broussard, Albert S. *African American Odyssey: The Stewarts, 1853–1963.* Lawrence: University of Kansas Press, 1998.

Browning, Elizabeth Barrett. "Aurora Leigh." In *Works of Elizabeth Barrett Browning.* C. S. Francis, 1857.

———. "Mountaineer and Poet." In *A Selection from the Poetry of Elizabeth Barrett Browning,* 2nd ser., new ed., 2:87. Smith, Elder, 1886.

———. "The Poet." In *A Selection from the Poetry of Elizabeth Barrett Browning,* 2nd ser., new ed., 2:28. Smith, Elder, 1886.

Bulwer-Lytton, Edward. *Clytemnestra: The Earl's Return, The Artist, and Other Poems.* Chapman and Hall, 1855.

———. "Essay No. X—Hints on Mental Culture." In *Caxtoniana: A Series of Essays on Life, Literature, and Manners,* 103–14. Harper and Brothers, 1863.

————. *Zanoni: A Rosicrucian Tale.* 3 vols. Saunders and Otley, 1842.

Bureau of Education. *Co-Education of the Sexes in the Public Schools of the United States.* Circulars of Information. No. 2–1883. Government Printing Office, 1883.

Burkett, Randall K., et al., eds. *Black Biographical Dictionaries: 1790–1950.* Microfiche 88, no. 211. Chadwyck-Healey Inc., 1987.

————. *Black Biography 1790–1950. A Cumulative Index.* 3 vols. Alexandria, Va., 1991.

Burns, Robert. "To a Mouse." In *The Complete Poetical Works of Robert Burns,* 31–32. Cambridge Edition. Houghton Mifflin, 1897.

Byron, George Gordon. "Childe Harold's Pilgrimage." In *The Poetical Works of Lord Byron with a Memoir,* 4:1–304. Houghton, Mifflin, 1882.

————. "Don Juan." In *The Poetical Works of Lord Byron with a Memoir,* 10:35–417. Houghton, Mifflin, 1882.

The Cambridge Biographical Encyclopedia. 2nd ed. Edited by David Crystal. Cambridge: Cambridge University Press, 1998.

Campbell, Thomas. "Hallowed Ground." In *The Complete Poetical Works of Thomas Campbell, with A Memoir of His Life, and an Essay on His Genius and Writings,* 166–69. Appleton, 1854.

————. "The Pleasures of Hope." In *The Complete Poetical Works of Thomas Campbell, with a Memoir of His Life, and an Essay on His Genius and Writings,* 3–33. Appleton, 1854.

Cardinal, Denise. "National Education Association." In *Encyclopedia of Education,* 2nd ed., 5:1769–71. Farmington Hills, Mich.: Thomson Gale, 2003.

Carlyle, Thomas. "Burns." In *Carlyle's Essay on Burns with Selections from Burns's Poems,* edited by Wilson Farrand, 1–67. Longman's, Green, 1896.

————. "Life of Burns." In *Life of Robert Burns,* pt. 2, 12–52. American Book Exchange, 1880.

————. *On Heroes, Hero-Worship, and the Heroic in History.* Edited by Archibald Mac-Mechan. Atheneum, 1901.

Casey, Edgar. "Quotes, Wisdom, and Sayings." Pearls of Wisdom. 2017. www.sapphyr.net.

Cavendish, Richard. "Robert Bruce and the Scottish Church." *History Today* 60, no. 2 (2010): 9.

"Centennial Celebration in Mobile." *Mobile Register,* 5 July 1876, 1.

Clarke, Edward H. *Sex in Education; or A Fair Chance for Girls.* James R. Osgood, 1874.

Cobb, William. "William Pickens." In *African American National Biography,* edited by Henry Louis Gates Jr. and Evelyn Brooks Higginbotham, 6:38–40. Oxford: W. E. B. Du Bois Institute for African and African American Research at Harvard University and Oxford University Press, 2008.

Cooper, Brittney C. *Beyond Respectability: The Intellectual Thought of Race Women.* Champaign: University of Illinois Press, 2017.

Cowper, William. "The Garden: The Task." In *The Works of Cowper and Thomson, Including Many Letters and Poems Never Before Published in This Country with a New and Interesting Memoir of the Life of Thomson,* bk. 3, 70–77. Grigg, Elliot, 1849.

————. "Table Talk: The Task." In *The Works of Cowper and Thomson, Including Many Letters and Poems Never Before Published in This Country with a New and Interesting Memoir of the Life of Thomson,* bk. 5, 3–10. Grigg, Elliot, 1849.

———. "The Winter Morning Walk: The Task." In *The Works of Cowper and Thomson, Including Many Letters and Poems Never Before Published in This Country with a New and Interesting Memoir of the Life of Thomson*, bk. 5, 85–93. Grigg, Elliot, 1849,

Cronk, E. C., ed. "Missionary Education through Ear-Gate." *Missionary Review of the World* 41, no. 4 (April 1918): 289–96.

Currie, Stephen. *The Liberator: Voice of the Abolition Movement*. Farmington Hills, Mich.: Lucent, 2002.

Danville Riot, Nov. 3, 1883. Report of Committee of Forty with Sworn Testimony of Thirty-Seven Witnesses. Johns and Goolsby, 1883.

Darwin, Charles. *The Autobiography of Charles Darwin, 1809–1842*. Edited by Nora Barlow. New York: Norton, 1958.

———. *The Descent of Man, and Selections in Relation to Sex*. 2nd ed. John Murray, 1874.

De Staël, Madame. *Corinne; or Italy*. Translated by Isabel Hill. Standard Novels No. 14. Richard Bentley, 1838.

Dewey, John, and Evelyn Dewey. *Schools of To-Morrow*. E. P. Dutton, 1915.

Dickens, Charles. *David Copperfield*. Project Gutenberg e-book.

———. *Posthumous Papers of the Pickwick Club*. Chapman and Hall, 1909.

Dorman, John Frederick, comp. Virginia Revolutionary Pension Applications. Vol. 25. 1976. Library of Virginia, Richmond.

Dryden, John, trans. *Virgil's Aeneid*. In *The Works of the English Poets, from Chaucer to Cowper; Including the Series Edited with Prefaces, Biographical and Critical, by Dr. Samuel Johnson: and the Most Improved Translations*, 19:358–461. Printed for J. Johnson, 1810.

Du Bois, W. E. B. *The College-Bred Negro*. Atlanta: Atlanta University Press, 1900.

Dunbar, Paul Laurence. "Life." In *The Complete Poems of Paul Laurence Dunbar*, 8. Dodd, Mead, 1913.

"Edison Never Was Tempted." *National Electrical Contractor* 16, no. 4 (February 1917): 79. Edison's quotation reads, "I have never had the time, [not even five minutes], to be tempted to do anything against the moral law, [civil law or any law whatever."]

Eliot, George. *The Mill on the Floss*. Thomas Y. Crowell, 1920.

Emerson, Ralph Waldo. "Essay V: Love." In *Essays*, 1st ser. Thomas Y. Crowell, 1890.

———. "Poetry and Imagination." In *The Complete Writings of Ralph Waldo Emerson*, 2:727–50. William H. Wise, 1929.

Eubank, Thomas. *Key to Harvey's Practical Grammar*. 7th ed. J. R. Holcolm, 1885.

Farrar, Louis Berkhof. "The First Epistle to the Corinthians—Christian Classics Ethereal Library." www.ccel.org/ccel/berkhof/newststamrnt.xiii.html.

Fisher, Dorothy Canfield. *Self-Reliance: A Practical and Informed Discussion of Methods of Teaching Self-Reliance, Initiative and Responsibility to Modern Children*. Indianapolis: Bobbs-Merrill, 1916.

Fletcher, Robert. "The Poet—Is He Born, Not Made." *American Anthropologist* 6, no. 2 (April 1893): 117–36.

Foster, Frances Smith. "A Narrative of the Interesting Origins and (Somewhat) Surprising Developments of African-American Print Culture." *American Literary History* 17, no. 4 (Winter 2005): 714–40.

Gardner, Eric. *Black Print Unbound: The Christian Recorder, African American Literature, and Periodical Culture.* New York: Oxford University Press, 2015.

Gates, Henry Louis, Jr. "The Trope of a New Negro and the Reconstruction of the Image of the Black." In "America Reconstructed, 1840–1940," special issue, *Representations,* no. 24 (Autumn 1988): 129–55.

Geiter, Mary K. "William Penn." In *Oxford Dictionary of National Biography: From the Earliest, Times to the Year 2000,* edited by H. C. G. Matthews and Brian Harrison, 43:557–66. Oxford: Oxford University Press, 2004.

Goethe, Johann Wolfgang von. *Faust.* Translated by Anna Swanwick. George Bell and Sons, 1879.

———. *Hermann and Dorothea.* Translated by Ellen Frothingham. Robert Brothers, 1879.

Goldsmith, Oliver. "The Deserted Village." In *Goldsmith's Poems,* 25–37. H. Maxwell, 1800. Microfiche 131, Evans 37530. Early American Imprints 1639–1800.

Goodare, Julian. "Mary [Mary Stewart]." In *Oxford Dictionary of National Biography: From the Earliest Times to the Year 2000,* edited by H. C. G. Matthew and Brian Harrison, 37:77–93. Oxford: Oxford University Press, 2004.

Goodnow, Marc N. "The Church and Recreation." *Churchman* 114 (15 July 1916): 81.

Grant, Ulysses S. "Reconciliation." https://www.virginiahistory.org/collections-and-resources /virginia-history-explorer/lee-and-grant/reconciliation.

Gray, Thomas. "An Elegy, Written in a Country Churchyard." In *An Elegy Written in a Country Churchyard.* Collier, 1799, 1–8. Microfiche 131, Evans 35562. Early American Imprints 1639–1800.

Green, Elizabeth Alden. *Mary Lyon and Mt. Holyoke.* Lebanon, N.H.: University Press of New England, 1979.

Green, Hilary. *Educational Reconstruction: African American Schools in the Urban South, 1865–1890.* New York: Fordham University Press, 2016.

Harlan, Louis R., and Raymond W. Smock, eds. *The Booker T. Washington Papers.* Vol. 3. Champaign: University of Illinois Press, 1974.

Harper, Frances E. W. *Iola Leroy, or Shadows Uplifted.* 1892. Reprint, New York: AMS Press, 1971.

Harris, J. *Benevolent Institutions: Department of Commerce Bureau of the Census 1910.* Government Printing Office, 1913.

Hayden, Robert C. "Morgan, Clement G[arnett]." In *Dictionary of American Negro Biography,* edited by Rayford W. Logan and Michael R. Winston, 452–53. New York: Norton, 1982.

Hemans, Felicia. "A Poet's Dying Hymn." In *The Poetical Works of Felicia Hemans,* new ed., 392. Phillips, Sampson, 1850.

Hendricks, Wanda. "Wells-Barnett, Ida Bell." In *Black Women in America: An Historical Encyclopedia,* vol. 2, edited by Darlene Clark Hine, 1242–46. Brooklyn, N.Y.: Carlson, 1993.

Henry, Patrick. "The 'Liberty or Death' Speech and the Clash with Dunmore, 1775." In *Patrick Henry in His Speeches and Writings and in the Words of His Contemporaries,* compiled and edited by James M. Elson, 72–84. Lynchburg, Va.: Warwick House, 2007.

Holland, Josiah Gilbert. *Kathrina: Her Life and Mine in a Poem.* Sampson Low, Son and Marston, 1869.

Hollister, C. Warren. "Henry I." In Britannica.com.

Holmes, Oliver Wendell. "The Chambered Nautilus." In *The Complete Poetical Works of Oliver Wendell Holmes,* 149. Cambridge Edition. Houghton Mifflin, 1895.

Holt, Rackham. *Mary McLeod Bethune: A Biography.* New York: Doubleday, 1964.

Hopkins, Pauline. *Contending Forces: A Romance Illustrative of the Negro Life North and South.* 1900. Reprint, New York: AMS Press, 1971.

Hoskin, Michael. "Herschel, Caroline Lucretia." In *Oxford Dictionary of National Biography, From the Earliest Times to the Years 2000,* edited by H. C. G. Matthew and Brian Harrison, 26:822–25. Oxford: Oxford University Press, 2004.

Hoyt, Wayland. "The Prayer-Meeting Service." *Homiletic Review* 29, no. 5 (May 1895): 445–51.

Irving, Washington. "Rural Life in England." *Saturday Magazine* 3, no. 70 (3 August 1833): 42–43.

Jamieson. *Minden Armais: The Man of the New Race: A Memoir.* American Printing, 1890.

Johnson, Karen Ann. *Lifting the Women and the Race: The Lives, Educational Philosophies and Social Activism of Anna Julia Cooper and Nannie Helen Burroughs.* New York: Garland, 2002.

Johnson, Samuel. "Rasselas; a Tale." In *The Works of Samuel Johnson, a New Edition with an Essay on His Life and Genius,* 2:1–44. Henry G. Bohn, 1850.

Johnson, Samuel, and Alexander Chalmers, eds. *The Works of the English Poets, from Chaucer to Cowper; Including the Series Edited, with Prefaces, Biographical and Critical, by Dr. Samuel Johnson: and the Most Approved Translations.* Vol. 19. Printed for J. Johnson et al., 1810.

Johnston, Emma L. "Vocational Guidance thruout the School Course." *National Education Association Addresses and Proceedings of the Fifty-Fourth Annual Meeting Held at New York City July 1–8, 1916* 54 (1916): 645–48.

Keister, Lisa A., and Darby E. Southgate. *Inequality: A Contemporary Approach to Race, Class, and Gender.* Cambridge: Cambridge University Press, 2011.

Kitto, John. "Saul of Tarsus." In *Daily Bible Illustrations; Being Original Readings for a Year on Subjects from Sacred History, Biography, Geography, Antiquities, and Theology. Especially Designed for the Family Circle,* 8:92–97. Robert Carter and Brothers, 1881.

Knowles, Michael David. "Saint Thomas Becket." In Britannica.com.

Lamb, Daniel. *Howard University Medical Department: A Historical, Biographical, and Statistical Souvenir.* Freeport, N.Y.: Books for Libraries Press, 1971.

Lavender, Catherine J. "Notes on the Cult of Domesticity and True Womanhood." Prepared for students in HST 386, "Women in the City," Department of History, College of Staten Island (CUNY), 1998. https://csivc.csi.cuny.edu/history/files/lavender/386/truewoman.pdf.

Lee, Jarena. *The Religious Experience and Journal of Mrs. Jarena Lee Giving an Account of Her Call to Preach the Gospel.* 1849.

Lindley, Susan Hill. *You Have Stept out of Your Place: A History of Women and Religion in America.* Louisville, Ky.: Westminster John Knox Press, 1996.

Lindsey, Christopher F. "Robert Fulton." In *Oxford Dictionary of National Biography: From the Earliest Times to the Year 2000,* edited by H. C. G. Matthew and Brian Harrison, 21:177–78. Oxford: Oxford University Press, 2004.

Longfellow, Henry Wadsworth. "The Arsenal at Springfield." In *The Poetical Works of Henry Wadsworth Longfellow*, 1:122–23. Houghton, Mifflin, 1880.

———. "Autumn." In *The Poetical Works of Henry Wadsworth Longfellow*, 1:13. Houghton, Mifflin, 1880.

———. "Birds of Passage: Flight the Fourth, Charles Sumner." In *The Poetical Works of Henry Wadsworth Longfellow*, 1:330–72. Houghton, Mifflin, 1880.

———. "Christus. A Mystery, Part Two: The Golden Legend." In *The Poetical Works of Henry Wadsworth Longfellow*, vol. 2, pt. 3, 513–762. Houghton, Mifflin, 1880.

———. "Evangeline: A Tale of Acadie." In *The Poetical Works of Henry Wadsworth Longfellow*, 1:145–86. Houghton Mifflin, 1880.

———. "Hyperion." In *The Works of Henry Wadsworth Longfellow*, edited by Samuel Longfellow. Houghton, Mifflin 1885.

———. "The Light of Stars." In *The Poetical Works of Henry Wadsworth Longfellow*, 1:7. Houghton, Mifflin, 1880.

———. "The Masque of Pandora." In *The Poetical Works of Henry Wadsworth Longfellow*, 2:89–804. Houghton, Mifflin, 1880.

———. "A Psalm of Life." In *The Poetical Works of Henry Wadsworth Longfellow*, 1:6. Houghton, Mifflin, 1880.

———. "Santa Filomena." In *The Poetical Works of Henry Wadsworth Longfellow*, 1:347–48. Houghton, Mifflin, 1880.

———. "Seven Sonnets and a Canzone." In *The Poetical Works of Henry Wadsworth Longfellow*, 2:886–89. Houghton, Mifflin, 1880.

———. "The Student's Tale: Emma and Eginhard." Pt. 3, *Tales of a Wayside Inn*. In *The Poetical Works of Henry Wadsworth Longfellow*, 1 and 2: 374–486. Houghton, Mifflin, 1880.

Lynch, Hollis. *Edward Wilmot Blyden: Pan Negro Patriot.* Oxford: Oxford University Press, 1964.

Macaulay, Thomas Babington. "Essay on Milton." In *Macaulay's Essays on Milton and Addison,* edited by James Greenleaf Croswell, 1–89. Longmans, Green, 1897.

MacCulloch, Diarmaid. "Thomas Cranmer." In *Oxford Dictionary of National Biography: From the Earliest Times to the Year 2000,* edited by H. C. G. Matthew and Brian Harrison, 14:15–31. Oxford: Oxford University Press, 2004.

Mackenzie, R. Shelton. *Life of Charles Dickens.* T. B. Peterson and Brothers, 1870.

Malins, Joseph. "A Fence or an Ambulance." 1895. www.poemhunter.com/poem/ambulance-down-in-the-valley-part-111.

Mason, J. F. A. "William" [Adelinus]. In *Oxford Dictionary of National Biography: From the Earliest Times to the Year 2000,* edited by H. C. G. Matthew and Brian Harrison, 59:37–38. Oxford: Oxford University Press, 2004.

Matthews, William. *Hours with Men and Books.* S. G. Griggs, 1877.

"McKinley Assassinated." In *Facts about the Presidents. A Compilation of Biographical and Historical Information,* edited by Joseph Nathan and Janet Podell, 8th ed., 297. New York: H. W. Wilson, 2009.

Meier, August. *Negro Thought in America: 1880–1915.* Ann Arbor: University of Michigan Press, 1988.

Meredith, Owen. *Lucile.* James R. Osgood, 1874.

Minutes of the 18th Session of the Georgia Annual Conference of the African Methodist Episcopal Church, held in Valdosta, Georgia, January 17–21, 1884. Atlanta University, The Black Culture Collection. Micro Photo Division. Roll 594, Section 300, pp. 1–31.

"Minutes of the First National Conference of Colored Women: Letters and Resolutions." In *Records of the National Association of Colored Women's Clubs, 1895–1992. Part 1: Minutes of National Conventions, Publications, and President's Office Correspondence,* edited by John Bracey Jr. and August Meier. Bethesda, Md.: University Publications of America, 1994.

Moss, Alfred J., Jr. *The American Negro Academy: Voice of the Talented Tenth.* Baton Rouge: Louisiana State University Press, 1981.

"National Association of Colored Women's Clubs." *Colored Alabamian,* 30 July 1910, 1.

Owen, Thomas McAdory. *Alabama Official and Statistical Register 1915.* Brown, 1915.

———. "Noah Baxter Feagin." *History of Alabama and Dictionary of Alabama Biography.* Vol. 3. S. J. Clarke, 1921.

Patton, John O. "Lucy Craft Laney." In *Black Women in America,* 2nd ed., edited by Darlene Clark Hine, 2:226–27. Oxford: Oxford University Press.

Penny, Virginia. *The Employments of Women: A Cyclopedia of Woman's Work.* Walker, Wise and Company, 1863.

Pitt, William. "Lord Chatham's Speeches on the American Revolution: Speech on the Stamp Act, January 14, 1766." *Old South Leaflets* 8, no. 199 (1908): 449–60.

Plato. "Laws." In *The Dialogues of Plato,* translated by B. Jowett, vol. 4. Macmillan, 1892.

———. *The Republic.* In *The Dialogues of Plato,* translated by B. Jowett. 1:591–879. Macmillan, 1892.

Plowden, Alison. "Grey [Lady Jane]." In *Oxford Dictionary of National Biography: From the Earliest Times to the Year 2000,* edited by H. C. G. Matthew and Brian Harrison, 23:856–59. Oxford: Oxford University Press.

Poe, Edgar Allan. "The Poetic Principle." In *The Works of Edgar Allan Poe with an Introduction and a Memoir by Richard Henry Stoddard,* 1:227–56 A. C. Armstrong and Son, 1884.

———. *The Raven and Other Poems.* J. L. Graham, 1845.

Polk, R. L. *Polk's Medical Register and Directory of the United States and Canada.* R. L. Polk, 1917.

Pope, Alexander. "Epistle to Cobham." In *Epistles to Several Persons,* edited by F. W. Batson, vol. 3, no. 2, pp. 15–38. New Haven: Yale University Press, 1961.

———. "Epistle to Dr. Arbuthnot." In *The Complete Poetical Works of Alexander Pope,* 176–82. Houghton, Mifflin, 1902.

———. "An Essay on Criticism." In *The Works of Alexander Pope, ESQ. with Notes and Illustrations by Himself and Others,* new ed., 2:313–92. Longman, Brown, 1847.

———. "Essay on Man." In *The Works of Alexander Pope, ESQ with Notes and Illustrations by Himself and Others,* new ed., 4: 1–159. Longman, Brown, 1847.

Porter, Annie. "A Great Danger." *Independent,* 27 December 1883, 2–3.

Porter, Noah. "What to Learn." In *Higher Education in America,* edited by Derek Bok, 166–82. Princeton: Princeton University Press, 2013.

"President Lincoln." *American Clay Magazine* 10, no. 6 (July 1915): 27.

Prior, Matthew. "An English Padlock." In *Selected Poems of Matthew Prior,* 41–44. Kegan, Paul, Trench, 1889.

Proceedings of the National Conference of Colored Men of the United States, Held in the State Capitol at Nashville, Tennessee, May 6, 7, 8 and 9, 1879. Rufus H. Darby, 1879.

Quintilian, "Oratory and Virtue." In *The Handbook of Oratory: A Cyclopedia,* edited by William Byars. Ferdinand P. Kaiser, 1901.

Richardson, Charles Francis. "How to Study: Poetry." In *Modern Achievement: Reading and Home Study,* edited by Hamilton Wright Mabie, 335–38. University Society, 1902.

Riddick, J. Hudson. *The Danville Riot, An Address by the Rev. J. Hudson Riddick, of the Washington Conference, Methodist Episcopal Church, Delivered in the Augusta Street Church, Staunton, VA, Sunday Evening, November 10, 1883.* Baltimore: Oliver W. Clay, 1884.

Rief, Michelle. "Washington, Margaret Murray." In *Black Women in America,* edited by Darlene Clarke Hine, 3:326–29. Oxford: Oxford University Press.

Roberson, Houston Bryan. *Fighting the Good Fight: The Story of the Dexter Avenue King Memorial Baptist Church (1865–1977).* London: Routledge, 2005.

Rollins, Judith. *All Is Never Said: The Narrative of Odette Harper Hines.* Philadelphia: Temple University Press, 1995.

Ruskin, John. "Of the Received Opinions Touching the 'Grand' Style." In *Modern Painters, of Many Things,* vol. 3. John Wiley, 1890.

Scott, Anne Firor. "The Ever-Widening Circle: The Diffusion of Feminists Values from the Troy Female Seminary, 1822–1872." *History of Education Quarterly* 19 (Spring 1979): 3–5.

Scott, Walter. "The Lay of the Last Minstrel." In *The Poetical Works of Sir Walter Scott,* Complete Edition, 1–41. Crowell, 1884.

Shakespeare, William. *As You Like It.* In *The Complete Signet Classic Shakespeare,* 839–75. New York: Harcourt Brace Jovanovich, 1972.

———. *A Midsummer Night's Dream.* In *The Complete Signet Classic Shakespeare,* 524–54. New York: Harcourt Brace Jovanovich, 1972.

———. *The Tragedy of Hamlet, Prince of Denmark.* In *The Complete Signet Classic Shakespeare,* 910–61. New York: Harcourt Brace Jovanovich, 1972.

———. *The Tragedy of King Lear.* In *The Complete Signet Classic Shakespeare,* 1174–226. New York: Harcourt Brace Jovanovich, 1972.

———. *The Tragedy of King Richard the Second.* In *The Complete Signet Classic Shakespeare,* 437–78. New York: Harcourt Brace Jovanovich, 1972.

———. *The Tragedy of Romeo and Juliet.* In *The Complete Signet Classic Shakespeare,* 479–523. New York: Harcourt Brace Jovanovich, 1972.

Shelley, Percy Bysshe. "A Defence of Poetry." In *The Complete Works of Percy Bysshe Shelley,* 7:109–40. Staten Island, N.Y.: Gordian, 1965.

———. "Prometheus Unbound: A Lyrical Drama in Four Acts." In *The Poetical Works of Percy Bysshe Shelley,* 98–125. Edward Moxon, Son, 1874.

Simmons, William J., and Henry McNeal Turner. *Men of Mark: Eminent, Progressive and Rising.* George M. Rewell, 1887.

Smith, James McCune. "Civilization: Its Dependence on Physical Circumstances." *Anglo-African Magazine* 1, no. 1 (January 1859): 5–17.

Spencer, Herbert. *Education: Intellectual, Moral, and Physical*. D. Appleton and Company, 1860.

———. "What Knowledge Is of Most Worth." *Westminster Review* 2, no. 141 (1859): 1–23.

Stanhope, Philip Dormer. "Letter XLVII." In *Letters Written by the Late Right Honorable Philip Dormer Stanhope, Earl of Chesterfield, To His Son, Philip Stanhope, ESQ. Late Envoy Extraordinary at the Court of Dresden, Together with Several Other Pieces on Various Subjects*, 1:153–54. J. Dodsley, 1793.

Tennyson, Alfred Lord. "The Brook." In *The Poetical Works of Alfred Lord Tennyson*, Complete Edition from the Author's Text, 136–39. Thomas Y. Crowell, 1885.

———. "In Memoriam." In *The Complete Poetical Works of Alfred Lord Tennyson*, 105–29. H. B. Nims, 1885.

———. "The Poet." In *The Poetical Works of Alfred Lord Tennyson*, Complete Edition from Author's Text, 16–17. Thomas Y. Crowell, 1885.

———. "The Princess; A Medley." In *The Poetical Works of Alfred Lord Tennyson*, Complete Edition from the Author's Text, 381–440. Thomas Y. Crowell, 1885.

Thompson, Kathleen. "Brown, Charlotte Hawkins." In *Black Women in America: An Historical Encyclopedia*, edited by Darlene Clark Hine, 172–74. Brooklyn, N.Y.: Carlson, 1993.

Thornbrough, Emma Lou. *T. Thomas Fortune: Militant Journalist*. Chicago: University of Chicago Press, 1972.

"To Edwin Chalmers Silsby." *Booker T. Washington Papers*, 11 February 1903, Container 1, edited by Louis R. Harlan and Raymond W. Smock, 7:69. Champaign: University of Illinois Press, 197.

Townsend, J. Holland. "American Caste and Common Schools." *Anglo-African Magazine* 1, no. 3 (March 1859): 80–83.

Wabuda, Susan. "Hugh Latimer." In *Oxford Dictionary of National Biography*, edited by H. C. G. Matthew and Brian Harrison, 32: 632–39. Oxford: Oxford University Press, 2004.

Wallace, William Rose. "The Hand That Rocks the Cradle Is the Hand That Rules the World." In *Beautiful Gems of Thought and Sentiments*, edited by Henry Davenport Northrop. Colins-Patten, 1890.

Washington, Booker T. "The Industrial Education for the Negro." October 1903, TeachingHistory.org. 10 Jan. 2016.

Washington, Margaret Murray. National Association Notes. Tuskegee University Archives. 1895.

Watters, Mary. *The History of Mary Baldwin College (1842–1942)*. Staunton, Va.: Mary Baldwin College, 1942.

Watts, Isaac. "Song XX: Against Idleness and Mischief." In *Divine and Moral Songs for Children*. Hurd and Houghton, 1866. E-book.

Welsh, Alfred Hix. *Development of English Literature and Language*. 2nd ed. Vol. 1. S. C. Griggs, 1883.

Welter, Barbara. "The Cult of True Womanhood: 1820–1860." *American Quarterly* 18, no. 2, pt. 1 (Summer 1966): 151–74.

Wertheimer, Molly Meijer. *Inventing a Voice: The Rhetoric of American First Ladies of the Twentieth Century.* Lanham, Md.: Rowman and Littlefield, 2004.

Wesley, Charles Harris. *The History of the National Association of Colored Women's Clubs: A Legacy of Service.* Washington, D.C.: National Association of Colored Women's Clubs, 1984.

Whittier, John Greenleaf. "The Angel of Patience." In *The Complete Poetical Works of John Greenleaf Whittier,* Household Edition, 96. Houghton, Mifflin 1883.

———. "At School-Close. Bowdoin Street (1877)." In *The Complete Poetical Works of John Greenleaf Whittier.* Household Edition, 416. Houghton, Mifflin, 1883.

———. "The Barefoot Boy." In *The Complete Poetical Works of John Greenleaf Whittier,* Household Edition, 195–96. Houghton, Mifflin 1883.

———. "In School-Days." In *The Complete Poetical Works of Whittier,* 407. Houghton, Mifflin, 1883.

———. "Mabel Martin." In *The Complete Poetical Works of Whittier,* 516–20. Houghton, Mifflin, 1863.

———. "To J. T. F." In *John Greenleaf Whittier,* new rev. ed., 245–46. Houghton, Mifflin, 1883.

———. "Trust." In *The Complete Poetical Works of John Greenleaf Whittier,* Household Edition, 170–71. Houghton, Mifflin, 1883.

Wilkinson, Frederick D. *Directory of Graduates; Howard University 1870–1963.* Washington, D.C.: Howard University, 1965.

Williams, Jeffrey R. "Racial Uplift." *American History through Literature 1870–1920.* 2006. Encyclopedia.com. http://www.encyclopedia.com/history/culture-magazines/racial -uplift.

Willson, Beckles. "General Wolfe and Gray's 'Elegy.'" *Nineteenth Century and After* 73, no. 434 (April 1913): 862–75.

Woodson, Carter G. "Kelly Miller." *Journal of Negro History* 25, no. 1 (January 1940): 137–38.

Wordsworth, William. "Lines, Composed A Few Miles above Tintern Abbey, on Re-visiting the Banks of the Wye during a Tour, July 13, 1798." In *The Poetical Works of William Wordsworth,* 2:160–65. Edward Moxon, 1857.

———. "Peter Bell." In *The Poetical Works of William Wordsworth,* 2:242–82. Edward Moxon, 1857.

———. "She Dwelt among the Untrodden Ways." In *The Poetical Works of William Wordsworth,* 1:250. Edward Moxon, 1857.

———. "To a Young Lady." In *The Poetical Works of William Wordsworth,* 2:193. Edward Moxon, 1857.

———. "Weak Is the Will of Man, His Judgment Blind." In *The Poetical Works of William Wordsworth,* 2:307–8. Edward Moxon, 1857.

Wynes, Charles E. *Race Relations in Virginia 1870–1902.* Charlottesville: University of Virginia Press, 1961.

Young, Edward. "The Complaint: or, Night Thoughts on the Life, Death, and Immortality." In *The Poetical Works of the Rev. Dr. Edward Young, with the Life of the Author,* 1:3–150. Printed for Benjamin Johnson, 1805.

Archives

Catalogue of the Tuskegee Normal and Industrial Institute. Tuskegee, Alabama, 1895–96. Normal School Steam Press, 1895. Tuskegee University Archives.

Kelly Miller Papers. Moorland-Spingarn Research Center, Howard University.

National Association Notes. Margaret Washington Papers. Tuskegee University Archives.

Record of Interments. City of Montgomery. Alabama Department of Archives and History.

Turpin Washington Papers. Goochland County Historical Society.

Index